POLITICAL PHILOSOPHY NOW

Modernity Reconstructed

José Maurício Domingues

UNIVERSITY OF WALES PRESS • CARDIFF • 2006

© José Maurício Domingues, 2006

British Library Cataloguing-in-Publication Data
A catalogue record for this book is available from the British Library.

ISBN 0-7083-1938-6 hardback
0-7083-1937-8 paperback

All rights reserved. No part of this book may be reproduced, stored in a retrieval system, or transmitted, in any form or by any means, electronic, mechanical, photocopying, recording or otherwise, without clearance from the University of Wales Press, 10 Columbus Walk, Brigantine Place, Cardiff, CF10 4UP.
www.wales.ac.uk/press

The right of José Maurício Domingues to be identified as author of this work has been asserted by him in accordance with sections 77 and 78 of the Copyright, Designs and Patents Act 1988.

Printed in Great Britain by Cromwell Press Ltd, Trowbridge, Wiltshire

Contents

Preface — vii

PART 1 FREEDOM

1. Freedom and Domination — 3
2. Projects, Dialectic and History — 28

PART 2 EQUALITY

3. Citizenship and Equality — 57
4. Inequalities and Real Abstractions — 71
5. Justice, Real Abstractions and the Return to Context — 93

PART 3 SOLIDARITY

6. Solidarity and Complexity — 115
7. The Fundamental Forms of Contemporary Solidarity — 132
8. Complexity and Mixed Articulation — 154

PART 4 RESPONSIBILITY

9. Social Theory and Responsibility — 173
10. The Transformations of Responsibility — 183
11. Responsibility Today: Horizons of Development — 200

Notes — 223

Index — 257

Preface

The goal of this book is to scrutinize the imaginary and the institutions of modernity in order to outline its horizon of possibilities today, as well as its impasses. I intend therefore to render in a broad and synthetic way some of the key categories of the imaginary of modernity, especially those that refer to how the relations and patterns of social life are arranged, and their institutional embodiment. The relations of the human species with nature unavoidably come out too. I have singled out four categories: freedom, equality, solidarity and responsibility. Apart from the last one, there is hardly anything new in this short list. Yet I develop my arguments so as to throw some new light on aspects of those categories and specify their interrelationship. Moreover the notion of responsibility plays a decisive role in this book, not only because it has not held centre stage, as it ought to, in previous and even current debates, but also because it allows for a deeper understanding of the other categories. In some measure the notion of responsibility brings out some of their intimate and sometimes hidden features.

This book is concerned with the imaginary of modernity, but the cognitive, normative and expressive aspects of social life cannot be discussed, except analytically and aiming at specific goals, in isolation from social practices and institutional arrangements. There is not a simple causality from the imaginary to institutions: social practices and institutions evolve *in tandem* with the imaginary and may even serve as the starting point, although always depending on practical forms of reflexivity, for transformations of the hermeneutic fabric of social life; and the development of institutions may generate forms of consciousness, values and norms. The junctures and disjunctures between imaginary and institutions produce tensions and impulses. Generally speaking, imaginary and institutions are distinct aspects of social processes and practices; they therefore intertwine, although often contradicting and blocking, perverting and spurning each other.

Rather than attempting the impossible task of amassing the enormous empirical material about early and advanced modern social life, I have decided to resort more directly to the social sciences theoretical literature. The book carries out a hermeneutic analysis of the modern imaginary, understood, according to Gadamer's standpoint, as making up a *tradition*, as well as aiming at an analysis of the main institutions of modernity in terms of social relations and patterns of behaviour.

Freedom is presented as a paramount element in our quest for transcendence and meaning in modernity; equality is taken to be on a par with it, but does not enjoy superiority, either in normative or in descriptive terms. I reject any opposition between 'negative freedom' and equality; nor do I accept its opposition to so-called 'positive freedom', especially in normative terms, although analytically this traditional liberal thesis has a certain amount of truth. Freedom and equality ought to go together if they are to prevail in modernity. Also problematic is the dissolution of freedom into a multiplicity of 'substantive' forms which are not inimical to far-reaching systems of domination and inequality. Solidarity on the other hand is discussed in connection with the complexity and plurality of contemporary societies and the emergence of a third phase of modernity, which I have called *mixed articulated modernity*. Finally, responsibility is introduced as the hidden rationale behind much of the modern imaginary, whereby the shortcomings and impasses of this civilization are dwelt upon and some alternatives adumbrated.

As dialectical counterpoints to these four main categories, a number of others are introduced, although by no means forming binary oppositions: freedom appears in tension with domination and dogmatism, equality at odds and entwined with inequality, while solidarity is entangled with exclusion, fragmentation or simply disarray, and responsibility in tension with itself – if it is utterly individualistic – or in opposition to sheer recklessness. Reason or rationality are equally crucial features of the modern imaginary and are variably and in manifold ways embodied in different institutional domains. They could offer occasion for an independent chapter but are instead present throughout, standing out at many stages.

These categories organize our daily lives and our normative and analytical activities as social scientists and philosophers. In the development of the exposition freedom comes first, not because it is more important than the other categories, but because of its prominence in the imaginary, followed by equality and only then by solidarity. However, this should not lead to a homogeneous view of the modern imaginary and institutions, since these categories possess multiple meanings. This diversity entails different possibilities of reading and ordering of the categories in logical terms, even while I shall try to make their meanings more precise in the course of the discussion. That notwithstanding, I deem the order followed here as appropriate to understand how they are hierarchically placed in our forms of consciousness and institutions, irrespective of the stronger or lesser presence of alternative imaginary designs and institutional variations vis-à-vis the dominant pattern. This is also the first reason why responsibility, both individual and collective, comes at the end of the book. The second reason derives, however, from my regarding this part as the place where I can more consistently discuss alternative ways across or out of modernity. This book is after all presented, in continuity with my previous ones, as a contribution to a critical theory of modernity. Here too, the theory of collective subjectivity plays an important role.

This book has as a general inspiration Hegelian–Marxist methods of categorial exposition. Yet, whereas trying to present a total and closed system of concepts is valid and necessary when we are dealing with topics of true (transtemporal) universality, this démarche cannot be followed here. I think that modernity has been accomplished, whatever its concrete contradictions and tensions: we are dealing with a completed historical development. Nevertheless, its unfolding carries on; continuities and ruptures are still in the making. They depend on us, individually and collectively. The exposition of the categories featuring in this book must take this into account and stay open, eschewing any attempt to foreclose in theory what remains contingent in life. One of the arguments I advance is that if freedom is to be taken as actually central for modernity its consequences must be thoroughly accepted and reckoned with. In addition, some of the explanatory and interpretative elements of each category are introduced only in a further chapter instead of that in which it figures with centrality. As usual in analytical constructions the reader is asked to be patient. This derives from the very structure of the exposition, since the categories are closely entangled in reality and the book is designed with a view to penetrate ever-deeper layers of social life.

At this point a caveat must be added: in no sense does this book intend to be exhaustive, an enterprise in any event very unlikely to succeed if we bear in mind the topics it grapples with. Modernity cannot be really understood via an exclusive concern with the West; no one should expect the development of the world to mirror that of the West, on whatever plane or dimension. However, rather than attempting the difficult dissection of the manifold aspects of modernity in its global coordinates, this book will be concerned with this Western universe, and that of the areas closely, though not exclusively, connected to it, such as 'Latin' America (where other civilizational influences have from the start been present). Moreover many of the issues and even imaginary and institutional elements that appear there have a considerable influence on other areas that give shape to global modernity.

This book is a rather revised and slightly condensed version of a book published in 2002 in Portuguese. Many people have helped me in this enterprise. Piet Strydom was very important for my first awareness of and later insights into the notion of responsibility. Frédéric Vandenberghe aided me in particular with his knowledge of German social theory. Isabel Ribeiro discussed important aspects of political philosophy. Maria Regina Maciel helped to refine my view of psychoanalysis. Mônica Herz suggested the decisive pieces regarding international relations literature. Jeffrey Alexander drew my attention to issues related to modern social solidarity and Gerard Delanty's advice was crucial for the final form of the text, also commented on in detail by Hauke Brunkhorst and Howard Williams. Huw Lloyd Williams has kindly corrected my English. Two stays in Berlin, at the North American Institute of the Freie Universität and at Humbolt Universität, in January–February 1998 and 2000, were important for my arguments about communitarianism and the sociology of law. I would like to thank Hans Joas and Klaus Eder for their kind invitations on those consecutive occasions. Friends and colleagues of the Social Theory Working Group of the Brazilian Association for Post-Graduation and Research in the Social Sciences (ANPOCS) at different stages contributed to the development of my ideas, the same happening with my colleagues at IUPERJ. This book results from a number of years of research, during which I could count on the steady and decisive support of the Brazilian Scientific Research Council (CNPq). I thank them all for the outcome, which does possess a collective dimension, although of course I bear by far most of the responsibility for its possible virtues and shortcomings.

Part 1

Freedom

1 • Freedom and Domination

A Modern Paradox

We live in a paradoxical world. Never has freedom been apparently so close at hand. Many things seem to be open to change. Friendship, sexuality, gender and age roles, group, ethnic and national identities are some areas in which we appear to be capable of choosing the way we live, in what some, a bit too hastily and sanguinely, have christened a 'post-traditional' society. However, economic and political institutions in particular seem to have evaded this contingent horizon. Domination, in contradistinction to freedom, is deeply entrenched in these domains, spilling over into social life as whole; other features of modern societies are also pervaded by domination; thereby a cluster of privilege and unfreedom is maintained. Added to the sphere of unfreedom is a self-inflicted harm deriving from a reflexive cancellation of reflexivity – what I call the *dialectic of freedom and reflexivity* – which is characterized by dogmatic identities connected to what we will study as disembedding and re-embedding processes. Hand in hand, domination and dogmatism dialectically oppose, and are entangled with, freedom in modernity.

The tensions within modernity have been interpreted in distinct ways, with each strand predominating in different authors, or in different works or phases of the same author. Much of twentieth-century social theory and philosophy has paid tribute to those tensions; sociologists have accordingly crafted theoretical frames to interpret them, including the opposition between 'freedom' and 'discipline' or between 'regulatory' and 'emancipatory' aspects of modernity.[1] That tension has caused fierce disputes in intellectual life as well as strains and contradictions within the body of work of individual thinkers. It is not merely as an intellectual issue that it should be understood; rather it is the stuff of much of social life, even more so today than at the beginning of the twentieth century, when it seemed possible, to many at least, that its two poles could be reconciled by means of a radical revolution. Perhaps those poles are today more separated than ever before. In spite of this, more recently, especially in sociology, domination has not received the attention it deserves.

There are many ways to define the word freedom, which has a multiplicity of meanings in daily life. Some basic forms of characterizing freedom have been its definition as (internal) autonomy, as negative, as positive, as the possibility of 'need satisfaction', as the possibility of self-expression (in an authentic guise). Instead of trying to encompass all definitions and uses of the idea of freedom, I will concentrate on some crucial strands of twentieth-century social theory and philosophy; I will then bring out some contemporary aspects of the problem of freedom and liberty. Domination, too, has many definitions, although it has been articulated much less in daily life, since its success depends precisely on ideological concealment, that is, through the translation of hidden sectional interests into false universal standards. In what follows I would like therefore to depict some of the principal ways in which the tension between freedom and domination has surfaced in social theory. In the two main strands I will analyse how cognitive, normative and expressive aspects are present and interwoven. In one strand we are conceived of as free subjects, in the other as subjected individuals. For both currents there is a sharp distinction cognitively, but regarding the normative dimension it is clear that freedom is posed as the main standard for the assessment of modernity. This is so irrespective of whether freedom is seen as living among us or not, although especially in this and the following chapter on the normative dimension, the regulatory side of modernity will be represented. Expressively the situation is similar to cognition. Some believe that we are free to build ourselves and our identity aesthetically; in fact we have no other option. For others such an outlook is a proof of how trapped we are, unable even to recognize what holds us captive.

Let me make clear that, despite this initial concentration on two intellectual strands, my aim is to reach out to the hermeneutic dimension of daily life. The intellectuals whom I will examine have elaborated ideas which simultaneously draw upon and refashion feelings and notions that are to be found in the daily practices and forms of consciousness which construct modern, especially advanced modern, social formations.

This chapter is in part an exercise in intellectual history. Nevertheless, it is presented with systematic intentions: its main goal is to help to pose a theoretical and political question that is crucial for critical theory in the twentieth-first century. I will take it up more explicitly in the next chapter. The possibility of freedom for human beings in general has not, for both social and material reasons, been very common in history. I want both to understand and to explain why freedom is an imposition for modern individuals and collective subjectivities but also something that drives us forward. A problem should not be concealed, though. That we live at least potentially in a post-scarcity era seems a reasonable argument, although this should not be comprehended too literally, since many goods will always be scarce; nonetheless we do not live in a post-domination era at all, and we run the risk of entirely giving up on thinking how this might ever be possible. This would probably mean that new meanings and motivations would have to become dominant. However, we must not, at least for the time being, be too pessimistic. There is still a good deal of productive movement in social life that derives from the tension I have signalled, that is, the tension between freedom and domination.

The two main strands of social theory and philosophy I will tackle are the following: that which stems from Nietzsche and, by stressing contingency and freedom, results in the works of Heidegger and Sartre; and the tradition of critical theory that starts with Marx and culminates in the Frankfurt School, which stresses the relationships of domination in which we are entangled. They are both onesided. However, through their radical slants they bring to the fore some basic tendencies of modernity, which must be sociologically explained and then synthesized in chapter 2. If we must stress contingency and freedom, we should not however lose sight of domination, which must be conceived of not merely as a result of rationalization, but as based on social stratification and collective projects.

Contingency and Freedom

Knowledge and values appear to have acquired an altogether contingent outlook in the contemporary world. If Kant (despite his 'Copernican revolution', which introduced finitude and criticism as two pillars of modernity) avoided falling into the realm of relativism and uncertainty through his construction of cognition and practical reason as universally valid, the late nineteenth century witnessed the collapse of his construction. In Hegel this had already become a problem, which he overcame through the subordination of historicity to the totalizing development of the Absolute Spirit. Marx did no more in this regard than to find a new 'universal class' – the proletariat – to be the 'bearer' of such transhistorical, universal knowledge. Nietzsche posed questions and produced answers that were the final blow to this kind of certitude.

I will not to go into greater detail with respect to those developments; they have been extensively analysed. Whether they stemmed from the pervasive power of the notion of *Kritik* – which corrodes all dogmatism, the 'death of God', leaving humankind bereft of universal and eternal standards – or the crisis of historicism and the faith in progress – which underlie the introduction of contingency into social thinking as an inescapable issue – will not be the focus here. Nonetheless, this last account is perhaps particularly fitting as an explanation of the situation: only when history is conceived as linear is it possible to think of it as undergoing a severance.[2] The (at least partial) discrediting of the widespread notion of progress and disappointment with the supposed perfectibility of humankind (in one way or another crucial for the Enlightenment) left history without a direction, unable to fill in the gap opened by the collapse of sacred universal standards offered by religion.

Nietzsche interpreted that situation, introducing ideas and problems for the following century. Relating it to the 'death of God', he identified a deep crisis which made the present empty due to the lack of signposts. The recognition of that implied 'nihilism'. According to Megill, this can be understood in two guises. We fail to respond to the opportunity offered by the world's nullity, thus regarding 'the devaluation of all present values as oppressive and burdensome' and pretending that nothing has happened. This implies a 'passive and anaesthetic attitude'. Or we embrace 'an active, aesthetic nihilism', which Nietzsche prescribes as appropriate for modern existence. We then dance upon the void, becoming 'the artists of our existence, untrammelled by natural constraints and limitations'.[3]

Lacking foundations and the Kantian optimism regarding universal standards of truth and morality to be established with recourse to critical thinking, we were forced to choose between two alternatives: either we took responsibility for that situation and became active creators of our lives, as *free* agents, or we adopted a timid attitude, returning to the 'dogmatic slumbers' of pre-critical thinking. During the twentieth century a number of key thinkers eagerly took up those problems both in philosophy and the social sciences.[4]

Weber, for instance, unequivocally a sociologist but for many contemporaries also an important philosopher, was heavily influenced by Nietzsche (although this should not be exaggerated) in terms of the latter's 'realist' view of social life, which put the phenomenon of *domination* at its core, as well as regarding the excessively human, arbitrary, subjective character of values. The influence of Simmel – who examined the contingent emergence of values in his *Philosophy of Money*[5] – may have been rather important in this too, even though the issue was pervasive in Germany at the time.[6] This was a main focus of Weber's research on world history and the singular position and aspects of Western modernity. The unforgettable passages of 'Science as vocation' bring this to the fore, when Weber speaks of pluralism and the struggle of idols as the fate of modern man.[7] Should we regard nationalism as the antidote, especially in the case of Germany at the beginning of the twentieth century, to that sort of poison, and as mirroring Nietzsche's supposed distaste for the weakness that pluralism brought about?[8] We can point out Weber's commitment to the 'destiny' of Germany as a Great Power and the necessity of choosing one's God in this polytheistic world, and even going to war for it, thus decidedly rejecting, like Nietzsche, the ethic of the Sermon of the Mount.[9] Yet within this investigation these must remain moot points.

Easier to pin down is the contradiction manifest in Weber between his view of history as necessarily contingent, in which the crisis of historicism is patent, and his stubborn rejection of there being any way out of modernity. This would progressively become a universal, worldwide force, vis-à-vis politics and economics, sociability or sexuality, although rhetorically he accepted the possibility of new prophets arising at the *close* only of the modern predicament.[10] We were free in general historical terms, in particular to choose our idols; nothing, however, could change the actual course of history and the inexorable process of rationalization that the West and eventually the whole world were doomed to undergo.[11]

Heidegger's work is conspicuous with respect to this problematic. It may be true that only in his later phase, after *die Kehre* (a radical shift in his thought), did the notion of crisis take hold of his thinking – a thesis which would become established with the increasing sway Nietzsche held over him.[12] But it is clear that a number of issues stood out in *Being and Time*. Along with an overwhelming sense of nostalgia for Being and the need to overcome the forgetting to which it was subjected by metaphysical ontology, alienation as well as the opposition between authenticity and inauthenticity in human existence (*Dasein*) play a paramount role in that work. They are related to the facticity of 'Being-there', to the contingency of its existence. Even if we do not accept the exaggerated assertion that *Being and Time* is but a sustained reply to Lukács's *History and Class Consciousness*[13] – which will be examined below – there are good reasons to perceive Heidegger as in part concerned with an alternative view to that Marxist book.[14] As we will see, Lukács spoke from the standpoint of the absolute lack of freedom prevailing in bourgeois society, which could be overcome only by means of a total revolution. Reification was conceived of, if not as the sign of a crisis, at least as the cipher for the degraded human condition, contrary to the promises of the Enlightenment. Heidegger's theses about the 'decay' (*Verfallen*) of Being-there, its absorption in *das Man* – the masses and daily routines and 'public' chatter (*Öffentlichkeit*) – and about inauthenticity are obvious attempts to deal with a similar problem. But to what extent do facticity and contingency entail a sense of freedom in *Being and Time*?

At a more general, philosophical level, the crisis of metaphysics and the possibility of the destruction of ontology allowed a renewal of the interrogation about Being.[15] In this regard there is a great sense of opportunity and new beginnings. However, it is doubtful whether his discussion of authenticity is indeed to be reconciled with the possibilities that our contingent thrownness into the world opens up.[16] What comes through here is that not all choices are equally good choices, not every 'project' (*Entwurf*) is similarly authentic, nor are all 'possibilities' actually interchangeable; more than that, perhaps only one choice is in fact authentic in terms of one's existence. Heidegger speaks of the 'decay' of Being-there in the world as a 'positive' possibility (that is, ontologically extant), not a corrupted state as such. He nevertheless goes on to show that this implies our being captured by the 'averageness' of *das Man* and our looking away from Being. This blocks the recognition of our 'authentic' possibilities, which are revealed only when anguish (*Angst*, 'fear') sets in, against the peace of mind we obtain when we are immersed in the taken for grantedness of our collective existence.[17] He goes as far as to suggest that the 'authentic openness' of Being-there regarding its possibilities is indeed the 'truth of existence', although, similarly to 'decay', the ontological 'facticity' of Being-there includes also 'untruth' (*Unwahrheit*) as a 'positive' possibility.[18] Listening to the silent 'call' (*Ruf*) of Being, only a 'decision' (*Entschlossenheit*) could free and allow us to assume our free being towards our possibilities, our 'situation' (of openness and ultimately death – the end of all possibilities). This decision is always a concrete one, but cannot be avoided if we want to live in authenticity and truth (that is, to assume our freedom on the ontological plane proper and not merely on the ontic, practical-ethical one).[19] Freedom would be thus ontologically constitutive of Being-there as such. However, we may legitimately wonder on which possibilities, and on what grounds, one should further 'decide', once that basic ontological decision was made. After all decisionism seems to sneak into Being-there's resolutions.

What inauthenticity means in 'daily life', in terms of proximity, might be reproduced in a different manner in 'historicity',[20] but in this dimension the range of 'authentic' choices seems to be seen by Heidegger as narrowly limited. This probably becomes nowhere clearer than in his writings of the period of the *Rektorat*, when he *decided* to be the first Nazi rector of the University of Freiburg. Although these texts may be seen as secondary within Heidegger's philosophy and although it may be suggested that Heidegger slides from the ontological to the ontic plane without adequate philosophical mediation, they do translate his more general philosophical concerns into politics. Not only do those passages make obvious the problems one might point to regarding his Husserlian phenomenological standpoint, as to intersubjectivity transplanted to the collective level and Heidegger's (at best) fall into alienation and *das Man*, but it is also evident that one choice alone was deemed by him 'authentic' for the German people in the face of the Füher's 'call' (an arguable category to be used in that context: was it so silent as in *Being and Time*?), which consisted not in a demand but merely in the offering of a 'possibility'. They should take it or else, it is implied, eke out a miserable fate, alienated from their true destiny and the renewal of the *Völk*'s will for 'self-responsibility'.[21] He thus returns to the never-really-argued definition which conveys the existential–phenomenological 'fate' (*Schicksal*) of the individual 'to-death' (as by the way in *Being and Time*) to be that of the true 'destiny' (*Geschick*) of a people as stemming from its 'decision for definite possibilities', which is 'free' first of all through sharing and 'struggle' (*Kampf*).[22] Be that as it may, at least in one dimension Heidegger's legacy for the understanding of modern individualism and social life was crucial, notwithstanding his repudiation of Existentialism and his increasing concern with Being alone.[23] The world seemed now to present an inescapable 'circumstance' to human beings: life was to be human-made and we ourselves had to take care of our destiny. Contingency indeed was fate.

Although many differences can be pointed out between Heidegger and Sartre, the main name of French Existentialism, it was the latter who spelt out the most far-reaching implications for human freedom of the former's ideas. One problem remains, however, which Sartre was not able to overcome, at least in the writings of his so-called 'classical' Existentialist phase. Following Nietzsche, Weber had pointed out the ultimately irrational character of human choices of values. In Heidegger there is hardly a criterion upon which to decide what should be taken as 'authentic' in life beyond the acknowledgement of freedom and which 'call' we should take at face value. This was in fact a problem that became all too obvious in his 'decision' to support the Nazis. Individual and ungrounded (in terms of rationality) *decisionism* was inevitable in the way in which Heidegger developed his arguments as stemming from facticity and contingency *and* as a flight from intersubjectivity, despite his 'mis-step' in the 1930s. Sartre's thought was plagued by the same sort of problem, perhaps even more profoundly. This means that freedom risks being swallowed by irrationality and voluntarism, in such a way that it does not leave room for the intersubjective construction of shared values and norms.

Resuming Heidegger's insights, Sartre took the issue of freedom in a radical direction. Whereas in the former nostalgia and authenticity still played an important role, Sartre dissolved this possibility. Even in his more engaged piece, *Existentialism is a Humanism*, Sartre tells us that there are no criteria upon which to decide which values should orientate our actions, although in an arguably Kantian twist he suggested that when we choose a course of action and values for ourselves this implies the whole of humanity, by setting universal standards.[24] More generally he stresses that we are condemned to freedom: we are not free to stop being free. Against this only two possibilities are suggested: behaving with a 'spirit of seriousness', as if values were given or desire related directly to the materiality of things, or in 'bad faith', therefore hiding from ourselves the responsibility of choosing, through social roles or supposed prior conditionings. This is however a burden from which we cannot escape. Our motives and drives are not things, since we always lend them new meanings. More technically he states that freedom stems from our capacity to 'annihilate', to bring about 'nothingness' (that is, 'néantisation'). Because consciousness is no thing, consisting basically in a 'lack of', we are always bound to break free from our 'essence'. We desire what we are *not*: freedom is, as he put it, 'the being that makes itself desire of being *in-itself-for-itself*'. The problem is that this synthesis is 'impossible' and in the gap between the 'in-itself' and consciousness qua the 'for-itself' causality is suspended, identity cracks up, absolute contingency is introduced, values are generated and freedom emerges.[25] His conception of freedom is entwined moreover with a view of the 'original choice' and the 'fundamental project' according to which they emerge from a 'pre-reflexive' position. All partial projects stem from the fundamental one – which can be on the other hand always recreated *ex-novo* – but possess a contingent aspect when they concretize it.[26] Sartre is by no means inattentive to the fact that we live in situations that place limits on and inform our action. But he wants to stress the *absolute, unconditioned* character of freedom, which he derives from the very constitution of consciousness – its 'nothingness'. If the 'being of man' – as such – is 'free-being', anguish is the 'consciousness of freedom', a 'reflective' and 'affective' state that stems from the 'fear' before the 'possibilities' of existence. We snatch ourselves away from anguish when we take a 'decision' which, momentarily, limits our possibilities.[27]

Sartre's thinking became increasingly close to Marxism, remaining nevertheless faithful to Existentialism. Perhaps a new opposition, namely between subjectivity and the 'practico-inert', reasserted the original divide between the in-itself and the for-itself, while the incorporation of a number of questions raised by Marxism created new problems for his concept of freedom. Sartre admitted, indeed correctly stressed, the structuring of society in classes and the fact that *scarcity and possibilities, hence freedom, are unequally distributed* (a point to which we will return). He was acutely aware of the 'objective' conditions that impact on the range of 'possibilities' available to individuals, even acknowledging a relationship between necessity and freedom. This is far from accepting, however, that freedom – which accounts for our *creative* capacity – does not pertain to every person in any situation; we continuously strive to accomplish our goals and thus contribute to the making of history, irrespective of whether we are aware of that or not (although he has now perhaps opened more room for reflexivity as regards the project). As he phrased the issue:

> We affirm the specificity of the human act, which cuts across the social environment retaining the determinations and which transforms the world on the basis of given conditions. For us man is characterized by the surpassing of a situation . . . the most rudimentary conduct must be determined in relation to real and actual factors that condition it and in relation to a certain object to come to which it tries to give birth. That is

what we name *the project*. Thereby we define a double simultaneous relationship; in relation to what is given, *praxis* is negativity: but it is always a matter of a negation of a negation; in relation to the object aimed at, it is positivity; but this positivity flows into the 'non-existent', into that which *has not yet been*.[28]

In a passage that contrasts with positions of authors, which I will examine later, Sartre emphasizes that at the heart of 'reification' the 'human agent' is still a 'constituting and dialectical totality'. Nonetheless, he also wants to define and explain social phenomena. He draws a (typological) distinction: 'groups' are active and based on shared 'praxis', even if the individual is mediated by the 'Other' in the constitution of intersubjectivity and his own subjectivity; 'collectives' are passive and captured by the 'practico-inert', by their 'Being', their 'essence', by the 'seriality' in which they find their 'unity' through the demands of an external 'common object'. There is no necessary order from seriality to groups or vice versa, but the former is marked by a 'degradation' in terms of the 'intelligibility' of its action for itself, with the same happening with respect to the relation of individuals with the groups they constitute, that is, the relation between 'constituting' and 'constituted' dialectic. In fact Sartre resumes the stark distinctions of his erstwhile works, which are now lent a dialectical twist: he opposes spontaneity, creativity and freedom to their denial, to passivity and exteriority, in other words, reification, even though the practico-inert is always present to some extent in the emergence of groups, which can become frozen as a 'serial' collectivity – a 'false unity'.[29] In so doing Sartre nevertheless presents a picture of social systems that is far too traditional and embraces the notion of a centred subjectivity, in this case a collective one, when he defines social 'groups', which evince intentionality and self-awareness, and, with negative overtones, 'serial' collectivities as their decayed substratum and often destiny.[30] He also resumes Hegel's insight into the intersubjective constitution of freedom and domination in the dialectic between master and slave, placing violence and struggle at the heart of freedom.[31]

Sartre upheld a much more open conception of history than Heidegger's, although it was, at the same time, heir to the philosophy of history and did not therefore make much sense after the invasion of Czechoslovakia (this probably being the reason for his leaving unfinished the second tome of the *Critique of Dialectical Reason*). He did not accept the notion of a macrosubject as the 'carrier' of history; instead

'History' was seen as a *totalization* – a process of 'diachronic synthesis' – without a *totalizer*, unfolding through the mediation of a multiplicity of struggles between distinct collectivities, from the transformation of 'groups' into 'series' and vice versa, with each generation looking for a new meaning to its own action and for the process as a whole. Each individual *praxis* was as such already 'totalization', new meaning, radical freedom, although it did not exist in a vacuum, since it had been conditioned by previous history and the praxis of others, also escaping the intention of the individual. However, Sartre thought that we could understand the direction of history, its intelligibility – as 'meaning' and 'truth'. This seemed to be, regardless of the obscurity of the formulation, the coming true of freedom, even though this was a 'totalization without a totalizer or a detotalized totalization'. As we could achieve such 'understanding' only as historical agents, the debacle of real socialism seems to have created an unsurpassable obstacle.[32]

Apart of course from Simmel's and Weber's approaches, these are basically philosophical accounts that identify something they are not really able to explain. Is freedom always present in social life as Sartre was prone to believe? If not, why has this topic become so prominent in modernity? Recent sociological accounts have readdressed these problems and emphasized precisely the theme of contingency and freedom in a number of ways, to some extent under the influence of Sartre himself.[33]

For instance, drawing upon Heidegger and Sartre – but, contrary to them, stressing contingency and freedom as typically modern, even 'high' modern phenomena – Giddens discussed the 'disembedding' mechanisms (associated with symbolic tokens and expert systems) which operate in modernity and lead to an exponential fostering of reflexivity, to freedom, to the openness of choice and responsibility, and to new tribulations, risks and opportunities for the contemporary 'self'.[34] Personal relations, love, eroticism and family life have thus become constructions that are no longer given in advance. He drew also upon Beck's similar theses[35] to arrive at those ideas, although in this German author the ecological crisis and the increasingly individualized labour market imply much stronger constraints for the life course and choices of collectivities and individuals. Giddens recognizes that 'risks' abound in this new situation, but is happy with, and underscores, the 'opportunities' that are opened up by this development. For Melucci, in turn, in a world in which systemic complexity has become paramount and demands high levels of contingency, we are 'caught up in the paradox in which choice becomes destiny', both at the individual and the collective level. He emphasizes how the possibilities and limits for autonomous reflexivity in connection with those choices hinge on an unequal distribution of resources.[36] In the next chapter I will draw on these concepts to provide a sociological account of freedom.

Let me stress for the time being that, despite the fact that the writers just discussed point to constraints and are themselves attentive to the limits of action, choice and freedom in human life and society, their overall emphasis is on the openness of the world, of identity, of social relations, of history. There are good reasons for this – and sociology took by and large too long to come to grips with phenomena philosophy had already disclosed. We do live in a world in which important aspects of our lives and relationships have become much more amenable to choice and intervention. We cannot plainly speak of 'detraditionalization' as some sanguinely do – insofar as modernity actually possesses its own traditions and phases. But it is correct to draw attention to the 'reflexivization' of this tradition, *although only in some of its aspects*.[37]

To press the point home, let me note that in those sociologists the issue at stake is not as general as in the case of the philosophers who inspired them and often had no precise empirical objects to investigate. The 'self', mainly in identity-building, personal relations, especially regarding friendship and family patterns, as well as social movements, geared towards gender, generational and aesthetic questions, have been the key topics under the scrutiny of such sociologists. A selection of examples, restricted to the authors singled out above, clearly shows this. Melucci, for instance, opposes the 'new' social movements to the old, arguing that the former concentrate on 'cultural' questions and the reconstruction of personal identity, being distanced from the transformation and exercise of political power. Giddens's own discussion of new 'lifestyles' refers mainly to personal relationships. Beck is concerned with similar issues. However, although also particularly attentive to problems and constraints derived from the functioning of economic systems (whose 'market model', due to its ever more brutal demands, implies 'a society without children') and critical of capitalism as well as of political systems (authoritarian democracy), he does not venture very far in terms of proposing solutions beyond enhanced citizen participation.[38]

The fact is that most changes in 'lifestyle' which are underlined by the authors who believe that freedom is writ large contemporarily do not venture to question capitalism and individualism, consumerism and privatism, bureaucratization and elitism. They abide by the patterns of existing liberal–modern societies, which confine narrowly the field that is open to reflexivity. A tacit surrender to the limits established by those restrictive institutions and cultural patterns is therefore ingrained in those movements and the work of those authors who analyse and at times take them at face value. It is beyond doubt that changes in family life, the emancipation of women, the greater plasticity of sexuality and the reinvention of race and ethnicity, among other highly reflexive transformations of identity, are important, must be welcome, and are valid in and of themselves. Overall, nevertheless, they fall short of challenging capitalism and elitist democracy. I will address this more directly later. Before that, let us dwell upon what the other strand of social theory singled out at the beginning of this chapter has to say about our modern world.

Reification and Rationalization

Modernity emerged as having at the core of its imaginary the emancipation of humanity from necessity and the clutches of superstition and domination. Individuals should be freed so as to fulfil their own natural condition. With many variations around this basic theme, the Enlightenment projected a society in which, through the demise of the Ancien Régime, progress and freedom would prevail. Things soon became more complicated. Whereas criticism had been previously directed against the Church and feudal conditions, the critical movements that later on faced the transformed conditions of life came frequently to denounce the very structures of modernity for having failed to implement its own project. The critical social theory which we will now examine, whose key problem is that of 'reification', figures prominently in this attempt at revision, although its theories have been crafted with increasingly desperate overtones, due to the closing of the 'space of possibilities' in their worldview.[39]

The trajectory of freedom in the mainstream of the German tradition of critical theory departed from Marx's early critique of civil society, and the project of emancipation implied both the fulfilment and transfiguration of the existing order. The Marxist immanent critique of capitalism held the social order to its own promises: rationality, abundance, the betterment of life and the end to exploitation and misery for all, not restricted to the ruling classes. But it did not question the Enlightenment project of combining human freedom and happiness with the scientific-technological progress of 'productive forces'. Only later on did the Frankfurt School denounce the perverse dialectic of that project due to its very entanglement with the domination of nature. More recently Habermas has attempted to reunite Enlightenment and emancipation by going back to the Enlightenment legacy of practical reason.[40] It must be borne in mind, nevertheless, that along with a rationalist conception of human actors, an aesthetic attitude has been crucial also for most of this strand of thought. It received this from the Romantics and particularly from Hegel. The problem was that, contrary to the currents which believed that freedom was an actual possibility for human actors, and aestheticism something to be practically implemented, critical theorists considered this impossible. They reckoned that the basic structures of social life in modernity – which equals capitalism for most of them – placed limits on human freedom and in fact turned it into its contrary, namely unfreedom and alienation. Criticism was intended precisely to expose these shortcomings and help to overcome them.[41]

From Hegel to Marx and beyond, creativity (as an undercurrent) and alienation have held centre stage in social theory.[42] Hegel portrayed the unfolding of the Absolute Spirit as a process of self-creation by a self-positing subject that objectified itself in the course of history. This process of self-creation and achievement of knowledge about itself was not simple: the Spirit became alienated in its exteriority until it was able to become reconciled with itself in a final synthesis that would happen only at the end of the whole process, which had thus a *telos*, a predetermined target. Marx rid his ideas of this idealist construction and substituted for it the human concrete subject struggling for survival in a material world. Labour was seen as the creative activity of the subject. Yet, here too we are faced with the problem of alienation. Marx's development in this regard was complex, from his youthful writings to the mature work, and I do not intend to reconstruct it here; instead I will briefly concentrate on the role of subjectivity under capitalism and the theory of the 'fetishism of the commodity', which was extremely influential in the following decades. Marx shows human beings as powerless agents who cannot but submit to the logic and the representations of the relations of production of capitalist society.

Modern capitalist society was characterized by a stiff logic as a 'natural–historical process', which developed according to 'law-like' tendencies and antagonisms. The individual was merely a 'bearer' (*Träger*) of economic categories and class relations – the working class was obviously subordinated to the power of the ruling classes, but also capitalists and landowners were understood by Marx qua de-individualized 'Persona' at the service of economic processes. It did not make sense therefore to attribute responsibility to individuals who were not creators but 'creatures' (*Geschöpfe*) generated by those processes, although it was possible for them to elevate themselves above society in *subjective* terms. A complication arises insofar as Marx stressed that he was trying to grasp the capitalist dynamic in its pure form, beyond contingency and superficial disturbances, and it is clear that he was carrying out a *theoretical reconstruction* of that mode of production, without direct correspondence in social reality. This might be read as implying that the individual's lack of freedom was, in real life, not as absolute as it seemed in the theoretical construct. In any case, these practical relationships were connected to the forms of consciousness that prevailed in capitalist society and had their 'cell' (to resume Marx's phrase at the opening of chapter 1 of *Capital*) in the 'fetishism of the commodity'. According to him, commodity assumed a mystical character. Instead of perceiving the market as the locus of the relationships between 'men', this fetishist form of consciousness presents those interchanges as relationships between commodities. Analogy in this case should be made with religion, which is deemed something autonomous, but is in reality a product of the human mind. For Marx these thing-like and naturalized elements produced a closed whole and meant an absolute lack of freedom. Individuals were unable (when isolated) to bring about change beyond the logic of that 'mode of production'. Only the 'free association' of producers, in a communist society ensuing from the revolutionary activity of the working class, would bring the realm of freedom and spontaneity down to earth and make true the promises of modern civilization.[43]

The immanent critique of modernity, which was taken to task over its own internal tensions, found in Marx its main architect (though Hegel was the first great intellectual to tackle its limitations and one-sidedness, in a rather conservative way). Others such as Simmel and Weber contributed to the critical theory of the twentieth century. Simmel suggested a Hegelian reading of modernity according to which the 'tragedy of culture' stemmed from the fact that 'subjective culture' produced a world of 'objective culture' which, in its complexity, evaded the possibility of being reabsorbed and recognized by its individual creators – which meant that, contrary to Hegel's conception, there was no synthesis waiting ahead.[44] Simmel was more influential for critical theory in his indirect appropriation of some of Marx's themes in *Capital* (once again harking back to Hegel), linking the abstract character of the commodity to other phenomena such as formal logic and modern law, which share that empty and abstract outlook – although Simmel placed weight on more encompassing 'metaphysical' factors and was adamant that money also meant individual freedom, since it allowed people to break free from personal controls (as incidentally was recognized by Marx).[45] In turn, and in part certainly with Simmel's example in mind, Weber depicted modernity as a civilization in which instrumental and formal rationalizations enjoyed the upper hand and emptied social life of meaning, although the general introduction to his sociology of religion (as well as his manifold studies) presented a more pluralist reading of the process of rationalization. Bureaucracy and law, economics and politics were put under the spell of an unavoidable process of an ever more adequate adaptation of means to ends and deductive thinking, which disregards the specific contents and situations that they face. We had been locked into an 'iron cage' from which there was no way out (except, maybe in the long run, as seen above, if new authentic prophets ever appeared).[46]

In a piece of enormous influence in the social theory of the twentieth century, Lukács combined these 'post-Marxist' theses with Marx's former ideas, once again bringing together an aesthetic perspective and a dismal view of the possibilities for its fulfilment. Lukács started from a Hegelian reading of Marx (although he did not have on that occasion the opportunity to read his first, more philosophical works) which had a rich aesthetic flavour. He understood humanity as a collective, self-positing subject which expressed itself in the world; its development eventually reached capitalism, in which it became alienated. In a world shot through with 'reification' (*Verdinglichung*), people were absolutely powerless and formal–instrumental rationality would prevail until the working class – the subject which could alone fully comprehend the objectivity of that world – inevitably dealt a final blow to the existing capitalist society.[47] If Hegel's sway is self-evident in *History and Class Consciousness*, Weber's influence, and to some extent Simmel's as well, is unmistakable. This sort of Marxism made the Third International shiver, leading Lukács to an abjuration of his book – an abjuration in which, to judge from his later development, he believed to a considerable degree.

In the world of reification there was no room for autonomous action, for 'praxis'. The effects of the capitalist mode of production reached far into all spheres of social life, its seeds lying in the 'structure of relationships of the commodity', the 'original construction of all forms of objectivity (*Gegenständlichkeitformen*) and its corresponding forms of subjectivity'.[48] The fetishism of the commodity is here the decisive inspiration for Lukács, of course. The *real abstractions* connected to the commodity form pervade all economic, juridical-political and spiritual levels of capitalist society. This thesis was coupled with a reading of Weber that gave absolute pride of place to formal–instrumental rationality. In Marx, short of revolution, there was hardly any room for freedom; in this Hegelian–Weberian rendering of his work not even a little bit of it was left. Instead of behaving creatively, social actors were doomed to a contemplative attitude.[49] Fragmentation and specialization were key words in that process of rationalization, along with the possibility of *quantifying* everything, which meant at once a narrowness of view and the glossing over of all particular contents of whatever object.[50] Everybody was caught in this movement, which for the first time in history had genuinely transformed society into an integrated totality. Although we phenomenologically encounter 'isolation' and 'atomization', these are mere 'appearance' (*Schein*): underneath we are compelled by that 'rational calculation' which stems from the 'movement of commodities in the market' and sets in as 'unitary laws', a natural law-like phenomenon that determines the 'fate' (*Schicksal*) of all members of society.[51] Lukács was so sure of the absolute lack of freedom in this society, perhaps, that he did not bother to raise it explicitly; it played a decisive role as a negative, tacit issue.

The critical theory of the Frankfurt School, of Adorno, Horkheimer and Marcuse, appropriated those ideas in its own way. Although the problem of the individual, its 'rationality' and 'spontaneity', was from the beginning – during their most Marxist phase – a motivating force even for critical thought itself,[52] it was to assume increasing centrality in the course of the development of their thinking.

As is well known, Adorno and Horkheimer altered their approach away from the Marxism that, especially in the case of the latter, furnished the core of their ideas in the initial period of the Institute for Social Research in Frankfurt, during the 1930s. The surrendering of the working class to capitalism, the emergence of fascism and especially Nazism, along with the Stalinist, 'totalitarian' character of Russian 'socialism', convinced them that modernity had definitely gone astray. Nothing could save it. *Dialectic of the Enlightenment*, a short and dense, beautiful and painful book, was the outcome of this line of reasoning. It pointed to the absolute lack of freedom and choice, spontaneity and imagination under the spell of formal–instrumental rationality – whereby 'praxis' fails or goes under due to 'reification' and thinking is denied as 'ideology', although, strangely enough, they were able to identify and denounce this.[53] The programme of the Enlightenment had been the 'disenchantment of the world', dissolving myths and substituting knowledge for 'imagination' (*Einbildung*). However, it had itself become myth in its unfolding though, an entity and force alien to its creators, who originated it in their effort to fight a threatening environment. Abstract thinking was its 'tool', they say, whereby an analogy is drawn between mental categories and the social practices entangled with the movement of the commodity. 'The new' (*das Neue*) could not therefore emerge, constrained as it was by the abstract categories of a 'totalitarian' way of thinking which refused and in the end tried concretely to eliminate that which did not conform to its internal structure.[54] Anti-Semitism was a brutal and radical, albeit rather 'normal', result of this sort of historical development – dramatically showing how there was no room for freedom and no space for difference.[55]

It is manifest that the Marxist–Hegelian and Weberian impulse was present in the book although, for instance, they never quoted Lukács. The materialism of Marxism, its historical theory proper, played in contrast a relatively minor role in their worldview – a true *Weltanschauung* – which constituted a sort of tragic counterpoint to the development and 'cunning' of reason in history, references to the commodity form notwithstanding. These play a major part only in their discussion (written mainly by Adorno) of cultural industry, which puts forward an abstract equalization of all contents and forms so as to turn everything into a commodity of easy acceptance for a pre-formed and idiotic consumerist 'public'. Cultural industry – a concept first crafted in the 1930s by Marcuse – is also inimical to freedom and creativity: it homogenizes and excludes difference, repressing the 'power of representation' (*Vorstellungskraft*) and the 'power of imagination' (*Einbildungskraft*), the same fate destined for 'spontaneity'. As a consequence there is no freedom, since all 'details' are defined in advance according to what is permitted or forbidden. Cultural industry is mere repetition, excluding novelty.[56]

A couple of years later Horkheimer resumed some of the book's theses in a series of conferences in New York. He opposed 'objective reason' – implying the achievement of harmony of a totality – to 'subjective reason' – merely formal (the terms were indeed used as synonymous) and geared to the adequacy of means to ends.[57] Democracy features as a particularly interesting topic in those conferences, receiving a very pessimistic and conservative assessment. Subordinated by subjective reason, democracy no longer had intellectual foundations. Most people have no 'personality' and function under external pressure to attain adulthood and responsibility. They mimetically imitate power, which explains why democracy, in such irrational company, cannot compete with authoritarianism, the only thing they understand.[58] More or less at the same time Adorno wrote the aphorisms of *Minima Moralia*, denouncing the 'totalitarian', repressive or 'integral' society, which gets hold of all forms of consciousness. This society was 'essentially' the 'substance' of the individual; no 'particularity' could withstand the power of the 'general' and emancipation could not occur: the whole 'stole' the 'power of freedom' from the individual, who was turned into a 'simple abstraction'.[59]

Years later, in *Negative Dialectic*, he broadened those arguments, connecting them to a view of knowledge and dialectic, with a decidedly anti-Hegelian approach. This was seen by Adorno as akin to 'unregulated' thinking, critical of the system – insofar as it was not captured by the general, hence remaining faithful to the 'particular', the 'non-identical', the 'heterogeneous'.[60] Moving in a very rarefied atmosphere, Adorno wanted to use reason – that 'negative dialectic' which refuses synthesis, totality, identity, the general, or even its (false) conciliation with the particular (which would be dominated) – against instrumental, totalitarian reason, against identity logic (a strategy which would be duplicated in his aesthetic theory, mainly with the concept of 'mimesis'). Many of the arguments of that book relate to knowledge, epistemology and similar themes. There are also insights into the relationship between freedom and determinism. In this book, his most complete treatment of philosophical questions, Adorno is at times curiously closer to Marx than in previous works. This occurred precisely at the moment at which Horkheimer chose the individual (and religion) as his axiological trench and adopted a much less sharp critical posture regarding actual social life,[61] although they shared a similar refusal of 'totalitarian' society and a dislike for the leftist students' movements of the 1960s.

For Adorno the principle of individualization of bourgeois society – the 'law of the particular' in which the 'generality of reason' was connected to the individual – and the tenets of liberalism failed to consider the intertwinement of individuality with society. Hence freedom could not be really understood.[62] Adorno criticizes Existentialism and Sartre in particular (of whom he thinks higher than the 'depoliticized' Germans) for falling prey to 'decisionism', which cannot see 'social relations and conditions' as furnishing the 'occasions (*Anlässe*) for action', since the 'absolute freedom of decision' is as 'illusory' as the absolute and world-generating 'I'.[63] In relation to Marx's theory of value Adorno states that freedom was created by social processes – as a 'function of the interchange society' – and was also cancelled out by them – since those processes worked over the heads of the individuals and subordinated them.[64] Adorno argues that freedom had been since the eighteenth century the most direct interest of philosophy, under the express mandate of the bourgeois class. But that interest is contradictory: it turns against the old subordination and searches for a 'common format' to conciliate 'freedom and subordination'. A new guise for the latter was accomplished by means of bringing the former to the rational level, 'away from the empirical domain' (*von der Empirie entfernt*), in which it is not to be realized (*verwirklicht*). The alliance between the 'teachings of freedom' (*Freiheitslehre*) and 'repressive praxis' takes philosophy always further away from a 'genuine insight into the freedom and unfreedom of the living' (*das Lebende*). This insight is precisely phrased in a passage in which Adorno notes that 'freedom of will' and 'determinism' are, contrary to usual opinion, both moments of social life, coming together in the process of individualization; they both 'proclaim identity' (which is the category he wanted to combat in order to rescue the 'particular', the non-identical). Freedom becomes 'concrete' only in 'resistance (*Widerstand*) against repression'.[65]

In a somewhat dubious passage, where he *emphasizes human action*, or at least in some way underplays the workings of the system, Adorno denies any inevitability to that outcome. It is true that freedom becomes an 'old' category. This is no 'fatality' though; on the contrary, 'resistance' – as it seems, to the 'integration of society' – explains why this is so. And he goes even further, stating that freedom is conceived of in such an 'abstract–subjective' manner that the predominating social tendencies have no difficulty in making it innocuous. This deflection of freedom from social reality implies however that it does not 'lose . . . its power over people'.[66] It is unlikely that Adorno held any optimistic expectation in this passage, or at least it would have been at most a very mild and circumspect hope. The fact remains, nonetheless, that it can be read as the maintenance of a fundamental normative element in the imaginary of modernity, one that spurs people further on, in the midst of other tendencies and contradictions, domination and meaninglessness. I will return to this issue in the next chapter.

Marcuse's work is much more concretely orientated and politically engaged. The demise of the working class as a revolutionary agent provided the backdrop for his argument; society was 'capable of containing social change', blocking the surge of new institutions and 'modes of human existence'. It showed a 'totalitarian tendency'. Technology had yielded 'new, more effective, and more pleasant forms of social control' and become the 'great vehicle of reification'. This stemmed from a *choice* between historical alternatives, being the result of 'the play of dominant interests'; it truly gave shape to a 'project', as he put it, explicitly utilizing Sartre's concept, which had at its core the domination of nature, whose effects spread across the whole of the social world.[67]

> We may distinguish between true and false needs. 'False needs' are those which are superimposed upon the individual by particular social interests in his repression: the needs which perpetuate toil, aggressiveness, misery, and injustice. Their satisfaction might be most gratifying to the individual, but this happiness is not a condition which has to be maintained and protected if it serves to arrest the development of the ability (his own and others) to recognize the disease of the whole and grasp the chances of curing the disease ... Most of the prevailing needs to relax, to have fun, to behave and consume in accordance with the advertisements, to love and hate what others love and hate, belong to this category of false needs.[68]

What might be the situation of freedom in such a disheartening world?

Freedom at that point could be defined only negatively – as freedom *from* the economy and its controls, *from* politics, over which we have no actual leverage. It should also be seen as intellectual freedom *from* mass consumption and indoctrination. But there were powerful forces against freedom: individuals were 'kept incapable of being autonomous' and 'liberty' had been turned into a 'powerful instrument of domination'. Contrary to the prevailing opinion, the 'range of choice' was not the decisive element for the 'degree of human freedom', 'but *what* can be chosen and what *is* chosen by the individual'. In that alienated state people recognized themselves in their commodities and 'introjected' social controls. A *mimetic* identification of the individual with society ensued as a product of scientific management and organization, beyond the borders of the company. In the face of this dreadful decay the mind lost its *inner* dimension – precisely the locus of *negative thinking* – and was left only 'one dimensional thought and behaviour', with no grain of transcendence to sow the seed of change. Politics mirrored – and actively promoted – this civilizational blockage. Even the Communist Parties had left their radicalism behind and the working class had been integrated within capitalist society as 'sublimated slaves'. The welfare state constituted a 'state of unfreedom', insofar as it was administrative and restrictive. 'Positive thinking' was 'tolerant' of human misery and enforced by no 'terroristic agency', but by the 'overwhelming, anonymous power and efficiency of technological society'. 'Happy consciousness', which believes in the rationality of reality, reflects the 'new conformism'.[69]

Even in those domains where freedom was seemingly coming to rule, such as in sexuality, we found merely a simulacrum of freedom – what he named 'repressive desublimation', which diminished erotic energy in favour of a direct intensification of sexual energy. Besides it was instrumental for commodity production. Pleasure became integrated into society – and was no longer antagonistic to it – becoming therefore 'harmless'. Genitally 'localized sexuality' and the 'performance principle' instead of a polymorphous sexual constitution of humanity prevailed and aggressiveness was 'rampant' in social life, with a problematic increase, against Freud's hypothesis, of *both life and death drives*. The only hope and possibility for freedom lay in the actual 'irrationality' of social life and its resulting 'struggle against society' as an element of 'choice' and 'decision', in favour of 'polymorphous sexuality' and fantasy.[70]

At that point Marcuse held a very pessimistic view of the possibilities of social transformation. This was considerably altered in the following years. At least in Vietnam, Cuba and China there was an ongoing revolution that was trying to eschew bureaucracy, guerrilla forces in Latin America had the same impulse towards liberation, ghetto populations were revolting against the system and student opposition swept the world, capitalist and real socialist alike. A 'great refusal' was on the rise, although none of those movements offered a revolutionary alternative to the integrated working class. We should, however, also be aware of the counter-revolution in place, which was to a great extent preventive.[71]

Habermas took up the ideas of his predecessors in German critical theory and tried to escape from their most pessimistic conclusions. I have analysed most of his ideas elsewhere.[72] Let me just sketch here his main theses. In his *Habilitation* thesis he tried to evoke the bourgeois public sphere (precisely *die Öffentlichkeit*), before its decay due to mass society and the commodification of all social spheres, as the realm of freedom and rational debate.[73] Some years later he would resume Horkheimer's efforts at laying epistemological foundations for critical theory – both holding positivism as the main enemy. Habermas rephrases the Enlightenment's quest for *emancipation* as the 'interest' (rationally grounded and pursued, his discussion of psychoanalysis leaving no doubt about that) which underlay critical theory – side by side with the 'interest' in control of the empirical-analytical social sciences and the 'interest' in understanding typical of hermeneutic approaches.[74]

His main book took his critical standpoint further. According to him evolution has uncoupled the systems of the economy and of politics from the life world with which they were originally intertwined. This corresponds to two processes of *rationalization*, the first 'communicative', culturally and institutionally woven, as well as linguistically mediated and dwelling in the life world, while the second would be 'purposive', instrumental and connected to those 'self-steered' systems coordinated by media such as *money* (the economy) and *power* (the political-administrative system). However, if this was a 'normal' phenomenon, the relentless expansion of those self-steered systems has entailed a 'colonization' of the life world, the attempt to place the latter under the imperatives of reproduction of the former. This brings about 'pathologies' linked to the deficient reproduction of personalities, culture and institutions, together with a reification of life forms and identities which commodity exchange processes and the imposition of patterns by the bureaucracy of the welfare state produce. And yet Habermas discerned only a few, maybe only one agent – the feminist movement – that could yield real change in late capitalism and modernity, embodying in 'institutions' the cultural potential already available in the advanced 'structures' of consciousness resulting from social evolution in a universalistic and reflexive direction.[75] It is clear, incidentally, that Habermas wants to tackle the problem of freedom in daily and cultural life and appropriate in his own, rationalistic way the life-world concept which appeared in Husserl's phenomenology and was, albeit never named as such and also rather distant from a sharp dichotomy between subject and object, pivotal for the whole of Heidegger's structure in *Being and Time*. By emphasizing its reflexive openness in modernity, he wants in addition to break free from its background conservative character, its taken-for-granted facticity, which becomes amenable to change through communicative action, dialogue and 'discourse'.[76] This consists moreover in the kernel of his support of a deepened – and rather rationalistic – continuation of the 'unfinished project' of modernity.[77]

More recently, that is from the beginning of the 1990s onwards, Habermas has evinced some more optimism and basically relaunched critical theory as a theory of democracy, insisting on communicative power and the importance of the 'interstitial' public spheres against that process of colonization.[78] His move towards a 'merely' radical democratic theory – which has moreover strong normative, rather than empirical, undertones – is hardly convincing, I think, although the deflection of the whole political spectrum to the right explains why he has probably felt it necessary to do so, as the outstanding public name of progressive intellectual politics in Germany. Yet this meant in practice relinquishing most of his insights into the impasses of modernity, although social life has become much bleaker in the last decades. Only in his more recent discussion of biotechnology does that critical edge seem to surface again.[79]

More generally, how has this situation been sociologically theorized? A number of well-known authors have had recourse to the Frankfurt School's ideas since they were first presented, especially from the 1960s onwards. Habermas has many followers today, but one can say that their approaches suffer from the conceptual and political problems of the original theory. Other authors are much more critical or pessimistic. In particular consumerism has held centre stage in the gloomy diagnosis of late capitalism. According to Baudrillard, for instance, even the 'id' – the heart of desire and imagination for psychoanalysis – has already been colonized by consumerism, with the amorphous 'masses' entirely dominating the desolated landscape of contemporary society. America offers a mirror of the future of the world tomorrow.[80] Jameson's arguments are similar in many regards and share the same thesis about consumerist 'postmodern society'. Besides there is no sense of history or future. This lack of *telos* has entailed the closure of the imagination vis-à-vis the possibility of different options.[81] It is not difficult to see that these approaches, which are not dominant in sociology, leave little room for choice and freedom. One could suggest that for them we live in a meaningless world, in which freedom and choice are merely ideological artefacts and appearances. The riddle of Weber's thesis about the 'loss of meaning' (*Sinnverlust*) in modernity, which for Habermas is not well interwoven with his thesis about rationalization, is probably to be found in this connection.[82] That is, although we apparently have all options open and can choose whatever values we fancy, in practice instrumental rationality makes these values sheer epiphenomena, powerless and colonized by 'consumer choice' and instrumental rationalization. Thereby we lose the possibility of *transcendence*, which is a key component of the definition of freedom in modernity. I will return to this below.

A difficult conclusion to avoid if such arguments and empirical considerations are taken into account is that, even in our personal paths – in the intimate dimension as well as in the economic and political domains – we are far from capable of acting with actual autonomy, irrespective of how excessively deterministically and onesidedly Marxism has, from its founders to the Frankfurt School and along with Weber and others, portrayed the human plight in modernity. But we must also be attentive to the fact that domination must be grasped in much more sociological and historical terms, not as something entailed by the development of reason and rationalization per se. Domination must be seen as a relationship between collectivities in which one or some of them exercise power over other collectivities, appropriating social resources. The relations between classes, genders, races and countries are today the most prominent in terms of domination. If they are somehow connected to instrumental rationality, they must not be causally deduced from them. Although Marx was not correct in his understanding of the development of the productive forces as the element that was in the last instance going to free humanity,[83] there is no reason to reverse his ideas and state that such development necessarily entails domination. The projects of collective subjectivities must always receive pride of place when such a discussion is advanced.

2 • Projects, Dialectic and History

Projects

As we have seen in chapter 1, for some authors human existence, and human existence especially in modernity (if we take into account the sociological literature), has become the realm of contingency and freedom. Astonishingly enough, for others the opposite is true: we are prisoners in a jail from which only total revolution could free us (while others do not even reckon on this possibility: for them we are simply doomed). For the former, even though they accept that freedom is not necessarily confined to personal life, this is where they usually place it. For the latter, the workings of the economy and the political system and/or the processes of rationalization connected to or which underpin them either completely block or at least threaten the possibility of freedom in all social dimensions. I do not think that these two views are totally justified. An apocalyptic conception of social life and history is untenable, although sometimes the degradation of important aspects of the contemporary world makes plausible the desperate perspective which authors such as Adorno, Horkheimer and Marcuse upheld. In a more sober mood we must recognize that there are indeed spaces of freedom today. On the other hand it is plain to see that the restrictions which economic and political systems impose upon freedom are tremendous and that it would be naive to disregard them. Nevertheless, I do not think that this can be fruitfully understood merely with recourse to Habermas's colonization thesis. Those systems cannot be indicted alone for the problems of unfreedom and meaninglessness. The hermeneutic fabric of social life (what is conventionally known as the realm of 'culture') and the interests entangled with it should be taken as decisive in this regard as well.

Modernity promised freedom to everyone. The Enlightenment made it its dearest friend. Modernity had however, in the Western, male and bourgeois project which was also part and parcel of its origins and unfolding, domination at its heart. I will focus on inequalities and classes later on, as well as on civil rights as a support for capitalist private property, and the 'sexual contract' that underlies social life in modernity. Suffice to say here that domination is a multidimensional feature of our societies. This is something of which Marx and Weber especially were acutely aware, although contemporary sociological theory tends to avoid this issue. Today, yesterday's powerful forces are marshalled to sustain relations of domination.

The goal of this chapter is to find a sociologically based explanation for the stronghold of freedom in modernity, despite or also because of powerful counter-tendencies, as well as to understand why and how projects of domination are woven by collective subjectivities. Conservative projects and the dialectic of freedom and reflexivity will be crucial for my argument below. But also a minimal definition of freedom, or more precisely, of freedom in its modern guise as distinct from and opposed to privilege and its importance as a value which orients and motivates agents in modernity will provide the main thread of argument in this chapter. My aim here is twofold. First, to search for the obstacles preventing the realization and expansion of freedom, which we will find in the external domain, with conservative collective projects, and within the internal dimension, with the dialectics of freedom and reflexivity. In the case of the former it will be clear that domination such as those projects envision is directed against the specifically modern conception of freedom – that is, as the erasing of privilege – and on the other hand against the opening of lifestyles. To allow for a deeper understanding, a basic definition of freedom in modernity must then be introduced. This will buttress an explanation of its relentless dynamic in social life and in the modern imagination, which I will articulate to the specific content of the notion of *transcendence*. Whereas in chapter 1 I critically reconstructed the main ideas of those two fundamental currents of twentieth-century thought, I intend now to select a number of analytical issues whereby *agency*, individual actors and collective subjectivities will be brought out in relation to freedom and domination. I will link the issue also to *history*, accentuating its contingent aspect rather than assimilating theses derived from the philosophy of history.

Let us dwell upon the concept of *project*, which will play a crucial part in subsequent developments. Both rationalistic and decisionist or voluntaristic perspectives must be rejected. We must keep away from the view of projects as either a rationalist or a teleological (historicist or functionalist) construction, always systematic and supposing clear ends as well as a self-sufficient and clear-cut consciousness that delineates and controls them. But we must avoid the opposite pitfalls. If projects are not proposed and carried out by a clear consciousness and a centred collective subjectivity, they do not derive from an absolutely arbitrary, totally groundless 'choice' either. Besides, nor are projects woven in an utterly 'pre-reflective' mode, in which consciousness is linked merely to a diffuse being in the world, nor do choices and 'fundamental' projects encompass and originate all future moves of individuals, let alone those of collectivities. Choices and projects are socially grounded and cannot be thought of as disconnected from previous social conditionings and memories, without detriment to the labour of creativity, of imagination, in their making. They vary due to this constitutive and relentless creativity as well as their interaction with other individuals and collective choices and projects; they are sometimes abandoned and may be discontinuous, being always contingent in their unfolding and succession. Thereby both freedom and domination acquire a human and social intersubjective aspect. I thus depart from the philosophy of history and acknowledge the wills and wishes as well as the contingent accomplishments of the human species. However, choices and projects do not consist in blind decisions and openings to the future either. While intellectuals and leadership frequently play a key role in the articulation of projects and 'choices', all participants in each one of them contribute reflexively to their making.

Therefore if projects depend on the *concrete possibilities* that are offered in each situation, a comprehensive concept of individual and collective reflexivity must be supposed in order to grasp them. I have elsewhere explored this issue in relation to the concepts of memory and creativity and proposed the following distinctions: while we must theorize indeed a form of reflexivity which is rationalizing, in that it is systematic (whether instrumental or communicative), we must also perceive that it is based on other more pervasive ones. These are those which I have defined as practical reflexivity – which may be discursively organized, but is not systematically exercised and is in fact that which we use mostly in our daily life – and as non-identity reflexivity – which is rooted in the 'id' (cf. Freud and Castoriadis), standing as the main source of our capacity for creative undertakings. They are all interactively and symbolically produced.[1] By no means can we control the outcomes of the exercise of reflexivity. And although heightened freedom may call forth a stronger exercise of reflexivity as creativity, the workings of the 'id', with its desires as well as fears, our practical attitude towards the world, as well as our rationalized response to the impulses underlying the former, may lead to a refusal of freedom and thus to the use of our memories in such a way as to close the alleys, let alone avenues, to our own possibilities of creative exploration of freedom, and those of others, both individually and collectively. Doubtless, this can only be carried out through creative recourse to reflexivity, but it is often precisely this recourse that in the last instance one wishes to cancel out.

Conservative Projects and Freedom

We must therefore be careful to separate rationalization from its (often, though not always) deleterious effects and the relationships of domination that are established between collectivities plus the projects engendered to maintain them. These two dimensions have been conflated in the accounts of much of Western Marxism, in its Frankfurtian strand, even in Habermas's attempt at rereading such problems, regardless of his widening of the notion with the introduction of 'communicative' rationality. In particular political systems and the decision-making centres of big corporations and financial markets remain elusive for the ordinary citizen of low-intensity contemporary democracies. Domination, which has not really been prominent in sociological theory, must return to centre stage, since those relations of power between collective subjectivities, split between ruling and ruled ones, play a pivotal role in the configuration of modernity, although power relations today have often become impersonal, multifarious and disembodied.[2] Moreover, contemporary social systems – especially those configured as 'societies' – possess a hermeneutic fabric that embodies domination schemes that are no simple by-product of the development of a historically all-encompassing rationalization process. In daily life – to be sure with differences easily grasped along class, as well as racial, ethnic and gender lines – actors frequently sustain exactly the same sort of privatist and utilitarian as well as authoritarian attitude that is central for those systems. Not only is Habermas's separation of life world and systems theoretically deficient – a point I have dealt with elsewhere – the life world is not by any means simply the locus of sheer universality, liberty and reflexivity either; other, much less noble traits are also present there. Unfreedom is deeply ingrained within our own desires and expectations in all spheres of life, although in some of them there is perhaps more flexibility and people can impose sharper limits to the transformation of freedom in privilege and demand solidarity, respect and acknowledgement which are more difficult in the economy and in politics insofar as they face great and powerful systems as isolated individuals. Conservative projects draw precisely upon those less noble cultural traits and often upon the sense of powerlessness of individuals and collectivities.

While there is apparently no direct causal link between conservatism, or at least acquiescence to the bureaucratic and exclusionary features of politics and to the exploiting essence of capitalism, on the one hand, and the defence of traditionally modern (or even pre-modern) forms of sexuality, family life as well as similar and related concerns, on the other, there is an obvious historical association between them. It was not by chance that North American reality during the 1980s was the outlawing of abortion, 'creation science', and other concerns of the 'Moral Majority', with high-tech mystification, gene technology, and weapons of technological gigantism. This strange mix – with neoliberalism and political conservatism performing a key part – proved capable of attaining a certain level of stability and even becoming a seductive model for other areas of the world.[3]

In fact both sides of the mix stem precisely from a refusal of freedom and may indeed appear isolated. But this refusal of freedom in general provides at least an 'elective affinity' and often a weak causal link between them. Market economics and liberal political systems are in principle open to contingency; however, as institutional and motivational traditions, they have blocked changes everywhere they reign, whereas ruling classes and associated political 'elites' – that is, ruling collective subjectivities overall – have frequently made an effort (usually connected to the role the family can play in social stability and in the achievements of its older as well as younger members) to bring them together. In order to accomplish this they must *eschew freedom* in both domains, as part of their modernizing plans and offensives. It may well be the case that this is a rather appropriate answer, from conservatives of different colours, to the increasing complexity of social life and the problems unleashed by the free development of each system, which then creates problems for other subsystems – in the case in point changes in morality threatening the stability of political and economic systems, and, to a lesser extent, vice versa. Phenomena such as specialization and differentiation may be responsible for both efficiency and sharpened confusion and strains, since modernization in one sector may disrupt processes elsewhere.[4] This however is not a 'systemic' problem, nor is the resulting inflexibility of modernity a by-product of it, although of course changes in those patterns must take account of the opportunities thrown up and the constraints imposed by enhanced societal complexity, they stem from options (hinging on either 'practical' or 'rationalized' reflexivity) of collectivities. Those choices are socially and politically mediated, irrespective of how stark and voluminous unintended or unanticipated effects are shared as barely controllable constraints. And as far as we can tell they come in wholesale packages: research – whether in Britain in the late 1940s or in Brazil in the 1990s – shows that conservative attitudes ranging from sociability and sexuality to politics and economics do not appear in isolation, but *in tandem* with one another.[5] Perhaps, as has been suggested in a study about Chile as an exemplary neoliberal society, this is due to a mechanism of dislocation of fear (connected to feelings of heightened helplessness) from the destructiveness of more aggressive market dynamics to the moral sphere.[6]

Although this is not always the case and regardless of how elusive the connection between these domains remains, it is very common to find racism, sexism, homophobia, neoliberalism (although right-wing populism complicates this equation – in any case in practice implying the support of big capital), and an often highly restrictive view of democracy as well as related phenomena and attitudes going merrily hand in hand. It is useful to stress once again that it is therefore into the cognitive, normative and expressive patterns of social life as such, that is, into the 'hermeneutic dimension' of social systems, into a 'cultural' backlash – thus not merely into the overall predominance of 'instrumental reason' or the 'colonization of the life world' – that we must look so as to understand contemporary blockages of freedom, since projects are decisive in this regard. To some extent the workings of what I will soon examine as the dialectic of freedom and reflexivity is important for the defensive formulation of conservative projects which aim at preventing social change. But it must be clear that these are usually devised to maintain class, gender and racial stratification and subordination, as well as bureaucratic domination, and that usually the opposite is true regarding projects that have freedom as their goal.

At this stage it is imperative to note finally that, in contradistinction to what happened with previous traditions, modernity has severed the tie that linked freedom to the possibility of domination over others (a point I will further elaborate upon in part 2). Modern conceptions imply the *universality, inalienability* and *indivisibility* of freedom, in contrast to its *plurality* in previous times (which in fact constituted *privileges*, according especially to eighteenth-century and early nineteenth- century authors). This unity now tends to have been dissolved once more. The first form in which this was phrased introduced the distinction between 'negative' and 'positive' freedom: while the first would imply merely 'freedom from', the second would more strongly demand 'freedom to'. They might therefore be incompatible in many respects, while the former (to a great extent underdetermined) does not even possess criteria clear enough for its own concretization and might often hinge on the exercise of the latter to create situations for its own enforcement.[7] More recently freedom received a dangerous formulation whereby it was defined simply as multiple and *not inimical* to, but instead compatible with, large-scale systems of domination, in Sen's globalizing developmentalist perspective which points to 'capabilities' as discrete 'empowerments' that provide for 'substantive' freedoms.[8] It is thus against that original and peculiar modern conception of freedom that conservative projects have fought, even while they appear in a liberal guise. The concentration on 'negative freedom' or on the 'plurality of freedom' allows for the reproduction of domination and privilege, as against institutions and projects that can substantiate the actual realization of freedom in contemporary modern social formations.

Disembeddings, Projects of Freedom and Transcendence

How is it, then, that freedom has been imposed upon us, despite systems of domination being so prevalent? Which conceptual construction could explain how it has become something from which we cannot escape, at least in many spheres of life, especially regarding our personal lives, in individual and collective terms? Why are projects that aim at advancing freedom in reality so important and widespread?

Giddens introduced the concept of 'disembedding' of agents from their specific, more localized contexts of existence, as crucial for an understanding of modernity. He wanted to reformulate the Hobbesian–Parsonian 'problem of order' in terms of levels of 'time–space distantiation'. Space and place usually coincided and relations of co-presence, face-to-face interactions, wove social life in pre-modern societies. The emergence of modernity turned 'place' into something 'increasingly phantasmagoric', swept through by influences from afar which decisively contribute to give it shape. To a considerable degree disembedding processes are a consequence of those transformations, allowing and pushing agents to cope differently with their identities. Disembedding mechanisms are of two kinds: 'symbolic tokens' – money standing out in this regard, and here Giddens obviously draws upon Marx's *Capital*, and also upon Simmel's *Philosophy of Money* – and 'expert systems'. He agrees with Marx that money offers an empty and abstract 'impersonal standard' (as 'the universal whore'), finding in Simmel the thesis of its instrumentality for time–space distantiation. On the other hand he thinks that we should focus on the technical and professional systems that structure much of the contemporary social environment. We possess little knowledge of those structuring processes (as Weber incidentally stressed in his discussion about rationalization and the social accumulation of knowledge). Those expert systems also remove social relations from the 'immediacy of context'.[9]

Initially those processes of disembedding were staged at the national level, especially, as we will see in part 2, through a connection between citizenship and 'real abstractions'. They cannot be confined to that level, though their dynamic increasingly overflows onto the global plane. The severance of the link between 'place' and 'locale', to resume Giddens's expressions, proceeds to embrace the whole world, and freedom is thus potentially set within ever-wider social, institutional coordinates. A 'compression' of time and space, or as I prefer to put it, a *reconfiguration of space–time*, which becomes compact although remaining heterogeneous, and due to which people are now exposed to influences from great distances in their daily life, becomes therefore a constitutive feature of social relations and individual and collective identities. Many institutional obstacles remain in terms of the circulation of people at the global level, which has been in any case enormously intensified, and citizenship is far from being established at this level; however, the contemporary imaginary of modernity has produced a link between freedom and globalizing influences which encompass the whole planet and the whole species. The globe appears as a field of experimentation and resources to be drawn upon.[10]

Giddens merely describes conceptually those mechanisms in parallel, but at times their common 'abstract' character comes up as a sheer coincidence, since he provides no unifying explanation. It is particularly important in theoretical terms to pose the question of what precisely characterizes those disembedding processes in modernity, beyond mere uprooting, a process present since the beginning in all human societies. Are disembeddings open to theorization in individualistic terms, as Giddens, and Simmel before him, suggest, or should we take into account a more collective dimension, as Wagner does?[11] I believe that the answer to this implies a more collective conceptualization and that it is therefore worth having recourse to the theory of 'collective subjectivity'.

In modernity stable identities have lost their place in the long-term processes, usually connected to slow rhythms of change, in which individuals and generations passed their time on this planet rooted in specific contexts. We are required much more frequently and intensely to reconstruct our identities and social relations, to define who we are, what we expect and must do, with whom we should get along with in life, shorn of secure bases even in taking those decisions. This is the actual reason for the changes in beliefs and the stress on contingency that so typically characterize modernity, and the predicament recognized by the philosophers I have examined in chapter 1. Indeed, freedom is not exerted in a vacuum, nor are our identities and social ties independent from other people's influences. In any case, compared to previous historical periods and civilizations, our situation implies a much stronger need to take our own choices in our hands, reflexively in a more systematic – that is, rationalized – or practical way. In such a situation of dislocation from more restricted contexts of social interaction and identity fluidity, both on the individual and the collective levels, the processes of symbolic interchange and communication are intensified and widened, from the local through the national to the global level.[12] One possibility that arises from this is often an acceptance, sometimes a commitment and at times projects that strive for freedom, as we saw with Nietzsche, Heidegger and Sartre, as well as with Giddens himself and Melucci. We face the contingency of our lives head on. We may also decide to expand it, for ourselves and for others, and are thus thrown onto the stage of politics, whether in more restricted or in broader terms. But another possibility also exists.

Freud noted that a close relationship exists between 'anguish' (or 'fear', if we disregard, as I think to a great extent we should, his not-always-maintained separation between *Angst* and *Furcht*), 'danger' and 'helplessness' (*Hilflosigkeit*). The first is a reaction to the helplessness of the individual in a traumatic situation, for which the prototype is the helplessness of the very young baby, incapable of action and having to deal with all sorts of new stimuli. In situations of danger and fear – created either by the internal pulse of 'drives' (*Triebe*) or by external elements – this sort of reaction is repeated and may become a structuring feature of the 'I' (*Ich*). Objects can nevertheless be introduced as cushions for feelings of anguish.[13] Indeed, identities can do the same job, providing strong moorings for subjects and allowing for a reduction of the sensation of danger and associated anguish. Often, therefore, the more traditional and stable identities seem to be, the better they seem to fit the needs of people in situations perceived as of dangerous and of helplessness. This happens with respect to personal relations – including sexual and marriage ties – all the way through to various collective endeavours, including class and religious identities. Modernity has multiplied situations of helplessness in which the basic and abstract identities of citizen and free worker that we will examine in part 2 have not been sufficient to lend people stable identities. But we must here further distinguish between an ontological condition of 'helplessness' in which humanity as a whole seems to dwell, especially in the face of the powers of nature, and the specific modern conditions of disembedding. Freud, who deemed religion an 'illusion' that universally helped to overcome that state of helplessness and acute insecurity, with its accompanying anguish, discussed the former.[14] The latter certainly includes this aspect. It must be seen in a more ambivalent way, though, insofar as it actually throws us into a situation of far-reaching contingency, but in so doing opens room for freedom and types of identity which are possibly more fulfilling. Hence we can build a bridge between Sartre's conception, seen in chapter 1, according to whom anguish would be 'consciousness of freedom', as fear in the face of our possibilities, and Freud's, who intertwines it with helplessness. We are deeply helpless when we become free, and anguish, as fear in the face of that which we must choose, decide, stems from this situation of contingency in which our identities are no longer a priori given.

In his later work, however, Freud did not link helplessness to the infant's lack of control over his or her body; rather it had to do with the silent and self-destructive workings of the death drive and thus the lack of control of the person over internal processes of which we are not even aware. The death drive was noisy only when it was directed towards the outside, coming out as aggression against other people. Freud derived from this a deeply pessimistic view of our potential for self-destruction and mutual extermination, which he saw as both unsurpassable and as something that generates intense disquiet, unhappiness and anguish. Eros – the life drive that brought people together also in social life – was the only force working against it.[15] This is not the place to assess Freud's metapsychology and such an unsettling hypothesis. However, it is plausible to suggest that the tougher society is on people, the more that aggressive potential will be directed towards it and people will tend to be violent in the very re-embeddings they promote so as to master meaning and anguish, their helplessness.

Why *religion, as a modern answer to modernity*, has become a way out, an option for the re-embedding of so many desperate populations across the globe, should give occasion to ponder the problematic developments of this civilization, especially at the turn of the twentieth to the twenty-first century. So-called (usually religious) 'fundamentalisms', which are in fact rather modern, though they draw upon previous, non-modern social memories (that is, traditions), must be understood in these coordinates. The *social* reinforcement of scarcity and hopelessness, along with helplessness, must be taken to task. The same applies to a great extent to the lasting importance of 'compulsive monogamy' and of 'romantic love', despite their repeated failures to deliver what they promise.[16] That is not to say that religion and love – which may both allow individuals to rise above immediacy, egoism and solitude – cannot provide settings for true meaning and transcendence. What should be understood is that, inasmuch as they become entirely closed and compulsive, this immediately puts them at odds with other deeper currents in modern social life. This deprives them of the possibility of fulfilling their aims positively: they become merely defensive, frequently shoring up the threats of looming freedom and reflexivity which surround their in fact fragile – though frequently ferocious and noisy – strongholds. Even conservatism as a 'disposition' rather than a creed or a doctrine, more as an explicit choice or as mere habit,[17] may be included in this sort of attitude towards freedom. To some extent it is understandable that people often prefer to remain as they are instead of enthusiastically embarking on the fast vessels of modernity. When however this becomes the manner in which people relate to the world in principle we are likely to be already halfway towards rejecting an open relationship with the changing contours of modern social life. Violence, if Freud's second view of helplessness is taken into account, may also be a way to respond to the increasing openness of modernity: bereft of strong moorings and beset by the reinforcement of scarcity and hopelessness, people may easily turn to violence, perhaps intertwined with dogmatism and compulsion, as for example when youths join extreme right wing movements.[18]

Disembedding mechanisms have in principle made us more capable of choosing our morality, our identity, our patterns of social relationships, which have become more contingent. They have nevertheless by the same token produced helplessness and a sense of disorientation which many, especially those bereft of power (economic, social, symbolic, etc.), may find difficult to deal with. We all need to answer reflexively the demands of freedom; there is no way out of this, as Sartre correctly implied. But the choice we make of morals, identity and relationships may work in the direction of cancelling out the very openness that gave us that choice. The anguish and fear brought about by modernity may be tackled by an individual or collective recourse to anti-reflexive, usually 'traditionalist' forms of re-embedding. Individuals and collective subjectivities draw upon different resources, according to distinct and varied interests, in a more open or closed manner, and can either further their own freedom or cancel it out. That is what I have called the dialectic of freedom and reflexivity. It can take place in any domain of social life, in a totalizing way, as religion is prone to do, and may connect several of these domains. This may explain the recurrently perceived connection between conservative elements in several dimensions, without a necessary causal link between them being supposed. A more general mechanism, that is, the processes of disembedding and re-embedding, underlies these processes. But more restricted and even contradictory positions regarding different dimensions can be taken, even perhaps implying allegiance to closed re-embeddings in only one or a few domains – 'compulsive monogamy' and 'romantic love' seemingly are the most common expressions of such a possibility, along with religion.

Our inner experience of time (which in turn contributes to the rhythms of the social systems which we weave together as collective subjectivities) must also be taken into account vis-à-vis such processes: the complexity of contemporary social life (which I will explore in greater detail in part 3) may elicit different responses. Anxiety, due to an excessive concern with the future, is one answer; the attempt to run after everything in order to catch up with time, thus disowning both past and present, is another; and a concentration on the past as a shield against anxiety may provoke depression, but also a form of manic militancy that makes us blind to the array of possibilities the present holds (indeed the option of 'fundamentalism'), which sometimes, however, demand hard choices, as well as the relinquishing of at least parts of the past and the acceptance of finitude as regards the future.[19]

That said, it must be emphasized that I do not mean that only a hermeneutic, identity-orientated and anxiety-taming aspect should be attributed to those processes of re-embedding. Cognitive and normative patterns play a fundamental role in concrete re-embeddings. Instrumental rationality is writ large as well in both dimensions of identity formation and of practical relationships. Differentials of power (symbolic as well as material, regarding for example wealth or politics) come into play when re-embeddings are at stake in a more or less decentred way, even if this is not evident for those who take part in them, and whether or not they represent the main motivation for that particular practical or rationalized choice. But it may also be that re-embeddings are carried out with instrumental goals in mind, either for the whole of the collectivity or for its leadership (irrespective of whether it was consensual or whether or not the whole collectivity was aware of it). Probably all these elements are present in re-embedding processes and they should be seen mainly in analytical terms, since they cut across the gamut of concrete social phenomena. It is unlikely that any of them would appear alone in a specific social process.

This cluster of elements provides only part of the picture, for though freedom has been imposed upon us, at the same time it has animated much of modern life. In fact, locked into this world, modern subjects have found in freedom the element that gives meaning central to their lives and enterprises upon the earth. Many dimensions have been touched by its spell; at an elementary level it appears in the dignity and the autonomy (however one wishes to phrase it) that has become in large measure central for free individuals in everyday life, for the justification of political participation and in general for the cultural tissue of early modernity and thereafter. Thus, conceptions of freedom and equality in modernity entwine with the universal 'dignity' of human beings, the realization of our specific potential, in opposition to previous and inegalitarian notions of 'honour'; this happens at the individual but also at the collective level.[20] If we look back we learn that individualism, or rather the valuing of each individual and thus a desire for self-realization and autonomy – in all dimensions – emerged with Christianity. It turns up in the two Western paths – one typical of north-western Europe and the United States, where freedom was intertwined with the pair science–conscience and norms were internalized in the latter (culminating in Kant's view of autonomy), and the other, alternative version characterized by the Iberian American greater independence of conscience from social norms.[21] But collective subjectivities have also been taken by its propelling power and individuals find meaning in modernity often only insofar as they are part and parcel of such collective demands for freedom. Revolutions and anticolonial struggles had freedom therefore at their core, but more circumscribed movements have developed with a commitment to the same demand, whether in explicit or merely implicit terms, although there is no comprehensive study of the topic in social science literature.[22]

Freedom has become essential for our identity in this regard, notwithstanding the emergence of other possibilities, which are usually defensive. If identity can be seen as corresponding to what we can expect from the world, to what we can and should do therein, which entails what and how we can know about it, all this is also enmeshed in the concrete practices of individuals and collectivities. As seen above, freedom already exists in some measure in this world or as something to still be achieved in a future state of affairs. Of course, historical teleological accounts have been entirely discredited in recent decades: nobody, or more precisely, only a few people – neoliberals and religiously minded people above all – believe now that humanity or society is moving towards some pre-determined stage. Freedom cannot be an exception in this regard. Nevertheless, can we not identify some sort of teleological directionality in history, linked to the unfolding of a number of cultural presuppositions which, generation after generation and in many different and transformed guises, have served as guidelines for social action and collective movement along the last centuries? Can we relate freedom to this sort of approach?

Transcendence has been, at least for some millennia now, a key problem for human beings and especially since a rupture of the sacred order of social life. Humanity has had to deal with the problem of evil in theodicy; the means to live a different life or alter this one, in the world or outside it, have taken on paramount significance. Whether and to what extent the great world religions have individual and collective liberation at heart is something that cannot really be decided here.[23] That transcendence has always meant freedom, from the body and the world, suffering, injustice and unmanageable stimuli, is a hypothesis that sounds rather plausible. It is obvious in the collective struggle and hope for freedom of the Jews in the flight from Egypt and their search for the promised land, as well as in all ascetic behaviour aimed at escaping from this world which especially Buddhism, Hinduism and medieval Christendom valued extremely highly. This is at least one of the key elements of theodicy, manifest in the Christian *parusia*, the eschatological expectation of the return of Christ, and the more ambivalent hope in the breaking loose of the Apocalypse and the realization of the realm of God in its aftermath. Directed towards the world the desire for freedom and liberation has maintained its transcendent impulse, but it must now be achieved away from God and in the embattled human earthly condition. Especially since in-world asceticism and activism have become the dominant strand of thinking and feeling in modernity – either in their original religious clothes or without them – transcendence has had to be at least in part accomplished *here and now*.[24] It is not by chance that so much of sociology has been keen to identify freedom as pervading our world: this is simultaneously a yearning and a unilateral comprehension of modernity, a reflection of what goes on concretely as well as a socially shared desire, and a formative reinforcement, in the normative, cognitive and expressive dimensions, of modernity's imaginary. We swill see in part 3 another form of exercising transcendence, as the opening to the other, which is intimately entwined with the dialectic of freedom and reflexivity. As freedom in the world, however, it furnishes the particular, distinctive core of transcendence in modernity.

Of course the contradictory character of social life has meant that alternatives to flee from it and gain a detached and 'spiritual' realm of freedom have been legion throughout modernity – 'affirmative culture'[25] was only one of these possibilities, which would crop up again and again (for instance massively in the 'New Era' 'spiritual' or religious movements without asceticism). In the case of 'affirmative culture', according to which the realm of goodness and beauty had been realized under the sun, its brief existence (being eventually sublated by the cultural industry) was due to attempts to save the values promised by the ascending bourgeoisie from the competitive and brutal world it had instead built. A great deal of religious 're-embeddings' of the present, more of a collective or of an individualistic kind, go in the same direction of preserving a sphere of personal and/or collective realization out of this world.[26] But most of our endeavours have had to be unavoidably carried out *in this world*, in this 'vale of tears', which must be therefore transformed – and this is today pursued by many reformed religions (their 'traditionalism' notwithstanding). One cannot do that without freedom, however, which has generally become part and parcel of the social memories and traditions that have deeply reverberated in the soul of modernity.

Furthermore the disembedded character of individuals and collective lives and identities in modernity has pressed nothingness and meaninglessness home for humanity. If this is an inescapable feature of the 'human condition', it has become deeply accentuated in the last two centuries.

Freedom is in this respect an *imperative*, something *imposed upon us*, as well as a *project*, a *desire*. Thus if 'negative freedom' should be defined as an 'opportunity concept' (which allows us to explore varied possibilities and cannot be personally evaded) and 'positive freedom' as a 'capability concept',[27] we near a possibility of explanation for the stronghold of freedom in modernity and its connection to the hermeneutic and motivational tissue of social life. Freedom is in this regard what answers for our being capable of doing something, either by remaining unimpeded in doing so or by being able to take the chance of doing so; this is true in both the external and internal dimensions, namely in our dealings with external nature and other people and as regards our relationship with our internal nature, whether in terms of conscious desires or unconscious drives. This means as a consequence that *loss of freedom entails loss of meaning, insofar as we cannot transcend actual circumstances without being able to use our capabilities and to enjoy the possibilities that are open for us in the world*. As soon as we get stuck in given conditions, trapped in unfavourable arrangements, as soon as the historical and personal horizons are closed, we stare into nothingness, meaningless flies on our faces, and we are taken over by the malaise associated with this sort of development; we are annihilated qua individuals and collectivities capable of transcending our present lives, which are, almost by definition, since there is no way everything will conform to our values and desires, unsatisfactory, muddled with evil, unhappiness and so forth. We are *forced into* the construction of meaningful relationships and destinies, for ourselves, for and along with others, but we cannot build them if the capability for that is denied, inasmuch as freedom is not at hand. This either brings us down or throws us forward, since it is not able to erase our values and desires for what we are not (as yet) and can (whether realistically or not) be and become. To a great extent this has been the history of modernity, although I must once again recall its dialectic, whereby freedom and reflexivity may be self-cancelled, bringing about a rather problematic state of affairs which is mainly defensive, in spite of its often aggressive countenance.

We must, though, be careful not to take freedom excessively in the abstract. It does not exist in thin air. As both a capability and an opportunity concept, freedom is linked to that which we want (freely) to achieve. Our projects, our desires, our often-fuzzy moves through life, all stem from memories charged with emotions; they entertain a strong relationship with the individual and the social past. Freedom is neither unconditioned – as though it had no bearings in previous sedimentation or a prior causality – nor can it be seen as operating through individual actors and collectivities which aim at abstract targets. Freedom *to* is always freedom to do something concrete. To some extent it is true that we pursue freedom for its own sake, as freedom from excessive constraints, although this cannot be absolute, for we have our histories and we are enmeshed in social relations and contexts. However, freedom for its own sake may lead as much to meaninglessness as does the lack of freedom. For staring into emptiness is also a consequence of a lack of direction in life, for both individuals and collectivities, something to which freedom per se cannot be offered as a solution. In fact it would mean lack of identity, for what we can do arises for us from our memories and relationships, though re-worked through creative mechanisms that in the last instance lie in our 'id'.[28] A dialectical connection is to be found here. If freedom and reflexivity may be self-cancelling insofar as people cling to compulsiveness or foreclosed identities, it can also become meaningless if we cannot connect to life and previous meanings – transcendence requires a basis from which it can start its flight. We must accomplish transcendence in this world and that means that specific life courses are to be chosen. This may sound an obvious point, but in fact it is not; instead it is supposed to be a sobering one. Thereby freedom is put into perspective and into a human scale: to be humanly free, individually and collectively, is to take options which exclude, due to their specific contents, other possibilities. Not all meaning is allowed; finitude, albeit contingent, is an inescapable feature of human life and of social formations. We do strive for what we are not, for that which we lack. But things are not so clear-cut; the past lives in the present and is projected into the future, for that which we lack in some measure depends on that which we have.

In contradistinction, it is never irrelevant to stress a problematic aspect of the struggle for autonomy in modernity. According to the

Frankfurt School thesis, in order to gain autonomy in the face of a nature whose forces were overwhelming, humanity set out to dominate it, first through myth and then through the Enlightenment project. This entailed an enormous increase in its power, meaning however that we paid a price, since we behave towards things as dictators do towards people: domination lurks in the 'manipulation' of things as a necessary element.[29] Certainly the philosophy of history contained in this appraisal distorted the path the evolution of the species actually traversed. In modernity, nevertheless, things take place in large measure in this way. We can therefore, at least in part, summarize the project of modernity as the association of the quest for freedom and autonomy with the effort of rational mastery of nature, in principle foreseen as eventually absolute.[30] But this happens both in relation to nature and in relation to society, as the rational project the Nazis put forward for the Jews dreadfully expressed in its cold rationality. Domination, to say it again, is rampant in social life and our very conception of autonomy has some relationship with it. What must be borne in mind, however, is that autonomy qua freedom in modernity should in principle exclude the domination of persons over persons, although the situation of nature remains much bleaker. Autonomy and freedom would thus be open to everyone.

Unfortunately it must be stressed that freedom is not necessarily in contradiction to the repression of internal nature. Indeed that is what Protestantism and its secular offspring have taught us, insofar as the movement affirmed freedom externally but strongly denied it when the expression of internal nature became an issue, can be regarded also as a crucial element in the enforcement of external domination over people and external nature. Moreover, we may be free and equal, but either by placing limits on other people's behaviour, or adopting the attitude Ulysses sustained in order to defeat the Sirens, we are bound to cripple our own freedom. In order to keep control over himself and continue unscathed by the tantalizing effects of the Sirens' song, he ordered his subordinates to tie him to the ship and made them deaf to his appeals. For Adorno and Horkheimer this expressed the rational control of one's inner drives in order to dominate nature and other people. That is where the species revealed itself doomed, since the search for freedom and the use of reason, that is, the Enlightenment, was clearly and tightly connected to domination from that very beginning.[31] Whether or not this is the best reading of the *Odyssey* will not occupy us here. It can be used in any case as a warning in the face of a deep-seated tendency of modernity to couple attempts at autonomy with control and repression of nature and other individuals and collectivities, a problem which we are far from eliminating.

Another way to look at this has been through the role of experts and the lack of control people have over specialized knowledge, a point already raised by Weber. Foucault framed the issue by means of his notion of 'power–knowledge', whether in terms of the creation of 'docile bodies' through disciplinary power or of sexuality as 'sexuality' against the mere 'pleasures' of the body.[32] In another dimension, Beck has argued against a mere technical understanding of the role of scientists and science, demanding a politicized view of the issue, which includes counter-experts, although we cannot escape all specialized knowledge.[33] Freedom has been seen therefore as beset by specialists and specialisms which incorporate an ideal of reason gone astray. Giddens's notion of 'reflexivity', albeit loose and not at all well defined in his work about modernity, indicated both the knowledge of (abstract) 'expert systems' and 'lay' agents, who can actively handle and even challenge what is produced by the former. Such a 'double hermeneutic', whereby knowledge circulates in society taking on shifting meanings, summons the increased – or at least undiminished – freedom that individuals ontologically capable of reflexivity thus enjoy in 'high' modernity. This is not to say that reason has the almost absolute power to master the world the Enlightenment attributed to it, since reflexivity yields frequently unforeseeable consequences and a spiral that undermines strong rational claims.[34] As a consequence freedom is indeed enhanced by such movements, yet cannot escape the opaque fate the increased contingency of radicalized modern institutions necessarily entails.

All in all, freedom has therefore assumed in particular an expressive and moral outlook, as a demand to be fulfilled, or has operated cognitively as an as yet imperfectly realized state, which should be achieved in the future. Domination and the reflexive refusal of reflexivity accompany freedom, relentlessly imposing unfailing restrictions on its trajectory.

History and Meaning

Concrete conditions in social life, linked to specific sorts of individualization and disembedding, have played a major role in the expansion of freedom as an impulse in social life. Those processes may, however, be complicated by the existence of different values and the clash between the freedoms of different people and collectivities. Furthermore freedom has become, ever more indeed, a concept with multiple meanings. Sustaining a universalistic concept of freedom is hence a more difficult, but necessary business if it is to remain important and true to its original modern usage, thus being capable of offering a meaningful universe of values and practices for all social agents, without degenerating into one more possible strategy to defend privileges. Perhaps in 'high modernity' or in 'postmodernity' other values will rise and take the place of freedom as a general framework for shared meaning and motivation. But it may be also that the Weberian thesis about the loss of meaning will be proven ever truer if nothing replaces freedom in that role, and this term freedom is in turn made hollow for most members of society who would then regard it as merely a new name for the appropriation of collective resources and opportunities.

To an extent the widespread privatization and mutations of the state already go a long way in this direction, with 'social fascism' slowly becoming entrenched in many spheres of social life,[35] frequently, if not almost always, in the name of freedom. This occurs even when democracy in its minimal – and in some degree irrelevant – requirements is maintained. This in fact explains why a superficial conciliation between freedom and authoritarianism, or, in more traditional terms, democracy and capitalism, takes place, contributing as well to a further enhancement of the multiplicity of meanings of this representational universe. One might suppose that the tension between the two main imaginary significations of modernity – the aforementioned 'project of autonomy' and the quest for rational mastery, the domination of the world – a dynamic force in modernity, may have been spent by an excess of defeats and utter failures of the former.[36] This would mean that the imaginary of modernity might suffer a complete reversal, implying a perfect match between Adorno's and Horkheimer's most pessimistic passages and actual historical developments. Hitherto though, despite shifts of significance and threats and counter-tendencies, that tension answers for what little remains of meaning in our spiritually depleted lives. Let us hope that will not be our 'fate', and that this sort of silent 'call' for a nihilism that promises not even an eternal return of domination, but a simple and relentless reproduction, will be resisted, along with its twin brothers, dogmatism and compulsion. Intellectuals still have a role to play in this context, denouncing the shortcomings and drawbacks of the contemporary social world and counterfactually proposing new ways for our common affairs, not as rational master schemes, but as ideas that may be appropriated by collective subjectivities in their daily struggles for dignity and freedom.[37]

By no means is this teleology part of the intentional development of history by humanity or even merely of the 'ruse of reason'. It has nothing to do with the development in history of the concept of freedom and the Absolute Spirit in a way reminiscent of Hegel's philosophy of history nor with unavoidable developments which derive from the way in which a number of issues are culturally organized in a given civilization, as Weber at times seems to imply. First, because we would be snared into an untenable position: how could freedom possibly be derived from a necessary development that would cancel out 'choice' and contingency? This thesis would be aporetical, not to say self-contradictory. I warn the reader at this point that the concept of collective subjectivity must not be confused with the collective *subjects* of idealist philosophies, which were retained by Marx, Lukács and the Frankfurt School.[38] This warning clarifies the role of freedom in modern civilization. At most collective subjectivity comes close – in the longitudinal dimension – to Sartre's conception of history as 'totalization' without a 'totalizer' (that is, an organized collective subject) or 'detotalized totalization' (as discussed in chapter 1). That would not do either, since Sartre held a strong view of the directionality of history, its 'truth' and 'intelligibility'.[39]

Although desires and projects of individuals are crucial for the demand for freedom, it is certainly not only on individual actors nor by any means merely on the aggregation and the so-called 'emergent effects' of individual actions that light should be shed when we speak of freedom as a recurrent yearning and project in modernity. Collective subjectivities of many kinds struggle and clash when following their dispositions and interactive inclinations, in a *more or less decentred way* (that is, in a more or less organized way and having greater or lesser self-awareness and identity), with or without clearly defined projects (in other words, intentionality), for or against the pursuit and widening of freedom. It is the *collective causality* (a basic *property* for their constitution qua social systems) which they exert upon one another, with recourse to memories they share more or less extensively and which they creatively refashion in the course of their interaction, that eventuates in a direction of history. However, this is not in any circumstance absolute, nor has truth or anything similar. It is traversed by a number of contradictions and tensions that can deflect it suddenly in an another direction.

We have seen that domination and blockages to the exercise of freedom are rampant in modernity, although they are not outspokenly voiced that frequently. That notwithstanding or precisely because of that, it may be said that the concrete movement produced by collective subjectivities, even if usually rather naively or sceptically, has practically and socially sustained a characteristic sort of *immanent critique* of those authoritarian tendencies and blockages. This can be empirically observed in the intertwinement of individual desires, projects and struggles with several collective ventures, such as working-class and socialist, feminist and anti-racist, sexual, youth, third-age and lifestyle movements, as well as revolutions and anti-colonial struggles. It comes out also in the myriad of yearnings and endeavours we can discern in daily life, once again individually and collectively articulated, regardless of the greater or lesser level of centring the collective subjectivities concerned may evince. In contradistinction, what must be discarded is the traditionally modern idea that the rational mastery of nature (internal or external) will ever be possible in absolute terms. Freedom will always be exercised within limits, natural and social, which vary according to our capabilities and definite social arrangements.

The systematic rationalized reflective understanding of this manifold process – its 'comprehension' – is therefore not totalization, but part of a 'double hermeneutics' which, in connection and sometimes in tension with it, helps to interpret and constitute one of the meanings history possesses and may contingently prevail in the course of its development. That tension may be somewhat negative if it sets rational standards for the action and movement of individuals and collectivities, which cannot in fact be fulfilled; it may be positive too, insofar as those rational standards spur people on, and especially if intellectuals aid in the translation of those aspirations and yearnings for freedom into hermeneutic and institutional patterns, which may help dreams to come true. As I have argued elsewhere, prospective counterfactual thinking is of overwhelming importance for critical social theory in general and particularly today.[40] How to facilitate the exercise of freedom is in this respect decisive.

We have some sort of cognitive, normative and expressive development; it has at least in some part become institutionally embodied. We cannot however talk of 'regressions' and 'pathologies', contrary to a strong tendency within contemporary German social theory, in which also the concept of 'learning' has become ubiquitous.[41] First because 'reconstructive' approaches are problematic in their intention to establish particular developments, as though there could be a universal yardstick with which to judge whether a development is 'normal' or not. But those terms are pointless too if what is meant is the fulfilment of any sort of the hermeneutic-moral and motivational potential available in modern civilization.[42] As reification theorists, the theorists of power and those of class (today corporate) society have endeavoured to show, there are other potentials and powerful tendencies, inimical to universalism, reflexivity, justice, freedom and equality. This does not mean either that we 'unlearn' anything, since the concept of 'learning process' presupposes that there are forms and contents to be learned at both the philogenetic and the ontogenetic levels. This would obviously suppress contingency, and freedom as a consequence, as a factor in historical development. Once we take contingency and freedom seriously and rigorously, we cannot plainly speak of 'regressions' and 'pathologies' and 'learning', except rhetorically.

In order to describe and theorize this trajectory of freedom, we could think of the decentred teleology of collective subjectivity in the latitudinal and longitudinal dimensions of social life. Holding common, though in several respects differentiated, presuppositions and memories, different types of human collectivities have sustained more or less intentional projects, consistently implying freedom as a leading force. Therefore neither 'objective' nor 'subjective' reason nor rationality is supposed as commanding the course of evolution. Adorno and Horkheimer's explanation for the objective prevalence of subjective reason, which is transformed in an obscure way into systemic formal-instrumental rationality, is questionable in historical terms, whilst Horkheimer's categorial separation between objective and subjective rationality (with him melancholically espousing the former, its historical defeat notwithstanding) insufficient.[43] What I propose here is a historical-contingent appraisal – though possessing evolutionary implications – of the emergence of an intersubjective reflexive process in which freedom as a motivational goal and a hermeneutic element (open to several interpretations) stands out. While that process includes rationalizing reflexivity (that is, systematic moments, in which intellectuals are by and large engaged) it should not be seen as a progression of rationalization that would have an objective character – which is in contrast to Habermas's implicit theory, based on Piaget and Kohlberg, despite his explicit reconstructive intentions.[44] *Freedom has been a contingent creation of the species* (even though it probably rests on some of its anthropological or ontological possibilities) in the course of its individual and collective interactions, leaning upon our reflexive and at times rationalizing faculties. It is not the outcome of an independent, objective development, but the specific result of crossed social processes that have brought transcendence down to earth in modernity (its restricted emergence among the Greeks in antiquity probably being explained by other factors).

Once again it is worth stressing that many other leading motives, sometimes antagonistic to freedom, also played a role in historical development in the same period. Overwhelming evidence can be mustered and a good case made to show that modernity is not committed to the realization of freedom, let alone its coming true. Many other vectors are operative in modern history, which push us towards varied forms of domination and the closure of the historical horizon. In addition, the loss of the historical dimension that features in usual portraits of 'postmodernity' probably makes 'consumer choice' the overwhelming feature of an individualistic and self-cancelling sort of freedom that has abandoned any drive towards transcendence and of a possible future of affairs for which liberty and the transformation of the world would be necessary conditions. *Accommodation* to the world, a sort of adjustment to its conditions, which, contrary to in-world activism, sees no irrationality, disorder or injustice in its constitution – a possibility which Weber explored in his comparative analysis of traditional Chinese Confucian ethic – does dwell with us and may become prevalent.[45] This might even be the case in societies which, in particular it seems in the Iberian American tradition, privilege internal freedom as regards social commandments, entailing therefore a less confrontational, more accommodating attitude which comfortably accepts and leaves the world as it is.[46]

With such caveats and provisos in mind, we can regard the species as a collective subjectivity which is shot through by many movements, causalities and dialectical processes, having, that notwithstanding, the desire for and the pursuit of freedom, at both the individual and the collective level, as outstanding levers of action and movement. The imaginary of freedom, serving as an ingrained social memory that is repeatedly refashioned, decisively contributes to the dreams and aspirations that motivate us today.[47] Once again I feel obliged to repeat that, in the face of power imbalances – due especially to an enormous concentration of power in the hands of corporate 'elites' and state bureaucracy – nothing assures us that it will prevail. It is unlikely, however, that it will not have a worldwide part to play in the near future. It thus appears reasonable to state the paramount importance of that particular value. In this regard the two strands of social theory revised above share the same sources, the same cultural background. In fact they are not merely witnesses to the desire for freedom. More than that, by means of a double hermeneutics they have decisively – and often intentionally, although other moves such as Heidegger's attempted allegiance with Nazism run against this – contributed to the unfolding of that broad decentred historical teleology of freedom, either affirming it or denouncing the limits modernity's in-built dynamic implied for the fulfilment of its own promises. I consider this a crucial source of critical theory in this new twenty-first century, as it was formerly as well.

If the social theories of the eighteen and nineteenth centuries – which were also the theories of the twentieth century – were connected to a considerable extent to the value of freedom, they were so in several ways. Whereas liberals usually stressed the desire for freedom by individuals (either in 'negative' terms as freedom *from* or in 'positive' terms as freedom *to*) having recourse to Hegel's syllogism of the general, the particular and the singular, Marx linked that liberal motive to the working class as the universal collectivity that would eventually be able to bring the realm of freedom down to earth. As pointed out above, the association of 'free producers' would finally open history to humankind's own creative endeavours. If Marx's project is patently exhausted, by both internal flaws and the changes in social life which have made the working class by no means an irrelevant collectivity but certainly not the almighty one he had foreseen, the same is probably true of liberalism. Moreover it cannot even realize for most individuals the 'negative freedom' it once promised, except within quite restricted bounds. Beyond theoretical arguments and the failure of socialism as we have practically known it, the actual misery of much of the global liberal world is plain to see after more than two centuries of institutional implementation. We need therefore to move beyond that stage, breaking free from the double bind of liberal and Marxist limitations.

This means that we need to mobilize the imagination to challenge the institutional arrangements that prevail in our societies and the cultural patterns that set avenues for motivation and social relationships. Political and economic institutions prevent us, at least most people even in advanced modern societies (let alone the periphery), from being really free to make use of the freedom which the contingent ways of life into which we are thrown today offer us, since power differentials and insecurity are such a pervasive feature of most people's life. Furthermore the absolutization of those institutions implies the denial of our collective freedom (and responsibility) in the face of history. As I will suggest later on in this book, especially in part 4, the concept of collective subjectivity may offer some clues as to how to imagine new institutional arrangements, which may moreover foster a synergy with the hermeneutic and motivational dimensions of society.

Let me conclude this chapter with what may appear to be an exhortation, but is in fact a troubling doubt. In modernity, as I have suggested, we are either free creatively to imagine and try out more fulfilling ways of life or we are not free at all. Admittedly we can give up on this creative attitude. This will not make us less 'authentic', although this choice, at least for many of us at this stage, probably hinges to some extent on 'bad faith'. It will make us, however, less free in political and economic terms, and also in those domains in which we like to think of ourselves as 'reflexive' and experimental. The theories of reification have certainly overplayed the overwhelming power of (instrumental) rationalization, while most of them have already tended to forget imbalances of power. Yet they still have, unfortunately, much to teach us about the limits to freedom in contemporary modern society. The phenomena they describe and theorize do not belong to the past, remaining paramount in the structuration of the whole of our lives. At present we accept either the confinement of freedom into specific domains or its excessively narrow realization, and in some cases even its demise. If the argument of this chapter makes sense and freedom is to continue to stimulate our lives and thinking – with great urgency geared towards institutional dimensions – there is hope that a virtuous circle can be established and that this new century will not end with a taste of defeat as bitter as the last one did. Of course, this may be so, provided that freedom does not lose its meaning and thus its grip on our imagination and yearnings, whereby it would become just a gloss for all kinds of arbitrary and authoritarian behaviours and habits, rules and legislation.

Part 2

Equality

3 • Citizenship and Equality

Equality and History

We have seen that the modern concept of freedom originally presupposed, in its unified and exclusive form, and in its refusal of domination and privilege, the equality of all subjects, of all the actors involved. Equality has therefore already been brought to the fore to some extent. We will grapple now specifically with it and its negative counterpart, inequality, which cuts across the dimensions of class, race, gender, ethnic, national and many other forms of stratification of collectivities. Equality is expressed best nowhere else than in the underlying structure of modern law and the legal-rational state – in particular of course in the concept of citizenship. Our cognitive and normative attitudes towards other people, mainly within existing nation-states, are filtered in considerable measure by this general and abstract notion; even expressively equality has played an increasingly important part, especially due to its multiple meaning (which has lost some of its teeth) and in societies which still strive to build a more effective citizenship. I will argue, however, by resuming the concept of re-embedding, that especially for the expressive construction of personal and collective identity it appears to be excessively abstract and thin. There is a close connection between citizenship and freedom, rights and autonomy: we can attribute to the first elements in those two pairs an emancipatory aspect.[1] Nonetheless, citizenship can be conceived of at the same time as a reified form of equality, a repressive one even, which has to do with the 'real abstractions' formerly discussed. Throughout this and the following chapters the uneasy position of collective subjectivities vis-à-vis the notion of citizenship will become clear, not by chance connected to those abstractions, albeit sometimes in an obscure way. Strongly voiced in recent debates, *active citizenship* will be dealt with in the next chapter.

All basic rights, which allow for both freedom and equality, are defined in the context of citizenship, which will be therefore presented as an absolutely central category of modernity, both in the imaginary and institutionally. Crucial for a sharper and more ambivalent understanding of citizenship today, 'real abstractions' operate also to disguise inequalities, another crucial feature of modernity, by dismissing the concrete, specific, particular and contextual qualities of individuals and collectivities. Before moving into that I want, however, to consider de Tocqueville's ideas, since he introduced in social theory the idea that historical development implied the unstoppable march of equality. This, in my view, is a serious mistake, as is implicit in the former chapter from a historical perspective as well as in the modern close connection between equality and freedom.

De Tocqueville put a strong emphasis on the concept of equality or the progressive equalization of 'conditions' of social life. For him it was the core of the process of *democratization* in modernity, which he opposed to, or at least understood as threatening, the existence of freedom. His Romantic background entailed a view of history as the unfolding of processes that had an internal logic which would be accomplished by human design; accordingly, the fate of the world – indeed his world, the West – was to become democratic.[2] Therefore, while I have myself stressed that freedom is to a large extent the *telos* of development of modern civilization, he emphasized equality – and as a threat to freedom.

If we think of history as a process with only one and necessary direction, it is inevitable that a choice be made between two possibly exclusive *telos*. But that was not what I claimed as regards freedom. The meaning of history is manifold and its evolutionary unfolding is contingent. Retrospectively one can read freedom or equality as the *telos* of modernity, but that will at most constitute a dubious reconstruction. It is more interesting to devise different forces in this civilizational development, which furthermore possess multiple meanings, accepting that their expressions may be in tension with each other. In any case that was not what happened between equality and freedom in the early hours of modernity; on the contrary they sprang up tightly entangled as the values which orientated the Enlightenment view of social life. Notwithstanding its shortcomings in terms of the connection between negative and positive freedom, even utilitarianism, as already noted, took this for granted. Only later on has liberalism (Constant's ideas and Berlin's book are in this regard exemplary, as much as de Tocqueville's œuvre, albeit for different reasons) clearly separated negative from positive freedom or assumed an 'aristocratic' – indeed anti-democratic – aspect, or at least became distrustful of the 'masses' (opting as a consequence for 'elitist democracy'). Only later also has the left sometimes insisted on equality to the detriment of freedom, foregoing the insights of Marxism, original social democracy, anarchism and other socialist currents. Whether freedom and equality will prevail and move forward hand in hand, or will move connected, but at odds with each other (for instance combining homogenization, 'real abstractions', domination and privileges, a possibility which looms large today) is still to be seen. After all, the future is open, for good or bad.

Even in de Tocqueville's work there are different paths to democracy, as the long-lasting opposition he sustained between England and the United States, each in its own way, and France demonstrates. He expressed a more optimistic view of that process in his first book, which exposed the fundamentals of North American life, where he found a democracy that was not inimical to freedom, problems lurking as a menace notwithstanding. There he found intermediate bodies, which provided social and political life with forms of association and the possibility that the individual interest was 'properly understood'. People were thus directed to public life, hence away from exclusive concerns with privatism.[3] The latter was a permanent menace to freedom and whether that country would in future become a free or an authoritarian society was an open question. Unchecked by the power of freely associated individuals government would degenerate into tyranny, becoming similar to France and its strong, centralized state, which traversed the revolutionary period remaining unaltered from the Old Regime to the Republic.[4]

Two issues may be further detailed here. First, the hypothesis that the greater equality becomes, the more inequality is perceived as unbearable by people – for de Tocqueville the French Revolution came about because peasants had achieved a better and practically more equal status vis-à-vis the aristocracy.[5] This brings out a well-defined and certainly correctly identified mechanism of ongoing 'democratization' of social life as an explanatory factor, although it should not be taken as absolute and implying more than a teleology that hinges directly on how people interpret social life. That is, that bounded *telos* is tied in with the imaginary of modernity and with how it motivates people. It is not dependent upon 'Providence' as de Tocqueville seems sometimes to imply, whatever that might mean.[6] Secondly, more seriously and in contrast to the first issue, is his hypothesis of a link between equality, (bourgeois) privatism and tyranny, and the disappearance of 'public virtue'.[7] This was never substantiated: there is no precise definition of factors and mechanisms (even the meaning of those words is often elusive). One can argue that the history of socialism and the popular struggles of the twentieth century muster evidence in favour of his thesis. This is however both empirically and analytically wanting. Empirically one need only point to, for instance, the development of social democracy and many other popular and democratic struggles, as well as to institutional innovations in the course of the development of modernity; even the history of communism should be treated with greater subtlety. Analytically the previously mentioned argument about the articulation between negative and positive freedom contradicts his point: equality is necessary if freedom is not to be *corrupted* by privilege (as it was in de Tocqueville's nostalgic aristocratic past). It is beyond doubt, however, that privatism is potentially problematic and has been a practical causal factor contributing to the limitation of freedom. Phrased differently, this theme featured in chapter 2. A thorough identification of its causes, however, must wait for later developments in this book.

Rights and Citizenship

Following Cohen we can identify three elements as constituting the concept of citizenship: 'a political principle of democracy' involving 'participation in deliberation and decision making by political equals', which has been dear to civic republicanism; a 'juridical status of legal personhood', including a 'set of legally defined rights', the main preoccupation of liberals; and a 'form of membership' that underpins a 'special tie', affording 'a social status and a pole of identification' that can become 'a rather thick and important identity', generating 'solidarity, civic virtue and engagement', the focus of communitarianism. This provided the 'classical synthesis' of citizenship.[8] I will concentrate now on that juridical status. It has been the actual and to a great extent also imaginary *core* of citizenship, whereby it was institutionalized in modern societies and most people regard themselves in relation to each other and to the state. The last aspect, providing for social solidarity, is also crucial for modern societies, and will be analysed in later chapters. The first one possesses some importance in social practice, but consists much more in an ideal than in a reality – the institutionalization of modern citizenship in particular owes little to it. This does not imply its irrelevance; on the contrary, in part 4

I will attest to its recent expansion and muse over why it has not been a core notion and practice in modern societies.

Bobbio offers a good starting point to discuss citizenship as a juridical status, reconstructing the trajectory of rights historically associated with it. Rejecting the natural law conception of human rights as innate, Bobbio affirms a historical perspective and underlines the fact that they are intimately connected to a modern individualistic conception, with an inversion of priorities from the duties of the subject to the rights of the citizen. The religious wars that heralded the modern era played a decisive role in this, with the claim to the right of resistance against oppression and the right of the individual to some fundamental liberties, originally phrased in the frame of natural rights. The new conception opposed the Aristotelian view of society that presupposed an organic totality wherein the subject occupied positions that in turn defined fundamental rights. In the 'despotic state' individuals have duties and no rights; in the 'absolutist state' they possess private rights in relation to the suzerain. In the 'legal state' the individual, now a citizen, possesses public as well as private rights. But modern rights were not born all at once: civil rights emerged in the struggle of parliaments against absolutist suzerains, political and social rights from popular movements (an issue which has been given short shrift by some writers in the aftermath of the defeat of 'really existing socialism', but must be once again emphasized).[9]

In other words, the passage from an 'organic' to an individualistic conception rested on what Weber called 'rational–legal'[10] domination in the exact sense of imposing – at least in principle – general and impersonal, universalized state laws. These limited the power of the suzerain, initially with respect to the private rights of the individual and, later on, to his public rights. It may still be noted that widespread violence and a situation of permanent warfare, yielded by civil and religious wars, state absolutist authoritarianism, the brutality of the capitalist enclosure movement and disrespect of the traditional feudal rights of peasants, marked European societies just prior to the emergence of such rights discourse and were thus relevant to its inception. The authority of the legal-constitutional state, phrased through an individualistic conception, was an answer to that, in terms of controlling both society and the state.[11] And, while the formulation and the institutionalization of citizenship rested on the notion of rights, it imposed a sort of particular deviant identity that was directly managed, out of the legal system of rights and the contractual social pact, by the penal system: the 'delinquent' – perpetrator of violent acts, now starkly and strongly delimited – should be segregated and kept away from society to a variable degree and for a length of time, as well as submitted to a *quasi*-private discipline. This imposed identity entailed the deprivation of the citizen status.[12] In recent times, as we will have occasion to note, this movement has been dramatically reinforced.

Bobbio completes the analysis of the evolution of rights, hence of citizenship, with three elements: the conversion of the declarations of principle into 'positive rights', their 'generalization' (meaning their multiplication) and, in a much more problematic way (albeit a decisive one, at the level of both conception and discourse, due to its natural law basis), internationalization. Piecemeal 'specification' accompanies those processes. In the transition from the ideals of human rights to citizenship rights, that is, the rights of the members of specific national states, this process of determination was already present, moving further, nevertheless, in the direction of a greater specification in terms of gender, age or phases of life, or with regard to particular and exceptional states of the human species. Whereas civil rights possess what we might call an almost apoditical universality, in their reference and attribution, since they are either general or lose their specific meaning, political rights and especially social rights really share a lack of 'distinction' and 'discrimination'.[13] Everyone is equal with respect to freedom from intrusion of somebody else into the security of one's life and property, including one's labour power and the right to come and go; otherwise privileges of status would be at stake. We surely could bring up problems in relation to this characterization, insofar as the power of the male 'head' of the household (that is, patriarchy) until fairly recently subordinated women and children to the arbitrary will of men.[14] But problems in the development of political citizenship are more salient. The separation especially between 'passive' and 'active' citizens implies the exclusion of the latter from politics, their enjoying of civil rights notwithstanding. The situation of social rights is for Bobbio in any event more confused: although we can speak of three fundamental rights (to work, instruction and health care) it is not clear what is accounted for and legislated about when social rights come into the picture, in particular because differences between people have to be appraised in order for them to be implemented. A crucial distinction vis-à-vis civil rights and even to a large extent political rights appears when we have to grapple with social rights: instead of demanding the limitation of the power of the state it is the latter that lays claim to an active intervention in social life.[15] Bobbio notes that in this case what the Anglo-Saxon tradition somewhat equivocally names *moral rights* face problems of scope and generalization when transformed into positive, *legal rights*.[16] The notion of their universalization becomes questionable.

What exactly is at stake when we speak of social rights? What do we intend to ensure universally in terms of 'human' or 'citizenship' rights with this group of rights? Bobbio's account is influenced, although he lends it a historically orientated inflection, by the continental European juridical tradition, whose bases are rather abstract. Perhaps a more empirical approach, which details the rights of citizenship, will help to clarify some further issues.

Marshall's classical definition of citizenship – which shifted citizenship from the market, its previous main and pre-political point of reference, to the state, still within the conception of rights as a priori, and can be characterized as 'left-wing liberalism'[17] – was extremely influential in the ensuing debate about the topic; it included the three elements of citizenship, each of which emerged at different points in time and successively. For him we have a differentiation of rights whose existence, under very distinct guises, previously implied a fusion and were due to the individual as a consequence of particular status and functions. With their differentiation, specific institutions were established, which guaranteed, respectively: freedom and equal legal status for individuals among themselves and vis-à-vis the state; increasing open political participation, beyond the restricted franchise based on rent and exclusion that marked its beginnings; and finally the right to a 'modicum of economic welfare and security' and to take full part in the 'social heritage' and lead the life of a 'civilized being' according to prevailing standards in society.[18] From the point of view of the economy the first basic civil right was that to work, which freed the individual from duties based on custom, regarding the place where it should be carried out and the very definition of the labour that should be exercised, breaking also the subjection of the worker to personal relations of subordination. From their very beginnings freedom and citizenship were identical in the cities; through nationalization the close link between them was intensified. Hence a universal 'status' was established (although we must emphasize that for a long time the situation of women within the family remained quite unequal) in contrast to the differentiated status of the feudal period.[19] Alongside processes of differentiation, social *de-differentiation* in some dimensions was, I would like to add, crucial for the emergence of modernity. Citizenship is a conspicuous case of these modern processes of de-differentiation.[20] The history of political rights is more complicated, since their appearance and generalization were piecemeal: at first they were the privilege of the most powerful groups alone. Franchise was related to a threshold of rent or the possession of property, which supposedly allowed for a reflective and independent use of reason. At that stage political rights were seen as a mere derivation of civil rights. Nobody was, in principle, excluded from their exercise, but people had to fulfil those prerequisites of rent and property. Only later were women included as well.

Formerly the participation in local communities gave the individual prerogatives of assistance. Those forms of assistance were by and large substituted by the belief that individuals, once freed from the clutches of feudal relations, would be capable of sorting out their own lives (even the Poor Law and later systems, which in Britain regulated social assistance, were thought out in opposition to the concept of citizenship, since they tended to exclude precisely adult males). Step by step, however, labour legislation, state education, pensions and other social rights were consolidated as fundamental elements of citizenship, now in its social dimension. Thereby *the citizenship status is complete and universalized, and starts to entertain a tense relationship with class stratification.* While citizenship implies social equality, class conjures up inequalities, and the divergent development in capitalism has led to a growing tension between these two principles of organization of social life, although, on the other hand, class cultures per se take a long time to lose previous specificities.[21]

But this has happened only in a second moment, insofar as civil rights were crucial for the establishment of capitalism. In fact it was civil freedom that made it possible for *contract* to substitute for the unequal status system of feudal society (also based on a sort of contract, but between unequals). It is important to note as well that rights are seen in liberalism as a 'zone of discretion of the rightholder' – the paradigm here is property rights – whereby immunity and freedom from domination would be achieved. This placed rights at odds with communal life and the concreteness of social relations and collective endeavours.[22] Conversely the emergence of political rights conveyed a potential threat to capitalism to the extent that it allowed for the ascension of the working classes and their collective struggles, pointing to social rights. Moreover rights now took on a collective dimension – initially articulated to the juridical acknowledgement of unions as collective agents.[23] In fact some go as far as to identify social rights with 'industrial democracy'.[24] In any case this move represented a harsh blow to the individualistic concept of civil rights and the idea that only individuals were philosophically and legally capable of enacting contracts – it assumed a collective dimension through the action and formal recognition of workers' unions.

It is interesting that Marshall also attributes to distinct centuries the emergence of diverse clusters of rights, with a logic according to which they seem to unfold from one another.[25] For several authors this lends his piece a problematic evolutionary slant, which is further accentuated in the explicitly evolutionary utilization of his work, although even those who are critical of his understanding of historical developments only partly contradict the logic of his text when they focus on societies where the succession of citizenship rights was different to that of Britain and Europe overall.[26]

A difficulty stands out in Marshall's conception, though, directly linked to the definition of social rights. In comparison with the precise and concise definition of civil and political rights, that received by social rights is patently sloppy and strewn, mobilizing elements whose articulation is not immediately clear. Even more important is the extent to which they possess a universal character and must be furthermore attributed to the collectivity or individuals. Despite sometimes permitting individuals to have monetary gains due to some rights, the main deed of social rights was to free real income from nominal income, since services provided by the state increase the former without growth of the latter. In a precise sense either the state adds something to nominal income or guarantees a number of basic goods and services. There are however three factors which define in which measure equality is made effective through these provisions: whether the benefit is offered to all or just to a specific group; if it assumes the form of a payment in money or of a service; and how resources are collected to afford the benefit. Marshall treats in detail the first and the third questions, noting that benefits subject to means-tested schemes have an egalitarian effect which is manifest straight away, for they increase the income of only those who are placed under a certain threshold. But they also provoke discrimination and stigma. Brushing them aside has the effect of raising the income of those who are already better off and can now count on universalized benefits. That notwithstanding, he adds that we must take into account that the expansion of social services (which is also the case of social benefits) does not aim to equalize *rent* above everything: the main goal of social policies is to promote the enrichment of the substance of civilized life in general, the reduction of insecurity and risk, a certain levelling of the better-off and the worse-off; in sum, the fundamental question is *equality of status*. Moreover the quantitative aspect of benefits handed down as services recedes; it is now the *qualitative* aspect of citizenship that matters and what come to the fore are legitimate claims to it, with the demand for better services being strengthened. This, however, entails a problem Marshall mentions only en passant: growing and, preferably progressive, tax burdens – although, on the other hand, individual rights become more subordinated to a general plan which is never entirely capable of satisfying demands.[27]

After this general assessment of citizenship, let us consider two specific issues. The first refers to the 'principle of equity', which has been strongly stressed more recently and according to which equals should be treated equally and unequals unequally (although the term has often been used simply as justice or fairness or as synonymous with equality). It may be seen as consisting in a refinement of justice, but can take a very conservative guise once we accept established patterns and try to sort out only anomalies, inconsistencies and incoherences. Of course equity fits well together with means-tested schemes and may be mixed, as is usually the case with social policies, with more universal strategies. But it is in my view definitely deleterious to citizenship and works as a way to preserve large-scale social inequalities if it assumes a central position in social welfare – as is usually the case with liberal, 'residual' regimes, to make use of a category that will be introduced below. It is not by chance that it features prominently in neoliberal policies today (mainly in those of the World Bank in conjunction with relief and compensatory programmes targeted to the poor). Conversely, it is seemingly necessary in numerous cases – such as in terms of women and racially or ethnically discriminated collectivities – when there is need to remain simultaneously different and achieve equality, demanding therefore a particularized and focused treatment.[28]

Also holding centre stage here we find the problem of a reasonable balance between individual and collective rights, since social goods are always scarce (and in this regard we may adduce that it is very unlikely that there will ever be a society in which some level of scarcity, in some spheres at least, will not be present). Marshall suggests moreover that they become scarcer insofar as their variety and quality increase. Phrased in different terms, it is the question of the universalization of social policies that re-emerges. First it is worth noting that at this stage the minimal rights and basic patterns of citizenship (the 'modicum' of welfare) which underlay Marshall's initial definition of social rights have been displaced – his definition can be moreover interpreted in a minimalist way, given that those rights are heterogeneous, imprecise, and given also that there are distinct historical possibilities for satisfying them. Is it necessary to see only in the state the agency which must ensure, generally and in this case 'collectively', provisions for the needy (for instance in the case of habitation, a scarce and expensive good) and for the most capable (in the case, for instance, of higher education), when the right to equality of opportunity plays a decisive role? Or is the goal to provide for all, as an individual right, those goods conceived of as a universal right of the citizen? One of the main problems of Marshall's proposals appears here, since he calls for a 'fair balance' between the collectivity and the individual, but does not thoroughly examine how the issue should be translated in terms of social policy. He seems concretely to admit only inequalities that are neither hereditary nor dynamic – that is, which can be overcome by the individual once he or she is given conditions to do so.[29] In any case it is important to stress that it is clear that Marshall remains within the bounds of the traditional presuppositional universe of modernity and presents the collectivity – usually embodied in the state – and the individual as the poles of social thinking and policy. The fact that his notion of 'collective rights' is underdetermined only helps to compound the problem rather than solve it. It is curious to observe that his emphasis on the state and individuals – which has prevailed in the construction of the welfare state in Britain and elsewhere – runs counter to strong trends within British socialism, as well as to those which flourished in other countries, which stress *collective, cooperative* mobilization to overcome poverty and inequality.[30] *Intermediate collective subjectivities* had pride of place in those alternative conceptions; this is by no means the case in Marshall's plan, although he helped to introduce *solidarity*, as a (rather passive) connection between all citizens of a national society, at the level of social rights, as a key issue for mature modernity. I will return to this in part 3, as well as in part 4.

It is now instructive to enquire again about what welfare social policies really aim at, in the context of a definition of citizenship which – despite tensions and provisos, expansions and adumbrated solutions – is carved out by an individualistic worldview. As seen above, civil and political rights were originally based on notions that stemmed from modern, post-Aristotelian natural law. They referred exclusively to the individual and, rigorously taken, excluded the social aspect. Freedom was ensured to the subject of law – the natural individual, however socialized through the pact it had woven with other individuals; that was his possession from the beginning and the formation of society was intended only as a means for its conservation. Social rights were introduced with the view that it was necessary to remedy the evils society per se generated. That has made the subject of law an uncertain, somewhat obscure figure, especially in the definition of social rights as 'collective rights'. Underlying this conundrum one idea has played an important, though not exclusive role: the autonomy of the subject is enforced only insofar as social contexts allow for it – state functions should therefore be geared towards the establishment of that context.[31] What is the target of social policies? Who is the subject of law in such coordinates? What does it mean to transform 'moral rights', in Bobbio's terms, into 'positive rights'? How can the access to 'civilized social life', to resume Marshall's point, be guaranteed? Should we rest content to see rights basically in historical terms, giving up an attempt at conceptual systematization? I will try to work something theoretically in this regard later on, in terms of interpretation and explanation.

Let me for the moment just note that the welfare state assumed different forms and can be described according to a threefold typology: liberal (residual and following means-tested schemes), corporatist (based on work merit) and universalistic (which some would deem the sole one truly committed to citizenship). The United States exemplifies the first, although Britain is increasingly inclined towards it; Germany embodies the second (as in part do Italy and France); and the third has the Scandinavian countries as its main expression.[32] It is possible to state that the first, liberal model – and in a minimalist sense – has become dominant in 'Latin' America (after a period during which corporatism prevailed, through a model of 'regulated citizenship', notably in Brazil, and a pattern of 'cooptation-repression' vis-à-vis social movements).[33] A proviso must however be added: this must be understood as merely a typology, since most regimes are a combination of diverse principles that in this classification appear only in pure form.[34] It is interesting to stress that the universalistic criteria of citizenship as rights pertaining to any individual come up only in relation to the universalistic regime, with strong state intervention and the definition of the collectivity and *solidarity* at the nation-state level. Yet, if 'collective' rights, however fuzzy their definition (but all in all collective in the sense of ensuring generalizable outcomes with unevenly distributed means), are recalled to mind, the situation is immediately altered. Be that as it may, if there are different ways to view social rights in conceptual terms, pragmatically a key problem is to be reckoned with: in order to assure that entitlements and services are universally available they must be generous and attractive, otherwise there will be incentives for the most well-off to look for solutions in the private market.

But there is another, somewhat different way of seeing the issue. Capitalism and the modern state rely on a separation between private and public, and on the insulation of politics from the economy (although Keynesianism and the welfare state changed this to some extent). Especially in the private economic terrain, individual freedom, an untouchable principle of the modern order, is therefore secured. Everyone may do what pleases himself and must bear the consequences of his choices. If modernity promised increasing domination over nature and exponential production of wealth, it was presumed that, insofar as the individual was willing to prosper and made efforts in such a direction, she would succeed, this hinging also of course on natural personal endowment.[35]

The privatization and individualization of existence have thus consisted in two pillars of the legitimacy of modernity. They were questioned once it became clear that domination was not confined to nature, instead cutting across and contaminating society as a whole, since capitalism and social classes reintroduced it (racial problems and gender division being added later on). Beyond philanthropy, two far-reaching solutions were outlined: either revolution or social citizenship. The former would bring the realm of freedom to all in a definite and thorough manner, ridding us of domination and allowing for the fruition of the end of scarcity;[36] bowing to the power of capitalism, the latter searched – and searches – for a compromise capable of broadening the sphere of freedom without challenging head on the system of domination and inequality. This arrangement is, at best, unstable and can be undone at any moment. This is what has happened in recent decades and it is not yet known how to have it re-established, given the mutations of modernity during that period, which I will analyse in later chapters. Without reference to citizenship equality fragments in disconnected and discrete 'spaces', being reduced to mere 'equity' and articulated to small 'freedoms' that do not oppose domination. That is what comes up in Sen's approach, in spite of its obvious generosity, and in attempts at poverty reduction that lean on his outlook, which are typical of the present blend of globalization and neoliberalism.[37] This threatens the very idea of the unity of freedom and its wholesale rejection of domination, turning equality into a plurality of possibilities whose relationships are not clear and exhausting it in a pursuit of a relative levelling out of goods, resources, empowerments, 'rights', entitlements, etc.

The complicated connection of citizenship with solidarity and its present prospects will be taken up in part 3. I want now to examine precisely that aspect of equality which Bobbio himself – when he speaks of 'negative freedom, the first right acknowledged and defended' – sees as pertaining to 'abstract man'.[38] This includes the whole system of citizenship rights, though, in this case contrary to his opinion, since he also notes that when dealing with social rights we cannot help taking into account the 'specific differences' which are relevant to distinguish individuals or, to put it more precisely, 'a group of individuals from another'.[39] This is indeed true; I will however argue that real abstractions are crucial to understanding social rights, and will try to outline an original perspective in this regard.

4 • Inequalities and Real Abstractions

Citizenship and Inequalities

Citizenship offers an abstract way of defining agents, primarily as individuals who do not possess specific characteristics which would be in principle relevant for this central category of the system of rights, although qualifications have been introduced piecemeal in its phrasing and workings. Before delving into the concept of 'real abstractions' and its connections with citizenship a counterpoint to the world of citizenship and its basic principle of equality is necessary, so as to evince the dialectical tensions already pointed out with respect to all main imaginary and institutional categories of modernity. Inequalities will come to the fore in the paragraphs below. Thus the social life underling abstract citizenship rights will be emphasized. Having laid these foundations I will return to conceptual matters related to 'real abstractions', as theorized by Marx, Lukács and the Frankfurt School; the analysis of a crucial work of contemporary political philosophy, Rawls's *A Theory of Justice*, will help to specify this concept and its workings in modernity. I will then resume the concepts of disembedding and re-embedding developed in part 1 of this book to close my main analysis of the development of equality, inequality and citizenship. Rather than to commodity it is to citizenship that I will link 'real abstractions' – an innovative step in the utilization of this concept in critical theory. This will be done not in terms of its genesis, but thanks to the central role of articulation it plays in modern social formations. The postulation that 'real abstractions' originated in modernity in direct connection with citizenship is not what is put forward here. The genesis of modernity can be understood only in terms of multicausality and its multiple roots. Citizenship, however, is crucial for the imaginary and institutional establishment of modernity, since individualism, the market, the modern state and a whole series of other institutional and imaginary elements depend on it to operate, although the opposite is to some extent true. Even modern social inequalities, as seen with recourse to Marshall's work, depend on the institutionalization of civil rights, the founding aspect of citizenship.

Social inequalities are rampant in contemporary social life in all spheres: internationally between nations and regions, between ethnic groups, classes, (socially constructed) races, genders, between sexually orientated collectivities (although it is unlikely that we would always find a correlation between wealth or income and sexual orientation). Moreover equality cannot develop exclusively through citizenship. Regardless of how juridified social life has increasingly become, in personal domains and relationships, in the household, in cultural life, patterns of marriage and consumption, wealth and income are not always amenable to intervention by the state. Justice is a much wider issue than can be regulated by law. There is no legislation capable of compelling men to share equally the upbringing of children and domestic work, for instance. Much of contemporary cultural struggles around post-colonialism and anti-racism bypass issues of rights; although there are no established frontiers in this regard, as the contests around curricula show, those struggles concentrate on wrongs and identity – it is another face of the struggle for recognition that comes into play, as will be seen in a later chapter. Let me concentrate now on one particular issue which has not been especially favoured in recent debates in social theory: inequalities between classes, emphasizing the concept of 'real abstractions'. That is not to say that class inequalities – which in their modern form are linked to moral individualism, that is, emphasize the empirical individual subject as the fundamental unity of society in terms of both being and ought to be – are exclusive in modern societies. In fact, varying from society to society, this combination of social classes and individualism may be associated with other logics that organize the hierarchization of social relations and the social space. Hence these two models may concretely work 'as alternative symbolic orders, at times complementary, at times contradictory'.[1] In Brazil and possibly in 'Latin' America overall, although surely also in Europe and North America, this actually happens. Be that as it may, social classes in the way specified (bringing together inequality and individualism) turn up in modernity as a universal form of stratification, and it is upon them that I will therefore dwell in what follows. In addition, it must be noted that I refer here to social inequalities – that is, discarding those which stem from natural attributes. On the other hand, a usual confusion must be prevented: social differentiation (to be treated in part 3) and social inequality are distinct phenomena, which do not presuppose nor complement each other, contrary to what is sometimes stated.[2]

Marx's theory of social classes, featuring mainly the bourgeoisie and the working class, needs to be updated so as to describe accurately contemporary capitalism, a step taken by a number of authors in the 1960s and the 1970s, resulting in theories of 'corporate' or 'managerial' capitalism;[3] all in all, in its conceptual pillars, I regard it, to a great extent, as correct. Marxist accounts of class could therefore be used to support the developments I venture now. Let me choose another way of approaching the subject, though, so as to introduce inequality as the institutional counterpoint to equality in modernity. Inequality pertains also to the modern imaginary, however less explicitly, similarly to domination, which is always camouflaged. It must be emphasized that thereby domination is back in the frame, not as 'rationalization' *tout court*, but as resting on the more or less direct relations between social classes and other collectivities, namely, race, ethnic and gender stratification, to keep to a minimal listing of the most prominent ones at present, though new forms of inequality such as those related to knowledge and information should also be emphasized.[4]

The following discussion of classes draws upon Bourdieu. This simultaneously allows for and requires a discussion of the space–time dimension of social systems, which features outstandingly in his rendering of social inequalities. This will lead us directly to similar problems in Rawls's conception of the 'original position', which is initially past orientated and then becomes atemporal, overlooking concrete inequalities. Key issues related to the abstract character of citizenship will thereby come to the fore.

The identities people assume in modernity – through what was formerly theorized in this book with the concept of 're-embedding' – can in principle be neutral in regard to equality and inequality. However, they are likely to be somehow entangled with the stratification of society. Thus adopting a religious creed does not in principle entail commitment to any sort of position in the social hierarchy, although sometimes, for concrete reasons, this happens to be the case. Adopting class or gender, racial or ethnic identities frequently means, on the other hand, the acceptance, apology for or struggle against social hierarchies. Bourdieu has shown that brilliantly in *Distinction*, where he brings out the struggles for the classification of the 'social space', the strategies which the upper layers of society employ in order to keep their symbolic power and privileged position, as well as the, not always direct, possibilities of converting aspects of one's 'capital' (symbolic, material, political, social, etc.) into different aspects of power. Notwithstanding Bourdieu's imperfect and merely descriptive notion of 'capital', his contribution is very interesting in that it shows how people find their concrete places and identities in modern societies. For him the social space is highly hierarchized and consists in a field of struggles:

> In order to take account more completely of the differences of life style between the different fractions [of the upper classes] – above all in terms of culture – it is necessary to pay attention to their distribution in a socially hierarchized geographical space. Indeed the chances that a group may have of appropriating a given class of rare goods . . . depend on one side on its specific capabilities of appropriation, defined by the economic, cultural and social capital it can put to work to appropriate the goods under consideration, materially and/or symbolically, that is, on its position in the social space; and on the other side on the relationship between its distribution in that. . . . In other words, the actual social distance of a group regarding goods must integrate the geographical distance that depends itself on the distribution of the group within the space and, more precisely, on its distribution with respect to the 'focus of values', economic and cultural . . .[5]

I have elsewhere discussed how much the modern notion of social space, one that was until recently absolute and is as yet dominant in sociology, owed to Newtonian physics and its notion of a homogeneous space, which was separated from (an equally homogeneous) time. Therein discrete actors – that is, individuals in Hobbes's classical, pristine formulation of the problem which took hold of the modern mind – acted as atomic particles coming across one another in complete independence.[6] This view shares entirely the abstract conception of human beings and nature that was typical of the Enlightenment, along with that of time. They have furnished some of the a priori categories of reason, to recall Kant's view, or the 'parametric variables', according to Parsons,[7] which have in the imaginary as well as in some measure practically (insofar as they have helped to organize the world) framed the lives of those abstract beings who have become known as modern citizens. I have proposed also a different way of looking at this topic, whereby we must couple time and space, following modern tendencies in physics, in connection with Einstein's Theory of Relativity and Minkowski's further developments. Time thus becomes a dimension of space, whereby the latter comes to be seen as possessing four, instead of three, dimensions. Moreover, and this is a decisive step, space–time coordinates lose their homogeneous and universal character, both in the natural and the social dimensions, acquiring specific conformations and rhythms according to their regional existence and dynamics. This insight buttresses the use of Bourdieu's thesis, despite his usually structuralist talk of positions rather than relations between collectivities (a strategy that makes his 'relationalism' problematic) and a metaphorical rather than a conceptual notion of the social space. The social space may be therefore comprehended as a particular dimension of social systems, which is therefore crafted by various actions of individuals and movements of collective subjectivities, but which has class distinctions and struggles shaping concrete space–time coordinates that possess particular features, conformations and rhythms.

This allows me to suggest that two forms of imaginary and institutional organization of the space and time of modernity are operative. One of them is expressed in the model Bourdieu critically presents; the other, in the abstract form through which individualist citizenship covers social life. That is, whereas the space and time of citizenship are homogeneous – and, as we will see, time for it dwelt in the past, at least in civil and political terms – the space–time of social classes and collectivities overall, of specific, concrete identities and institutions, evinces plenty of concrete particularities of conformation and rhythm, of hermeneutic densities, affective investments, power relations and struggles, of material interchanges. We must always bear inequalities in mind: in modernity they consist in the other face of citizenship, that is, of formal equality. With the institutional features of 'really existing modernity' qua basically and unavoidably class societies, we cannot think of one without staring at the face of the other, unless we prefer to buy into ideological delusions. That said, though, I must warn the reader at this stage that it is not my intention to throw the baby out with the bath water. The abstract character of citizenship has enormous advantages and has brought many benefits to those subject to it. This is how, for instance, I am inclined to read Alexander when he tries to bring out how civil society generates itself and, in relation with other social systems, its own 'uncivil' or 'anti-civil' aspects, and how nevertheless its expansion in one way or another incorporates formerly excluded groups. This is, however, a real dynamic, which is opposed to an idealized vision of civil society as inserted in abstract space and time: concretely the space and time (or, as I prefer, the space–time) of civil societies include stratifications and exclusions which have only slowly been overcome or at least lessened in modernity.[8]

Abstraction, Inequality and Power

Rawls's account of justice offers a particularly important specimen of mainstream modern thought and can be of great help in further developing the problems presented above. In what follows I confine myself to the essentials of Rawls's argument and to what is here of direct interest. The counterpoint between equality and inequality will be deepened, and how the outline of the latter is clouded by abstractions will be brought out. Against the backdrop of Rawls's argument I will be able to resume the relationship between equality and power.

Let us start with his depiction of the original position. It turns out that, although he places himself squarely in the contractarian position, there is nothing in his approach really left from the natural law tradition in which that is rooted, except a strongly individualistic a priori. Rawls states 'that the original position is a purely hypothetical situation', not to be expected in real life. It merely accounts for our moral judgements and sense of justice, providing an 'analytic method', according to the 'procedure' of the contract theories.[9] Objective 'circumstances of justice' (cf. Hume) are those which render cooperation between people 'possible and necessary', featuring persons with 'roughly similar' 'physical and mental power', who are vulnerable and live under conditions of 'moderate scarcity'. While our endeavours always fall short of yielding absolutely satisfactory results, they are usually 'mutually advantageous'. The 'subjective' aspect is introduced by his definition of people sharing 'similar needs and interests' – or these being 'in various ways complementary', although claims to resources are usually conflicting. Moreover, although people are not strictly egoistic, Rawls assumes that they are aloof to one another's interests, a point – untenable in concrete circumstances – introduced to avoid strong moral assumptions unduly capable of tipping the balance towards an a priori conception of, say, solidarity.

This does not fit well with his assumption about the actors of the model as 'heads of family' who uphold some sort of interest in the destiny of their offspring (which would obviously entail a more encompassing conception of responsibility than is compatible with his hypothesis of mutual aloofnsess). He curiously sorts out this problem by modifying the 'motivation assusmption' and making the 'original position' timeless (or rather time becomes entirely abstract therein).[10] Moreover, not only is his theory 'abstract' in the sense of eschewing concrete aspects of social life: he consistently avoids the sphere of production too, sticking to justice as distribution.[11]

Whereas those 'circumstances', while not exactly concrete, still possess some flesh, his further depiction of the 'original position' is even more disembodied (claiming now the company of Kant): the very disembodiment of the position is what underlies the 'autonomy' of the subject.[12] In fact I would like to suggest that Rawls's argument as a whole depends on two *epochés*: first, in logical terms, on that which leads, due to the 'veil of ignorance', to a conception of individuals without interests and qualities in the original position; secondly, on that which gives pride of place to the principle of 'equal liberty' to the relative detriment of social equality. In the first case Rawls's bracketing off of concreteness is carried out in order to underpin his 'pure procedural justice'. The 'effects of specific contingencies' that bring about conflicts and opportunistic inclinations must be 'nullified'. Under the 'veil of ignorance' men have no knowledge of their actual situation in society and their more or less privileged position, even of the actual conditions of society, nor of their natural talents and capabilities, and their own personality. They must decide, making use of all possible general knowledge about social life and human psychology, which principles must govern their common life. Those principles can hence be evaluated 'solely on the basis of general considerations'. Thus 'no one is in a position to tailor principles to his advantage' and rationality is not allowed to cross over to narrowly defined egoism. Thereby Rawls wants to keep utilitarianism, with which he shares so many presuppositions, at bay. Besides, since, as will be seen in a moment, great disparities do not follow from the contract at stake, envy should not be ascribed to highly abstract 'theoretically defined individuals'.[13] If Husserl was after a disembodied mind in order to solve the problems of the modern Cartesian spirit in terms of knowledge, Rawls searches for disembodied persons in order to rescue the beset citizen of politically traditional modernity.

A charitable interpretation would suggest that Rawls is proposing almost a 'thought experiment' (however akin to game theory and its similarly abstract players); general principles of justice for a liberal social democratic state could be derived from this. But more problematic is his second *epoché*, which comes before the first one in the book's exposition. At this point he is working at a somewhat less abstract level, focusing on the liberties of 'equal citizenship' and the common system of justice that regulates their living together. He wants to discuss exclusively the 'basic structure of society' (regardless of how 'vague' he accepts this notion to be) in terms of rights, duties and advantages.[14] His argument moves in several (at times apparently incompatible) directions, but he spends a good deal of time trying to ensure that 'equal liberty' is given priority over 'equality of conditions' – something that he for instance phrases with recourse to a 'serial' or 'lexical order', which is similar to the notion of 'cybernetic hierarchy'. According to that order '[a] principle does not come into play until those previous to it are fully met or do not apply'. There is no need thereby to balance the two principles he singles out for his theory of justice:[15]

> First: each person is to have an equal right to the most extensive basic liberty compatible with a similar liberty for others.
> Secondly: social and economic inequalities are to be arranged so that they are both (a) reasonably expected to be to everyone's advantage, and (b) attached to positions and offices open to all.[16]

Whereas Rawls attributes to the first principle the main elements, the 'basic rights' of what I have called the civil aspect of citizenship (political liberty, freedom of speech and assembly, of conscience and thought, security of property and in relation to the state under the rule of law) he admits the ambiguities which abound in the second principle. But he is more interested in the argument of the 'serial' priority of the first principle over the second, an ordering which, despite the length of the book, is never in fact discussed in any detail, apart from several passages of, in my view, not very persuasive rhetoric.[17] It is taken for granted as a basic condition of modern citizenship, its basic right, and he assumes also implicitly that the first principle is always under threat by the second as such, and never due to its (that is, the second's) incomplete realization. The furthest he goes is to stress that inequalities are to be accepted only to the extent that they are 'to everyone's advantage'. If that is not the case, we have 'injustice', which can be defined simply as 'inequalities that are not to the benefit of all'. The 'difference principle' allows for less indeterminacy in the balance between those first two principles, insofar as it affirms the necessity of better prospects for the worse-off if something is to be carried out that is to the advantage of the better-off.[18]

All things considered, it seems clear enough that Rawls is able to perform a curious operation in fact typical of much of, say, 'progressive' post-Marxist liberalism. He attacks 'unjust' social inequalities, which turn up at the most concrete (however still highly abstract) level of his theory. They have however been to a great extent neutralized beforehand by his lexical, never argued, ordering of the principles of justice. Abstract citizens are thus logically prior to concrete 'men' (and women!) in situations of concrete social inequality and social hierarchy. They are also politically and practically prior to concrete persons since the conception of justice must orientate our institution-building undertakings. Even prior to that people are – absolutely disembodied and abstract – in the 'original position'. Rawls thereby sets the stage for a tight coupling between formal equality and actual inequality, tipping the balance, despite his democratic inclinations, explicitly and intentionally in favour of the latter. At this point his arguments look specious since he never offers any justification for his main contention in terms of justice. As indicated in chapters 1 and 2, freedom is to be thought of only in connection with equality. Concrete inequalities represent privileges in terms of capabilities and therefore distortions in the very principle Rawls is at pains to uphold – equal liberty. I do not want to suggest that this can be completely levelled out. However, the main institutions of society must be orientated to an overcoming of inequalities in order to make freedom equally possible to everyone. Whether this can be accomplished within the institutional settings of modernity is a different issue. Suffice to say now that Rawls manages to bring together both particular life situations and socially uneven positions and what will be analysed in a moment as 'real abstractions' – placing the latter in a paramount position. His atemporal definition of time is moreover decisive for that, as it is in general for citizenship, allowing for abstracting the concrete social space–time that is cut across by deep-seated inequalities.

Rawls's position also clashes with other ways of conceiving liberalism. For instance it is inimical to the contention that, if equality is to be ascertained in the political dimension, there is no reason why it should not receive the same treatment at the economic level.[19] Finally it foregoes the fundamental question that so crucially has lingered in the memory of political philosophy since Aristotle's day, regardless of its repression today, namely, which social arrangements are best for making the best citizen?[20] Rawls accepts the possibility of distinct economic structures, whether 'property owning democracy' or 'liberal socialism', both market orientated, insofar as this is better suited to securing liberty;[21] yet he never poses the question of whether we should think that equality is to be taken on an equal footing with freedom so that this interrogation might be properly answered. It could be claimed that equality is compatible with dictatorship and authoritarianism in general; a conservative reading of de Tocqueville easily lends itself to such conclusions. The landscape acquires different contours, though, if we sustain a general conception of equality and apply it to all social spheres, including the polity as well as the economy and other domains, such as the family. Equality is a condition of freedom for all. Otherwise we return to a pre-modern conception of freedom as privilege, which is indeed what we find in many spheres of contemporary social life. No attempt at differentiating 'freedom as equal liberty' from the 'worth of liberty'[22] can be taken seriously in this regard.

This is clear if we elaborate on the concept of freedom as capability, resuming what was preliminarily introduced in chapter 1. As Giddens noted, power is a concept that can be understood in two ways: either as the capability of an actor to achieve what he or she wants, even against resistance from somebody else; or as a property of the collectivity. Giddens upholds an integration of both approaches, although evidently favouring the former as regards the conceptualization of action. He then renders the capability to act, to 'make a difference' through the idea of a 'transformative capacity', while its relational aspect is phrased by means of the traditional expression 'power', to refer to 'transformational capacity' when geared to getting the compliance of other actors, a Hobbesian–Weberian heritage in terms of social thought.[23] This may in fact allow us to bring that individualistic definition of power closer to the alternative proposed by Parsons and, more recently, by Mann, who stress its collective character, although in distinct ways – Parsons emphasizing its cohesive aspect, Mann its contribution to the strength of a collectivity, regarding either nature or other collectivities.[24] This is so insofar as we think of the *collective transformative capacities* (in terms of 'movement', though not exactly of 'action') of collective subjectivities in the face of the natural 'environment' or in their relationship with other social systems. It should be borne in mind that Weber had precisely defined 'power' as the 'possibility' (*Chance*) of bringing about willed states of affairs even against the 'resistance' of others, and used this notion of power to introduce the idea of *domination* as the possibility of assuring the disposition of other actors to obey an 'order' (*Befehl*).[25]

Thereby the relation between power and freedom becomes evident, and arguments such as Rawls's have their foundations contested. If power is a capability, it is what allows us to be free, to be able to achieve our ends, to make our desires come true. However, if people possess different capabilities, once they have different power vis-à-vis each other, they cannot be equally free. One would be freer than others. But this conforms only to the conception of freedom as privilege, not to the conception of freedom as a prerogative of all individuals and citizens. In other words, *it is incompatible with equal liberty*. This happens because equality is very centrally a condition for the equal exercise of our capabilities, of power, that is, of freedom in modernity. The contrary of that results in privilege and domination – an outcome of which Weber was quite aware. This is true moreover of both individuals and social systems in terms of their relations with one another. Pushed too far this argument leads to absurdities: one might imagine that in all spheres of social life all persons and collectivities should have the same capabilities, which is not only unlikely, not to say impossible, but bound to entail authoritarianism in place of freedom. Differentials of power are probable and healthy in complex societies, provided they do not mean extensive and inescapable systems of domination. There is no reason, conversely, to justify them as keepers of liberty, which is seriously harmed when those differences are cumulative and imply very unequal capabilities to influence the social world, regardless of being covered by abstractly egalitarian mechanisms such as citizenship or the 'original position', which are oblivious to these concrete aspects of power.

It remains to be added that capabilities must be thought of within relationships and relational contexts. Power and capabilities, as well as freedom, do relate to individual actors and singular collectivities. However, this discrete focusing can be accepted only analytically. Individuals and collectivities exist only within interactive relations. Thus the power and capability, as well as, once again, the degree of freedom enjoyed by an individual or a collective subjectivity can be rated only vis-à-vis other individuals and social systems with which they are interactively enlaced. How the social setting is organized, including the resources and constraints that figure in the interaction and are available for each one's action or movement, plays a fundamental part in this respect.

I stated in chapter 1 that the *telos* of modernity is in fact freedom as a possibility of transcendence and a meaning-endowing element, notwithstanding the dialectic of reflexivity and caveats introduced with respect to the role of accommodation and adjustment to the world, in ideology and daily life. A divergence from de Tocqueville was introduced at that stage, although a brief account of his ideas was offered only at the beginning of chapter 3. Having brought this out, it is about time to adduce that it transpires from what has been elaborated that there is no reason to sustain the 'lexical' or cybernetic order according to which freedom should have priority over equality. They stand on a par in the imaginary of modernity. One cannot come true without the other in the institutional orders we may establish in our common endeavours. That is not say that freedom has not been frequently overridden by strong and ultimately absolutist demands for the equalization of conditions. This has indeed been the case in many instances of modern revolutions, often combined with an architectural and rationalistic conception of social life, let alone modern alternatives and reactions against those main imaginary and institutional modern patterns which were then intrinsically against both freedom and equality. More usually, however, it has been the case that this sort of development is associated in the first place with the very blockage of egalitarian developments by ruling 'elites' in previous periods – that is, with relentless efforts to keep entrenched and unacceptable privileges; with national domination and an ensuing overwhelming desire for national liberation; with peasant societies and a lesser level of social complexity.[26] While this denies the balance of freedom and equality which offers one of the steering motives of modernity, the process that leads to this drawback stems as much from the attempt to prevent it from coming into being as from the desire for equality per se. The fight against equality, as much as yearnings for its realization, must therefore be held responsible for imbalances between those motives in actual developments of really existing modernity.

Disembeddings and Real Abstractions

In chapter 3 I carried out a reasonably detailed examination of citizenship, which was then contrasted to the actual inequalities which are absolutely central to modernity. Let me venture to offer a theoretical explanation of some of the most general mechanisms underlying citizenship and the veiling of those inequalities. The concepts of 'disembedding' and real abstractions can be of much help here.

Before further developing the relationship between citizenship and real abstractions it is necessary to point out that the manner in which this will be treated here is true, however, for the core of modernity, that is, for Europe and North America, as well as for the peripheral countries that stem from Iberian colonization, which still in the nineteenth century established some basic features of citizenship, in variable degree and extension, as well as highly selectively. Regarding other paths into modernity things are somewhat different. Some countries may have imitatively absorbed real abstractions, especially through law and sometimes autonomously, as a condition for modernization, including the introduction of capitalism. Others had markets and varied forms of free or forced labour, as well as huge disembeddings of populations, as a prime force in modernization. While in the western core of modernity citizenship may be 'logically' seen as the axis whereupon real abstractions rest, colonialism and imperialism were in contrast the main elements of those processes and the introduction of those abstractions in the periphery. The scope of this book does not permit further exploration of this sort of issue which is, however, interesting to bear in mind. It is worth noting, nonetheless, that, although from the very start Iberian-colonized America was connected to the processes of primitive accumulation of capital, the transition to capitalism proper and the piecemeal development of citizenship were concomitant in this region.[27]

As seen in chapter 1, Marx pioneered the understanding of the mechanisms of disembedding (although he did not use such a wording) as key explanatory factors. They stemmed from the abstractness resulting from the social development that culminates in capitalism, featuring prominently in the notions of labour in general, of exchange value, of money; they first became organized within nation-states, soon taking over the world market.[28] As usual in Marxism, the development of the productive forces and the accompanying institutional arrangements are seen as directly responsible for the appearance of those abstractions, which would vanish in communism with the end of the dominance of the 'fetishism of the commodity'. More crucial for our discussion in this chapter, however, is his original analysis of the notion of 'citoyen', unfortunately brief and never resumed, in some part probably due to disease and a somewhat premature death. He took it to be an ideological disguise for the individualistic appetites of the 'bourgeois'. Membership in the state blotted out the 'living individual', who was concretely a capitalist, a worker, a landowner.[29] Class interests are fundamental for his thesis, but the economy is only rather indirectly at stake. Thus it is instructive to point out that citizenship, in a logical though not necessarily in a historical-causal manner, is at the centre of real abstractions. The abstract individual, or 'abstract man' (cf. Bobbio's expression in the previous chapter), is at the heart of modernity and of real abstractions. His rights, civil and political, lend substance, although rather slim, to the founding identity of the members of modern society. People are disembedded exactly by those mechanisms that historically so many authors have described: enclosures of common land, the constitution of a national space, new identities, the growth of cities, new relations of production and free labour. The basic institutional and identity expression of those changes materialized however in the modern individualistic concept of the citizen, which abstracts from all the qualities, including those space–time and relational ones, of the individuals and collectivities that comprise that unequal and differentiated society.

We have examined Lukács's rendering of reification in the foregoing chapter, his stress on the *formal equality* which overwhelmingly defined capitalist society, the indifference of form as to content, and the passivity in which individuals were unwittingly compelled to live. I will return to that in a moment, for citizenship includes as main features both abstractness and passivity. As we have seen, Adorno and Horkheimer also placed emphasis on that formal–instrumental aspect of rationality and its culmination in modernity in a set of empty and disembodied concepts – which had a very oppressive character: they were indifferent to content and hostile to difference. Let me add that citizenship was a target of the Frankfurt School as well. We saw that in Horkheimer's rather conservative account of democracy. Adorno was in this respect subtler, and spoke of the 'dissolution of liberalism' in the era of the 'integral society'. He argued that, if we yearned for an 'emancipated society', capable of bringing about the 'general' as the 'conciliation of differences' and not their oppression and domination, the 'bad equality' shot through present conditions should be denounced. There was no good in an at best naive affirmation of the 'abstract equality of human beings', which was far too much in accordance with formal–instrumental rationality.[30]

Citizenship is hence *abstract* insofar as those qualities are not embraced to underpin institutions and craft identities; but it is *real* since everything is now organized around that abstract character and the lives of people will be lived henceforth according to those institutions and identities, regardless of their particular qualities and social positions. The very notion of 'abstract labour' – so crucial for Marx's economic theory, including the 'fetishism of the commodity' – hinges on an abstract conception of the individual and the free abstract citizen. I do not want to suggest that citizenship alone is responsible for that; many other forms of consciousness are equally abstract and individualistic. Citizenship is nevertheless quite pervasive and institutionally structures the main frame of modern social life. Even for instance the 'fetishism of the commodity', if that is borne in mind, does not need to be seen as the substitution of people by things, but rather as the coming across of people in the market who take each other merely as abstract beings, as holders of commodities. Marx's economic determinism, irrespective of its milder form as compared to that of other Marxists, foreclosed the development of this sort of intuition, but it can be grasped this way if his own insight into the role of the citizen versus the bourgeois is not forgotten.

Since Marx's time, and in part certainly as a result of his criticism and that of other, usually socialist orientated authors (such as Marshall), many would scarcely doubt that class is a basic feature of the modern 'social system' and its institutional foundations. This does not mean however that really liberal, absolutely individualistically orientated authors and politicians recognize this feature of social life in modernity, as neo-liberalism has unfortunately shown in recent years. More often perhaps we encounter today, as well as from the very beginnings of modernity, an individualist ideology that precludes consideration of the class structuration of society and explains different social positions as either the result of casual fortune or of the efforts of the persons who have fared better. In other words, if inequalities are not acknowledged, individuals are taken as abstract beings – free citizens from the very beginning – who can in fact 'invest' more in their success. The access to the upper layers of society is justified by the cost or sacrifice demanded to move up. This removes the tension between the (abstract) 'human community' and its stratification, usually with the reinforcement of the idea of a functional role of that enhanced effort and performance for the increase of welfare, the 'common good' for the whole of society[31] – a position already encountered in Rawls's arguments. This still works as a form of ideology clouding the concrete class structure of society, which is perpetuated across generations and has by no means disappeared.

In Habermas's work real abstractions play a key part once again, but without finding any sort of relation with citizenship. A problem dwells therein, which will help us to deepen the issue. As seen in chapter 1, his dual theory tries to account for the differentiation of social life in the course of evolution into the 'life world' and 'self-steered systems', coordinated not through linguistic means, but by money and power. The problem arises insofar as, from a normal process, differentiation is distorted, bringing about 'pathologies' stemming from the uncontrolled expansion of those systems which encroach upon and colonize the life world. In a critical discussion aimed at providing alternatives to what he sees as the single-minded concept of rationalization of his predecessors, Habermas presents his own view of real abstractions. His target is to a considerable extent Marx, for whom the market appears only as a means of masking class domination. In a communist society immediate social relationships would be resumed and abstract labour and commodities would be left behind as a memory of human prehistory. Habermas wants to distance himself from such ideas and from the theory of value (in whose place he puts nothing, though, not even the neo-classical theory of marginal utility). For him the thesis of a transformation of concrete into abstract labour lacks 'precision' (*Bestimmtheit*) regarding the concept of 'alienation' (*Entfremdung*). Habermas states that Marx lacked criteria to distinguish between the 'destruction of traditional forms of life' and 'reification' (*Verdinglichung*) of post-traditional life worlds: Marx was blind to the double character of modern social life and could not account for actual processes of social differentiation, ending up with a nostalgic view he wrongly transplanted to the future. In addition Marx refrained from focusing on the political-administrative system when he discussed reification. Habermas recognizes that Marx grasped in part the differentiation of the state and of the economy also as a process of systemic differentiation, but does not give importance to that, for his emphasis is placed on the permanence and irreversibility – and *positivity* – of such a differentiation.[32] In contrast, the colonization of the life world produces alienation in terms of political participation and at work, especially in 'late capitalism'. Two dimensions are privileged in this thesis: the establishment of the welfare state and the crystallization of the citizen in the role of client and of the worker in the role of consumer; and the 'fragmentation of the consciousness' of subjects – taking over from 'false consciousness'. This is in fact the main vehicle of the new theory of reification. But the juridification of social life, corresponding to some extent to the dislocation of the typical social integration of the life world by systemic integration, is also crucial for Habermas: law is linked to the life world due to imperatives of legitimation dependent upon culture and institutional forms; however, it increasingly functions as a 'means of organization' for self-steered systems, intertwined with money and power. The institutionalization of bourgeois society depends on juridification and the welfare state deepens its control over society, bringing it to the core of social policy. Profound 'reification effects' are produced since law is used as 'means'. With this theoretical strategy real abstractions could thus be empirically analysed within a research programme that owes nothing to the theory of value. Amazingly, there is no hint at citizenship in this connection, not even when law is at stake, since it is to a great extent inserted into the life world and hinges on communicative rationalization.[33]

Most problems in Habermas's analysis derive precisely from his dual theory. Reification, as well as lack of freedom, would therefore come from outside culture – a standpoint criticized in chapters 1 and 2. A more unified, although not less plural, conception of social life would not necessarily see real abstractions as coming from outside culture; nor do we need to see them as forcefully negative. Citizenship, one of the pillars of modern society, stands with its claim to equality at the core of real abstractions; to support this claim it is mandatory that a separation of systems and life world is avoided, as will become clear, by means of contrast, when we dwell upon Habermas's more recent views. The 'abstract individual', alongside the 'abstract collectivities' produced by the welfare state bureaucracy through its several classificatory pigeonholes, institutes the basic real abstractions of modernity, 'early' and 'late' alike, although with some important differences and shifts to which I will turn in a moment. All modern social life is largely based on these institutional and identity features, regardless of their insufficiency.

Another perspective can be gained if we note that whereas the absolutist state featured only one individuality – namely, the prince or the king, the suzerain – and the whole of the population was kept anonymous, the modern rational state inverted the equation: power was now anonymous while all citizens were, whatever their abstraction and interchangeability, individualized.[34] The idea of time and space conceived of as abstract as the individuals in modernity and as furnishing the 'parametric variables' for their action is here relevant. The novel homogeneous nation-state, albeit with individualized citizens, could not have come into being without that abstract conception of time and space (and I will not insist on that as regards the capitalist factory, a common topic in the Marxist tradition). Citizenship thus hinges on that unification and homogenization, conquered through administrative means, which is typical of modernity. Law was born at that stage too, in the new guise of a legal constitutional order initially understood as possible and necessary due to the social pact of free individuals. The penal system from the beginning provided institutions and more circumscribed identities that evaded that logic, in independence from (but also in part in complicity with) the judicial system. Only afterwards was a broader recourse to administrative regulations and administrative, versus constitutional, law reintroduced.[35] It is curious to note that Habermas seems to overlook this distinction along with his disregard of the role of citizenship in terms of the production of real abstractions. Admittedly, it is likely that some aspects of that are changing today, as we saw in relation to globalizing conceptions of citizenship. Real abstractions have not lost their hold or strength, though: on the contrary, from a nation-state level they are thrown onto the planetary level, with an amplification of the ambivalences, positive aspects and problems it entailed already in that former situation.

The expressive aspect of identity must be considered in order that we grasp in greater detail the relationship between citizenship and re-embedding. From what we have seen it is already possible to suggest that citizenship is far too abstract to allow for an altogether satisfactory meaning-endowing personal and collective identification, especially after it was shown incapable of fully answering to mounting social problems. Its more recent recovery in the aftermath of the wreckage of revolutionary movements cannot change this: it is unlikely that the exclusivity of citizenship as an organizing principle will be long-lasting. The expressive acting out of citizenship emerges, without detriment to its cognitive and normative aspects, when we focus on solidarity and especially on 'active citizenship', on the virtuous participation of the citizen in the public sphere.[36] The surplus necessity of identity and meaning creation not fully answered by the abstract character of citizenship finds an outlet in those multiple, concrete re-embeddings. To some extent 'active citizenship' and perhaps especially philanthropic undertakings, which are typical of liberal social policy – both discussed in subsequent chapters – offer more concrete forms of re-embedding, since they are usually carried out in specific social movements and mobilizations.

One final aspect of citizenship in relation to real abstractions is in order: passivity. Citizenship cannot be disconnected from the struggles and mobilizations that made it possible, due to its partly moral and cognitive, but also expressive, features, which appear mainly with reference to solidarity and what was referred to above as 'active citizenship'. Modernity has shown that, if we want to be free, we must fight for this; that if we want to be equal, we must fight for this too. Our desires and practical struggles are the basis of the institution of citizenship. In this regard citizenship is *instituting*, and really possesses a collective dimension, bringing citizens together in their mobilization for rights. Regardless of whether it is handed down from 'above' as a strategy of control and incorporation by ruling 'elites' or conquered from below, by popular movements,[37] it is however institutionally phrased, in spite of republican conceptions, mainly in liberal, individualistic terms, as rights the *state* has to guarantee for every citizen. In this regard citizenship is (legally) *instituted* and entails *passivity*. A citizen owes the state and society little beyond compliance with laws, payment of taxes, respect for other individuals and, sometimes, mobilization for war. Citizenship allows further active participation, but only in a few situations does it require positive action.[38] That is why most obligations reveal a moral rather than a juridical character, and do not touch on the kernel of citizenship (although some obligations can surely be imposed by the state). That is not to say that we are doomed to repetition and passivity, to absolute lack of freedom and creativity. The iron cage we inhabit is, although not for everyone, sometimes rather elastic, if it is indeed bounded. This is particularly true in contexts in which public participation is fundamental to the conquest of democracy and citizenship, thus creating a tradition of engagement. But even in this case the form of organization of the liberal state and its underlying imaginary presuppositions limit the scope of possible active involvement and the concretization of active citizenship.

Qua citizens of either nation-states or, prospectively, of the world, we have nonetheless no obligations beyond a very minimum. We enjoy, or expect to enjoy, rights, which must be universally recognized as pertaining to individuals as such, independently of their concrete characteristics. Collective rights, which have been defined by welfare state administrative law, have also been conquered in harsh and sometimes violent battles. They too become ossified in taxonomic schemes in which these newly created collectivities have a rather passive part to play, although it could be argued that the whole universe of 'experts' of contemporary society – the specialists in employment and unemployment, family and marriage, habitation and health, youth and old age – are not just agents of 'self-steered systems' but are part of the ongoing development of the encompassing social hermeneutic dimension.

To put the problem another way we can return to Rawls. He writes that there is 'no political obligation, strictly speaking, for citizens generally', except to abide by the general and agreed to 'principles of justice', although those who hold office have 'the obligation to keep promises'. It is true that he adds that we are under a 'natural' moral obligation to help to establish just institutions if they are not as yet extant, when no great costs are involved. Beyond that, though, citizenship falls under the sort of principle that, differently from those intrinsic to a theory of justice, applies only to individuals and 'permissions' to act: the 'interesting class of supererogatory actions' – that is, 'acts of benevolence and mercy, of heroism and self-sacrifice', good deeds of course, but no one's duty. Utilitarianism cannot explain these acts, which are placed beyond at least the fundamentals of contractarian theories too.[39]

Summing up all that has been hitherto discussed, the following theses ensue. Modernity has entailed a brutal dislocation of individuals and collectivities from local contexts and more stable traditions, throwing them into the facticity of modern existence. In the national space, and eventually in the global one, individuals are abstract insofar as their rights – and, less importantly, duties – altogether overlook their concrete situations. An abstract equality constitutes their first re-embedding, individually and collectively, after they have been uprooted by those processes of dislocation associated mainly with the establishment of a market economy and the national state, and has broken the traditional ties of personal subordination, with their particular rights and obligations. These are universalised in their abstractness and citizenship becomes their main institutional as well as to a great extent imaginary configuration. This re-embedding as a citizen of a national state is not only abstract; the rather decentred movement of collective subjectivities is what brings it about as well. It is true that revolutions and the struggle for rights, civil and political, have depended on the intentional and usually programmatic mobilization of collectivities, and counted on intellectual developments that lend them coherence and identity, hence implying the movement of centred collective subjectivities often as a crucial element of the *instituting* aspect of citizenship. But after that founding moment, that is, once citizenship is *instituted*, the daily reproduction of citizenship and the recurrent embedding of generations of individuals in this identity and institutional cluster become much more passive.

Individuals are born potentially as citizens, sharing at least some of the basic rights society and the state are supposed to respect and protect. This is something that comes ready-made, just to be worn as a skin fitting every person. The same happens with the social aspects of citizenship. They must be fought for: most aspects of social policy now phrased as rights were conquered in the course of popular battles, regardless of the concerns of state and entrepreneurial 'elites'. Once in being they are imposed from the top–down on those who sometimes may agree with the definitions the state has crafted to embody the outcomes of those struggles in the *instituting* moment, but would perhaps prefer to have their particularities taken into account instead of being framed within wide and abstract pigeonholes, which they do not control after social rights assume an *instituted* character. Finally it should be added that, while the space–time dimension of citizenship as instituted is abstract and unchangeable – as well as disembodied, despite bestowing positivity on rights and some particular characteristics of social rights – the space–time of struggles and citizenship as instituting is concrete, particular, implying specific individual and collective paths in daily life and history. The latter is reversible, the former irreversible.

Real abstractions have been lent a deeply negative connotation in the tradition of critical theory from Marx to the Frankfurt School, including in this animosity also *quasi*-liberals, such as Hegel,[40] or liberals proper, such as Weber. Although liberals stress the gains of citizenship and hardly anyone would doubt the civilizational improvement it has meant in terms of freedom from personal ties of subordination, those critics emphasize its dark side: its emptiness, indifference to concreteness and specific qualities of social agents, its instrumental annihilating push, its hostility to difference, its imposition of passivity on individuals and collectivities. That is to a great extent quite reasonable. Habermas's erstwhile avoidance of the all-too-obvious link between citizenship and 'real abstractions' as well as his more recent move to relinquish this sort of theme (as will be seen below) are witness to the exclusively negative undertones those hermeneutic and institutional elements have received in the critical tradition to which he belongs.

Remaining however within this tradition – although conceived of in a broader and more ecumenical way – we need to resume the issue and, while holding fast to some of the ideas it has previously developed, support the theory of 'real abstractions' with a more suitable version of the concept. That is what I have tried to advance here. We must be more ambivalent towards them, and this may also be seen as a positive advancement of the programme of the Enlightenment of freedom and equality, without overlooking their negative aspects. In other words, a more dialectical approach is required in order to cope with the complexity of the problem. Without that, considering equality in all its different facets and even freedom not qua privilege, but as universalized, cannot be contemplated. In this respect the emancipatory element of citizenship must receive pride of place, neither against nor in spite of 'real abstractions', but *because* of them. There are probably other ways of phrasing what the West has conceptualized as 'human rights', or, more positively stated, in terms of law, citizenship rights.[41] They must be universal regarding individuals and collectivities, though, otherwise they will thoroughly miss their target. This means that they must be cast at a very general level to be able to embrace all the citizens of a state, regardless of how different they may be from each other, and hopefully the whole of the species, once again irrespective of the particular features of individuals and collectivities, ethnic, national or otherwise. Nevertheless, that does not necessarily entail a commitment to citizenship as found at present, either in classical or in 'postmodern' terms. We may look at it as beyond mere abstractness, hence lending it concrete aspects, and passivity, hence attributing a more active impulse to it. This will soon be clearer when we examine the contemporary functioning of law, whereas a complete account of the relation between citizenship, passivity and active participation will have to wait until part 4.

In part 1 of this book we saw that freedom and domination are interwoven in modernity in a basic tension: while the former is central for the imaginary, the project and many of modern institutions, the latter is powerfully affirmed against it, as a project and institutionally. The same sort of problem – initially studied here through two structuring features of the space–time dimension of modern societies and afterwards through a confrontation with Rawls's construction – comes up as for the relation between equality – condensed especially in citizenship as a 'real abstraction' – and the inequalities which cut across social life. If this demonstrates irremediable contractions within modernity it lends it great dynamic power and has always spurred the development of this civilization.

5 • Justice, Real Abstractions and the Return to Context

Law, Systems and Citizenship

Law has been one of the main expressions of citizenship in modernity. It has in fact evolved according to the transformation of citizenship, going from a formal conception, which has the past as its horizon, leaving the present as it is, to a substantive one, whose goal is the future, implying a strong intervention of the state into the social world. Civil (and political) rights are of prime importance in the first phase of modern law; social rights stand out in the second. In addition a more recent phase, connected to the crisis of the welfare state, has ensued. In this, law has its procedural, 'reflexive' character stressed (and procedural here means not only the 'due process of law', but also its production and even its everyday reproduction). Since it stands at the core of citizenship as an institution, recent mutations in law are probably a good place to make sense of what may consist in a sea change in the state of social relations and the evolution of citizenship. That is what I will endeavour to work through in this chapter.

Much of the sociology of law and jurisprudence has been at pains to make sense of these changes. Luhmann and Habermas claim to have introduced innovative ideas in this exhaustively investigated area. I do not intend to deny that entirely, but hope to show that too many traditional commitments mar their attempts. Having reached this conclusion, the work of other theorists, especially Eder and Garapon, and also a general view that points to the societal proceduralization of law both factually and normatively, will be dwelt upon as more appropriate to grasp contemporary social and legal change.

Luhmann claims to be crafting an entirely new paradigm for sociology, breaking away from the tradition that sees society in terms of a whole with parts as well as from individualistic conceptions. He is not interested in 'action' either, his theory featuring 'communication' instead. Originally he worked with the paradigm of open systems – his first approach to the sociology of law was cast in this mould. At the beginning of the 1980s he changed to the view of social systems as closed autopoietic systems, which do not really exchange inputs and outputs with their environment. In place of that he describes them as creatively producing themselves from their own elements. The external environment appears as 'irritation' to the system, which then provides answers by having recourse to its own internal structures and processes, although Luhmann introduces also the concept of 'coupling' (*Koppelung*) to describe the permanent points of contact between system and environment. Systems possess binary codes (in the case of law, *legal–illegal*) with which they structure their self-sufficient semantic. Society evolved in the direction of an ever-wider differentiation of systems and functions. Law (*Recht*) is only one, however crucial, 'subsystem of society'.[1] Luhmann's writings are at the same time ingenious and quite elusive and full of ad hoc solutions for (sometimes artificial and self-inflicted) problems that create challenges for his theory, which he is at pains to shore up to rid of inconsistencies.

He identifies the 'unity' of law in its 'self-reproduction': 'autopoiesis'.[2] Law is not an instrument of 'social control' or 'integration' (contrary to Parsons and Habermas). He is adamant to replace this with the idea of a temporal function of law, insofar as it allows for making 'expectations' 'stable in time', shrinking the 'freedom of behaviour'. Law has therefore motivational aspects and is directed to the future. But this should not be read as if law only solved conflicts; on the contrary, it creates them as well, within its own functioning.[3] That binary code 'legal–illegal' allows for the system's internal 'reduction of complexity'. Yet there is a further function which provides the system with greater flexibility: whereas law is *normatively* closed, it is *cognitively* open, and can be related to its environment while keeping its own integrity without becoming oblivious to other societal processes (although some sort of external influence and learning takes place after all). This prevents 'moral' values from being 'immediately valid' in legal systems. Hence 'justice' (*Gerechtigkeit*) and 'fairness' (*Billigkeit*) can be distinguished, since the former must care for its own 'consistency', contrary to the well-known *pluralistic*, non-consensual character of the latter.[4] Validity (*Geltung*) is attached to procedures, not to the contents that assume legal form. And the discussion about valid law is nonsensical, since law is valid per se; if it is not valid, it is simply not law.[5]

A passage without much consequence for his thesis (although further on he discusses consistency, discrepancy and redundancy) emerges when Luhmann suggests that '[t]he legal system follows in large measure claims to consistency'.[6] A process of *rationalization* is implicitly identified as a condition for the proper functioning of the legal system. Yet Luhmann refers this directly to closure and autopoiesis instead of trying to ponder the specificity of law. He is not far (here in particular as also in general in his conception of binary codes as prevailing in all spheres of social life) from the universalizing emptiness of structuralism and post-structuralism, with which he is as closely associated as with functionalism and systems theory. He could have drawn upon Weber,[7] without of course being necessarily faithful to his specific theses. There he could find a conception of modern law that is historical (and not merely 'evolutionary') and attempts to explore both its autonomy and enmeshing with other modern social processes. By no means do I want to deny the relatively autonomous character of law in modernity, or undervalue its importance, its expression in 'real abstractions' notwithstanding. But Luhmann's theory is at once too simplistic and too rigid to tackle it, especially his view of systems as closed and autonomous. Moreover, he comes very close to juridical positivism when asserting the valid character of any law once it has been enacted procedurally, as though nothing else mattered.

'Coupling' is at best an excessively loose concept; at worst it is only a pointless importation of a biological construct into the social sciences. That is indeed what some, such as Teubner, seem to have recognized, trying then to offer a more sophisticated and specific solution, also through an attempt at 'coupling' the autopoietic theory and pluralistic approaches to law and evincing sympathy for postmodernism. He does not nonetheless give up the binary code legal–illegal, which is transplanted to all societal *loci* of production and exercise of law. Greater flexibility is gained with such a move.[8] And perhaps an even stronger objection was raised from within the Luhmannian camp, from a democratic perspective: since we cannot speak empirically of a normative closure of the system of law (for it is influenced by money, politics, family mores, etc.), we should think of 'allopoiesis' instead of 'autopoiesis', although this in fact configures a *problem*.[9] But the conservative consequences of the closed systems comprehension of law are plain to see in the utilization of Luhmann's theory, for example to evaluate the import of public opinion vis-à-vis environmental questions upon the judicial system. It must be really limited in a Luhmannian perspective, since once it becomes too 'irritating' for that specialized societal instance it cannot be reckoned with and entails the retreat of the legal system from citizen participation; having gone too far, participation must be rolled back so as to be productive and acceptable once again.[10]

Habermas has proposed an alternative formulation, classically related to individual morality and the public sphere, although sharing with Luhmann the notion of a centralized and state-exclusive legal system. He tries to shift the problem of the legitimacy and rationality of 'elites' to the legitimacy of general will formation in the contemporary public sphere. Elsewhere he noted how much Luhmann's new paradigm is indebted to the 'philosophy of consciousness', due to its postulation of independent entities that only peripherally depend on their environment for their self-referred definition.[11] Habermas is especially committed to avoiding this outcome, in itself problematic and because of his attempt to surpass theories of law that are not only state-centred (which he accepts), but which see legitimation as something which applies exclusively to the state (and thus to governing 'elites').

The backdrop to Habermas's construction is twofold. With the debacle of 'really existing socialism' and the victory of liberalism – which has been unwilling to respect the underpinnings and concrete welfare forms of social solidarity – we have become aware of the contingency of modernity and the limits of reason. But the reverse of this more modest attitude must be found in a straightforward support and elaboration of the basis of the legal state (*Rechtstaat*) and the demand, which he believes is that of citizens themselves, for more democracy.[12] Habermas moves clearly onto the centre of the political stage. Sociologically speaking, he is interested in finding out how highly differentiated and complex, pluralistic and individualized societies can have their life world socially 'integrated'.[13] A stark theoretical turn lurks herein. It may be argued that he leaves behind the separation between life world and system, so central to the theory of communicative action, including his aforementioned (in the context of our discussion of real abstractions) definition of law as stemming from the life world normativity, only afterwards becoming a state medium put to the service of the 'colonization' of its originating arena; his general theory and conception of law would have overcome that stark split.[14] This assessment is far-fetched vis-à-vis what is explicit in Habermas's text. However, in substantive terms it holds a lot of water. The discourse theory featuring in the book's subtitle is in considerable measure responsible for this.

According to Habermas norms are crucial for both strategic and 'understanding oriented' action. Even when they appear as mere facticity they must be founded in 'intersubjectively acknowledged normative validity claims'. Law in particular is at the service of this socially integrative power, which also allows for the individual's 'freedom of action', historically embodied in 'subjective private law'.[15] This explains Habermas's confidence in communicative action as a form of surpassing the gap between 'facticity' and 'validity'. Communicative action does not nevertheless present any 'ought to' (*Sollen*) or specific contents for 'orientation'; avoiding the aspect of 'practical reason' that is heir to the philosophy of consciousness, communicative reason (*Vernunft*) refuses ethical totalities that include specific life forms. It is also decentred and not linked to isolated individual or state macro-actors, presupposing only the 'linguistic *telos* of understanding'.[16] Habermas is explicit regarding his historical debts and allegiances. He does not overlook the issues raised by the Hobbesian tradition and its focus on strategic action. But he is adamant on the difference between validity and facticity in this respect: the latter is not sufficient to establish the former, which can remain valid though not implemented. In contrast to that Hobbesian view which remains content with the freedom of contract and the right to property as the prototype for law in general, he draws upon Rousseau and Kant for the 'concept of legality' plus legitimation and democratic will formation. This is transformed into law, resting on the 'principle of popular sovereignty (*Völkssouveränität*), and underpinning constitutional deliberative processes.[17] Positive law serves the 'reduction of complexity' of modern social life by offering more stable expectations, in contrast to 'informal norms of action', also of a communicative and moral character. *Contra* Luhmann, Habermas claims that the 'code of law' is connected to the 'medium of everyday language' and the 'social integrative accomplishments of understanding' operating in the life world; but it also brings 'informations about its origin in a form in which the special codes of the power steered administration and the money steered economy remain understandable'.[18]

Subjective rights should not be simply referred to 'atomized and opposed (*entfremdte*) individuals'; they stem from the 'cooperation' of subjects who recognize each other's 'rights and obligations' as 'free and equal' 'law associates' (*Rechtgenossen*). A state-orientated conception of law is misleading: law hinges on the rights subjects mutually acknowledge.[19] Habermas is here laying the groundwork for a discursive and interactive theory of law. For this a distancing from the strategic conception of law is required. Whether such a portrait can be taken as an actual description of law under the liberal state is doubtful, though. We can assume that the overwhelmingly individualistic conception of the subject in modernity (communitarianism notwithstanding) represents a sort of 'false consciousness'. This is a plausible hypothesis indeed, which should be connected to the real abstractions analysed above, although Habermas is by no means interested in this: in fact he seems now to regard such abstractness as positive.[20] There is much to this idea; in my view, however, it cannot be so plainly stated (more on that below). Moreover the role of the state remains problematic in this perspective. In any event such a step leads to a deflection of Habermas's approach from simple contractarian theories of the state, despite many of their goals and idealizing vision being taken up by him.

This is, to start with, what we find in his definition of 'basic rights', which yield freedom of action at the same time as they suppose the free coming together of 'law associates'. These individuals have their autonomy protected by law; this autonomy is exercised in turn in the processes of 'opinion and will formation' whereby legitimate law is produced. Rights are nevertheless also dependent upon sanctions enforced by the state against their disrespect. This implies a link between subjective rights and objective law supported by political power, and its differentiation as 'legal domination'.[21] In a rather disputable sentence Habermas therefore justifies the state as a 'sanction capable, organizatory and executive power' (*Macht*) with the idea that the 'legal community' of citizens needs a 'force' (*Kraft*) to 'stabilize' its identity and to speak for the law. The state is derived not only from the 'functional' needs of the law system; it is contained 'in nuce' in, and is presupposed by, subjective rights.[22] The legitimacy of the state is rooted in 'procedures (*Verfahren*) of law enactment'. Whether this is the best way to grasp state power and citizen autonomy will be discussed below. At this stage it is important to note that Habermas is by no means describing a historical process. On the contrary he is, albeit without warning, trying to clarify the *logical* and *normative* conditions under which a legal state must be seen as legitimate in modernity. This however exacts its price, in the form of a conception of law which is too close to liberalism, disregarding precisely those problems he had identified in former works which his move to the left of the centre of the political spectrum has obliterated. Moreover the evolution of law from the liberal to the welfare state and beyond is strangely absent from his account.

His discursive conception of law rests on a prime distinction: while administrative power refers to the state, communicative power, a concept already aired in his analyses of Hannah Arendt's ideas, is closely entwined with his discursive conception of 'political autonomy'.[23] The rule of law is important for Habermas, but he does not embrace individualistic presuppositions. The 'proceduralization of popular sovereignty' and the relinking of the political system to the 'peripheral network of the political public sphere' go hand in hand with the intersubjectivity of opinion and will formation in the broader and pluralistic public sphere and civil society. Communicative power and influence are thereby generated beyond the establishment of frontiers between state and society (mainly the economic system) that is typical of liberal thought. Against 'elitism', Habermas stresses the importance of that differentiation between communicative and administrative power, as well as the participation of the whole citizenry and opening politics up to a permanent and participatory process.[24]

Habermas's contribution to critical theory can hardly be overestimated in this particular domain. Critical theory has consistently had difficulty in dealing with democracy and his is an important step to surpass this long-lasting neglect. Especially in an epoch in which hopes for far-reaching social change that could lend a different meaning to freedom, equality and solidarity seem to have vanished, his persistent defence of the rights of all citizens in the construction of really democratic polities is extremely relevant. I do not think, however, that his description of the origins and functioning of the liberal democratic state is accurate. In contrast to Marx – and to some extent to his former work[25] – he is strangely oblivious to the fact that the origins of 'subjective private rights' are closely connected to private property, in particular having trouble in recognizing that the state is not the benevolent outcome of the association of citizens. This is not true in historical terms, since rights and the public sphere were in fact snatched away from the state in the early hours of modernity – authors such as Marx and de Tocqueville stressed this long ago; nor is it currently true, since a structure of domination which is not responsive to the citizen is in place and, regardless of the amount of democratization of society and the state that may be brought about, we will probably have to reckon with its autonomy from democratic opinion and will formation for the foreseeable future. Moreover Habermas was not capable of definitively overcoming his confusion in the conceptualization of the state with respect to the relations between administration and politics.[26] The problem is not to be found only in the former: *domination over society* is a deep-seated feature of the latter, as we have been aware since Marx, the anarchists and Weber. Habermas nevertheless had more awareness of this question, although he had no actual solution for it. He has become excessively committed to the heritage of classical liberalism and as a consequence the theme of domination has receded to the back of his thought. Habermas is careful in any case to try to find a solution to the (basically implicit) problem of real abstractions: generally speaking and vis-à-vis law in particular he introduces concrete interests and inclinations as the prime mover of subjects in discursive communicative action, although individuals ought to strive to rise above those interests and reach a superior rational position by means of their communicative and distortion-free interaction.[27]

Luhmann was concerned with the particular problems of the actual functioning of justice, instead of with general problems of values and norms; in this way he was close to a broad movement we find within the sociology of law in the post-war period.[28] For all I have argued, I cannot see his theory as adequate for a conceptualization of social life capable of doing justice to its dynamic, to the problems faced by actors and collectivities, to the intertwinement of its spheres, as well as to the other aspect of law – namely, its relationship to general conceptions of justice – which was typical of previous sociological approaches to the subject. Habermas is in this regard, as well as with respect to a theory of action, far more interesting, although his construction falls short of a proper sociological view of law, for his normative and idealizing strategy in fact precludes this approach; besides, from what we can observe, he is not interested in the actual operations of law in society. A conspicuous absence from both Luhmann's and Habermas's approaches to social conflict – an absence that is particularly strange since the sociology of law and jurisprudence have been systematically concerned with this pervasive aspect of social life; although it comes up intermittently, it plays no theoretical role in their views. For Luhmann smooth systemic autopoiesis has no room for conflict, whereas Habermas is interested in consensus-building among individual actors.

Law, Pluralism and Context

After this detailed analysis it is clear to me that, in short, the two main sociological (and partly philosophical in Habermas's case) attempts at theorizing law at present are found wanting in many ways. They are incapable of grasping ongoing legal change, either vis-à-vis citizenship or with respect to its concrete workings, and especially the connection between these two domains. We should look elsewhere, I think, for approaches more suited to understanding historically and sociologically the problems we aim to grasp. The authors discussed below may help specifically in this direction.

Eder, who is concerned with the evolution of law and its manifold processes of rationalization, attempted to grasp its relation to social conflicts, especially regarding changes in the direction of procedural mechanisms. Communication and learning processes, similar to what happens in all German contemporary theoretical frameworks, feature in his work. This is however connected to an underlying notion of conflict and social debate: while conflict sweeps through communication – and is not necessarily geared to consensus-building, a hypothesis in which his debt to, and disagreement with, Habermas is patent – learning processes are the outcome of conflictive communication (pathologies coming about when this is blocked or carried out onesidedly).[29] Most of his discussion tries to find a proper response to shifting aspects of rationalization in modern law. He affirms that formerly, in its inception, law was procedural in that it eschewed hierarchical and corporatist structures, setting free a new type of communication among free citizens. Procedurality referred only to the 'narrow domain of the legal-constitutional rules' that ensured rights within the natural law model and was connected to the growth of the public sphere. Formal rationality dominated at this stage. In any case Eder pointed to political associations and the political struggles that mark the ascent of modernity as the carrier of the evolutionary processes that led to this societal form.[30] The welfare state witnessed the rise of substantive (*material*) rationality and the attempt of the state to tame class struggle, legally constituting and regulating collective actors. Explicit group interests came to the fore and, rather than in the public sphere, the sources of law were searched for directly in society.

'Regulative law' – in which 'command', a concept dear to many law theorists, in fact has prominence – is the expression of such a development, which however overburdens the system of law and leads it to impasses, especially insofar as dissent becomes the normal outcome of its operations. A new situation is created with the beginning of 'communication society', where we find a 'multiplication of collective actors' and the 'liquefaction of moral questions'. Social conflicts of many kinds now take on a legal form and the proceduralization of law is an answer to this multiplication of tasks: 'post-regulative law' becomes dominant so as to allow for the organization of demands in a legal form, and is subject to a strong symbolic use.[31] It turns out that, instead of a closure of the system over itself (as 'reflexive' and autopoietic approaches to law demand), the proceduralization of law means *greater openness to society*. Neither formal rationality nor substantive rationality has the upper hand: 'communicative rationalization' is now the main expression of the proceduralization of law, facilitating the legal expression of social conflicts and evolutionary social learning.[32]

Although Eder is not explicit about this, I believe that these processes, irrespective of the predominance each of them may enjoy at any stage, should be seen as successive waves of rationalization of law and its penetration into the social fabric. Therefore while the 'negative' proceduralization of basic rights remains in existence with the emergence of the welfare state, the latter, albeit weakened, has its substantive rationality and associated processes of juridification still at work amid the new wave of proceduralization, which deals with other social issues (ecology, reproductive rights, collective cultural rights, etc.). Social conflicts of a different sort operate at each stage, but their rationale has become to some extent detached from the struggles that gave birth to them and, perhaps putting the problem more precisely, rights and types of procedural rationality have found new carriers, supporters and interpreters after they were first juridically codified.

Other approaches to law and the state are more radical in their questioning (or even challenge) of much of their functioning. Some go as far as to suggest that the current debate, so central in Germany, about 'proceduralization' or 'reflexiveness' in law is a 'false debate'; others argue that the audience of juridical discussions has to leave the field of experts and return to citizens themselves and the public arena.[33] A stronger displacement of law towards society stands in part in their account.

In a complex and long book from which I pick up only what is of direct interest here, Sousa Santos projects a task for legal reasoning which, although recognizing the centrality of the state and accepting much of the modern imaginary, wants to break free from modernity, towards a new, postmodern 'common sense'. The pillars of regulation, for which law is crucial, expressed in the principles of state and of market, have already been strictly defined by modernity. He therefore chooses the principle of community as more promising for his emancipatory 'heterotopical' endeavour: in tandem with aesthetic expressive rationality (contrasted to cognitive and moral–practical rationalities, which were, likewise the principles of state and market, deeply colonized by instrumental rationality), it provides better, more creative tools for the construction of new forms of life and social coordination. More plastic and less colonized, the principle of community should be advanced bearing in mind three 'elements': participation, solidarity and pleasure. Social experimentation rather than order should be at stake.[34] Sousa Santos is especially interested in legal forms and procedures that minimize its bureaucratic and violent aspects, in favour of enhancing the role of rhetoric and persuasion. Although he is critical of most usual forms of legal pluralism, which can be romantic and disregard reactionary forms of legal practice, it is from their questioning of the state as the sole legal entity that he draws a challenge to the presumed state monopoly.

He prefers to refer to a 'plurality of legal orders' rather than to 'legal pluralism',[35] moving in two directions: into the infra-state level and onto the global landscape. For the latter he develops the strategy of a 'cosmopolitan' (instead of abstractly universalist) approach;[36] for the former, studied in particular through the relatively autonomous legal institutions of a Brazilian slum in the 1970s, he demands the reversal of that imbalance in favour of bureaucracy and violence, which grew steadily in modernity to the detriment of rhetoric. Consensus instead of coercion, 'wide distribution of legal skills', accessibility and participation offer the blueprint for an 'emancipatory legal process'. Under 'different social conditions' those characteristics would 'be desirable as an alternative to the professionalized, expensive, slow, esoteric and discriminatory state legal system in capitalist societies'.[37]

Since Sousa Santos not only discerns plural legal patterns and systems in contemporary society, but also stresses their virtues and the creative potential of such a plural order, one question should be asked: what is the relation between his – in my view correct – apology for the principle of community and the principles of equality and universalism that is typical of modernity in general and especially of modern law? This is a relevant question since that plurality of legal orders and, above all, the non-professional and almost 'folk' agents and procedures he envisages can easily degenerate into particularism and bias. While they consist in a thorny problem, the abstraction and formalization of modern law were antidotes against the discriminatory and hierarchical patterns – which were phrased not only through explicit formulation, but through the practice of justice – prevailing in non-modern societies. They must continue to be seen in such a light: the social fragmentation typical of the present 'glocalization' of capitalist 'flexible specialization' – moreover under North American influence in 'Latin' America, entailing ad hoc solutions or phenomena such as the internal legality of narcotraffic – evinces how much pluralism may have a perverse countenance.[38] That is not to say that Sousa Santos's reasoning and proposals are to be rejected; one must however be cautious with such a crucial principle of modernity that has been moreover so closely linked to the demand and vindication of equality – and equal freedom – in the unfolding of this civilization. I will return to that shortly. This is especially true specifically in countries – such as Brazil, the focus of his research – that only recently and in a piecemeal fashion have been making real efforts to build a universalized, but also more informal and lay-orientated, judicial system (the example of the reforms carried out almost everywhere in the West is here decisive), some of which have been evolving towards a value-orientated, less watertight system of justice (thus more similar to the common law tradition), although this remains state-centred and controlled.[39] However, even this dislocation seemingly points to the necessity of a different functioning of justice as an answer to social demands in a situation of changed forms of solidarity.

One more discussion of, and attempt at a solution for, the stalemates of the contemporary system of justice is offered by Garapon. He moves within the de Tocquevillean tradition and is implicitly concerned with the problems of disembedding and real abstractions upon which I have hitherto dwelt, although his phrasing of the issue is theoretically wanting. Most of the time Garapon is deeply pessimistic, yet towards the end of the book, in passages in my view almost in contradiction with the crux of his position, he finds reasons in present social life to expect improvements in its conditions.

Why has the judicial system become so important in democratic societies? For Garapon the judge in particular serves as 'a referent to the lost, isolated and uprooted individual', who searches in law for a last resort; when identities and politics are emptied and lose content and real power, judicial solutions come up as a way to mend authority and solidarity, preventing the 'explosion' of democratic societies. This is why judges become the 'keepers of promises'. Social ties are reconstituted – or rather people hope they will be – by means of recourse to the judicial system; instead of negative and punitive, law becomes positive and constructive of social relations.[40] Therefore we may say that for Habermas juridification is, in his original formulation at least (though not more recently), a pathological side-effect (its strength notwithstanding) of the development of self-steered systems. In turn, for Garapon it emerges as a central outcome of the very dynamic of atomistic, democratic societies. On the other hand, while for Habermas more recently this is an essentially benign process, Garapon insists on the double danger which looms on the horizon: the excessive demands upon law and the judicial system are detrimental – indeed a 'threat' – for both them and democracy overall. Through a confiscation of the 'sovereignty' of the citizen, justice may substitute for democracy – and in civil law countries judges may become a 'clericature' totally escaping democratic control – and become at the same time paralysed; in addition, far from facilitating 'harmony', justice is based on and produces conflict.[41]

There is much of interest in Garapon's interpretation. Nevertheless, it is rather disconcerting to find a very conservative slant in his reflections. He is to some extent correctly concerned with what might be called the pathologies of freedom. He goes further, though, and advances an implicit eulogy to 'traditional' societies. While identity as well as social norms and roles are conspicuous therein, we suffer in modernity, with its mobility and uncertainty, not from too much constraint, but from the 'absence of law', that is to say, a menace of anomie. As a consequence, on the one hand delinquency sets in, especially for the youth, as 'sociability by *default*'; on the other, the 'uncertainty of norms is compensated for by the growth of the penal'. This generates in fact the rising tide of violence. After all we live, due to the relaxation of social pressure and the lack of a 'common enemy', as though we were carrying out 'the war of everyone against everyone' – in the face of which the 'equality of conditions' is nothing except a poor 'abstraction'; human rights corrode all cultural and religious particularisms. Contact with the judicial system works as the last frontier against 'total disaffiliation'.[42] De Tocqueville, Garapon argues, was correct in identifying the 'transformation of man' by democracy – the 'equality of conditions'. In particular there came about the decay of authority, since nobody now accepts the influence of others upon themselves; hence democracy must always reinvent its traditions and authority, whereby it risks coming under the tutelage of the judge.[43] This means that, in the face of spiralling complexity, two problems come up. First, the well-known abstract character of law is forcefully applied to domains in which it tears social relations and empties them of their solidary content; secondly, since law has to deal with an increasingly heterogeneous society and the legislator cannot foresee to which cases, with all details, the law will be applied, an enhanced ad hoc particularism, undemocratic for neither universal nor dependent upon the citizen, is played out by judges.[44]

That said, how does Garapon expect to surpass the bleak situation of democracy and freedom, the obvious lack of civic virtue that provides the backdrop of his denunciation of the hypertrophy of justice and of the insidious sway of the media? While he speaks for changes in penal reasoning and values in order to reaffirm the citizenship of those temporarily excluded from social life (allowing for the overcoming of the 'identity problem' and their 're-inscription into the symbolic') and for a more modest role for the judge, Garapon's defence of procedural justice – a tendency that is already operative – is at times relevant and somewhat surprising if his pessimism in previous sections of the book is taken into account. Decentralized, partly de-professionalized, and geared towards bringing people together so that they can themselves at least in some part find their own common norms – he openly speaks of a 'movement of *multiplication of the instances of debate*' – non-bureaucratic, face-to-face relationships are posed as crucial for the remaking of social links now eaten away by atomistic individualism. Justice must aim at the 'self-reflection' of all parts involved: 'the state is made animator' rather than working from the top–down and with exclusivity. A 'transformation of democracy' is at stake. No longer deductive and a priori, law must find consistency in its own movement and in diverse, *concrete* contexts. The communitarian, voluntary and associative organization of social agents, in collaboration with formal legal officials (judges among them), is the main direction that points to a recovery of social authority and civic virtue, both essential for the survival of democratic society.[45] As we will soon see, as much as individualism, the increasing pluralism of social life underlies this sea change in judicial systems and this is in part the reason why neither formal nor substantive rationalization properly answer social demands at present. Greater penalization of the judicial system will be even less capable of doing the job.

An additional hypothesis may be submitted, thereby what may be called 'rationalizing legal analysis' could be checked. Unger defines it as 'a way of representing extended pieces of law as expressions, albeit flawed, of connected sets of policies and principles', whose 'imperfect approximation to an intelligible and defensible plan' is thought to be partly already in the law, lest someone imagine that the analyst is imposing ideal conceptions of welfare upon law and society. Conservative reformism or at best 'progressive pessimistic reformism', typical of social democracy or the North American cult of the Constitution, are the children of such a limiting, defensive, anti-democratic and unimaginative approach to law and social change.[46] 'Rationalizing legal analysis' and its double, 'progressive pessimistic reformism', cannot address the sources of evil, even while they are committed to supporting the 'weakest and poorest groups in society', precisely those likely to lose out in the 'political struggles over lawmaking'.[47] Even if it is absolutely mandatory to cling to the universalism of law, a more flexible connection between law, the judicial system and the manifold movements of the social world should be envisaged. In short, the solution suggested above is congruent with the strategy of overcoming the problems and dilemmas of the welfare and interventionist state through the 'legal control of social self-regulation'. Instead of attempts at merely increasing the effectiveness of that intervention or at delegalization – traditional technocratic–social democratic and neoliberal solutions, respectively – the state would coordinate social self-regulation, a move which entails also a broader and shared sense of responsibility – the topic of part 4 of this book. Thereby the hope is that the problem of (universal) justice would not be lost and freedom would be strengthened.[48] It can also be argued that such moves do not signify simply an end to juridification, but rather a deflection, a change of form and content. It becomes more indirect and more responsive to social agents.[49] But if it does not disappear, maybe we can hope it will be set back to some extent.

Moreover it should be stressed that procedural, 'reflexive' law is no panacea. North American legislation against sexual harassment demonstrates the problem: although the debate revolved around its codification in terms of formal law, supported by liberals who rally in defence of individual autonomy and freedom, or as substantive, more intrusive and authoritarian law, as many believe it is indeed, legislation against sexual harassment is mainly of a proceduralist character in that it transfers to employers the regulation and prevention of such behaviour in professional settings. However, its vagueness and the discretionary power of employers have made it very repressive. In order to avoid lawsuits and thus minimize costs employers opt for 'playing it safe'. The arbitrariness of the answers is even greater if we realize that powerful figures in the firm may escape unscathed whereas for others job loss may ensue from mere accusations of harassment.[50] Citizenship is hardly boosted with this sort of proceduralist, society-based enactment of legislation. Here it is correct to be distrustful and critical of forms of particularism in order not to let 'power accumulate in the hands of those who already enjoy it'[51] – although a pure and simple universalist and abstractly orientated attitude is really out of place.

We have come the full circle: starting this part of the book with de Tocqueville's assessment of modern equality, we have now revised the contemporary situation of the legal system (the concrete institutional form which has guaranteed the main elements of civil, political and social equality in modern societies since the establishment of citizenship as a cardinal principle, concept and institution of social life) negatively or in an interventionist way. A complicated problem faces us: how to maintain the universalistic character of justice, seeing in the state the locus of peace and consensus, conciliation and sublation, at the same time as particular interests are legitimated, conflict is accepted within the legal system and its dynamic is returned to the citizen rather than being entirely trusted to the hands of 'experts'? Can we overcome real abstractions – first of all should we aim to do that? This seems to be Sousa Santos's goal, although he does not really postulate it that openly; even Garapon takes this path. On the other hand, ought we to rest content with Habermas's almost liberal view of law, despite his acceptance of pluralistic conflict, to be sublated in a universal direction in a way that is never concretely explained, likewise the passage from particular to universal interests in Marx's theory of the revolutionary working class? Must state law be seen as the best, and even the only way to regulate society juridically, without regard to concrete ways of life and to the detriment of sociability and its own forms of regulation of conflict? Can we avoid the shortcomings and drawbacks of actual forms of legal pluralism while retaining their rhetorical and participatory character? The 'colonization' of social relationships by law, though it emanates from (that is, has its sources in) the cultural and social fabric of advanced modern societies, is a problem which we must recognize, not because it may become an autopoietic, closed system, but due to the transformation of the social dynamic into rules that in the end are undemocratically and rigidly imposed upon society. Instead of working as the keeper of freedom and equality, law lurks as that which reintroduces new hierarchies and prevents the free interchange of sociability. To some extent a strongly legislative and increasingly creative juridical system (implying judge-made law) is both inevitable and positive according to our present knowledge, insofar as it has been connected to legally bound intervention by the social democratic state in society.[52] Law enforced from above is of course especially dangerous in the domain of personal relations, although even here it should not be simply deemed detrimental, insofar as rights, equality and freedom are conquered simultaneously to the reification of subjects turned into abstract and passive beings. This dialectical and problematical dynamic, which can be as virtuous as it is vicious, stands at the heart of modernity, and has been unfolding ever since its inception, in its two, repressive and emancipatory, directions. Can we somehow and to a certain extent bring law back to its nest in social life without loss of universality and impartiality? A proper answer to that depends on whether we can empower its emancipatory aspect without overruling social agents themselves.

In the face of growing societal complexity and pluralism – which renders state-centralized law unable to help to articulate society, which needs enhanced legal decentring and complexity, a point which curiously escapes both Luhmann and Habermas – we need to think of new ways of tying together the increasingly looser threads of our common life. Problems pertaining to the specific realm of legality and the juridical system are important per se and demand particular solutions. Nevertheless, we need to explain the dynamic of citizenship and law with reference to broader social trends, as I will do in the following chapters; moreover we are probably wiser to look for remedies and solutions elsewhere, since the core problems identified as besetting freedom and equality are likely to find outlets in other dimensions, both in the imaginary and in the institutional universe of modernity. Especially in the particular domain of justice, although legal pluralism is of course, in a broad sense, operative and unavoidable, it is likely that the centrality of the state as the keeper for universalism and uniformity will remain crucial for the continuity of democracy, notwithstanding our need for institutional imagination and reforms that may propel legal systems towards informality and decrease bureaucratization, something which can be empirically discerned as being in the process of implementation in official juridical systems. The spread and penetration of law over and into social life, although problematic since real abstractions and passivity tend to be overwhelming and further compound the retreat into privatism and social anomie, can be positive insofar as they may be combined with and counteracted by an actual change in the functioning and objectives of law. Of course this certainly becomes more complicated with the intensification of globalization and the relative loss of power by the nation-state.[53]

One issue seems to be therefore uncontroversial: a new phase in the development of law, beyond procedural (formalist) and substantive law, is in process, although it by no means produces their effacement – rather they all coexist in contemporary society. That simultaneity brings about a heterogeneity that only increases that introduced by the parallel existence of formal and substantive justice. All in all procedurality appears to have taken the upper hand and is likely to influence the operation of those two other principles, bringing individuals and collective subjectivities face to face, in a more active way than formal and substantive designs, both reifying law. In this regard crucial changes especially in the normative – as well as, and partly as a consequence, in the cognitive and expressive – dimension of law come about, in that it becomes much more flexible and potentially open to elaboration by 'lay' agents. Also paramount are changes in the space–time character of law. Liberal modernity has implied formal, conserving and past-orientated law, based on a view of detached space and time in abstract and atemporal coordinates, within nation-state limits. State-organized modernity dwelt upon substantive, interventionist and future orientated law, unearthing a more concrete social space–time, comprising specific individual and collective paths in the short and the long term, although the pristine elements of citizenship remained beyond its reach. The present phase of modernity, under the aegis of procedural justice, shows a tendency to combine past and future in the argumentative and interactive arenas of the present. These arenas of course include, but are not confined to, the main legislative bodies, in that more concrete and localized space–time axes multiply, in spite of and alongside the permanence of the national framework (to a great extent informally or formally conditioning or regulating local processes) and of a growing body of international law (which may assume a procedural character as well).[54] Whether these changes will take a democratic direction is still an open question, since decentralization, de-professionalization, rhetoric and especially social inequalities can yield outcomes that betray the very project of equal freedom that is so central for modernity. The danger of colonization of justice by powerful and anti-egalitarian collectivities cannot be dismissed out of hand in this new configuration.[55]

Opportunities for the self-regulation of society are a possibility to be explored in such a situation. However, that does not mean that we should simply relinquish the universalist and egalitarian, both formal and substantive, civil, political and social aspects of law in relation to citizenship. The challenge is how to recombine them, breaking through reification. This is true in societies where the welfare state was only partially implemented or not implanted at all, the former being the case of France in Europe[56] and the latter that of most countries in America. In such circumstances a superimposition of problems comes forward and we will not be able to decline to face up to either of those two challenges – to build the bases of that state in many aspects while at the same time striving to surpass it.

The developments reviewed above are not processed uniformly, as regards intensity and characteristics, in the countries this book is concerned with (the West and the America of Iberian colonization). In some of them lateral forms of juridical pluralism may indeed be at work as a mechanism to tackle that which the official apparatus, in its formality and rigidity, is itself unable to solve. Nonetheless, both in terms of pluralization and of the sheer quantity and variety of issues posed to the juridical system, it is possible to discern a significant increase in social complexity. Which solutions are drawn up depends on how this process and its effects in the juridical system are assessed and plans put forward to overcome them. That is, automatic answers are not at stake; rather we are talking of endeavours mediated by socially exercised reflexivity. They are far from exhausting their potentialities.

In any case moreover, law alone cannot do the job of healing the fractures and withdrawals pervasive today in advanced modern societies. Other dimensions can and should be thought out from a rather distinct angle. The next chapters will lead us toward these different possibilities.

Part 3

Solidarity

6 • Solidarity and Complexity

Equality and Difference

I analysed in the last chapter the meaning of equality, especially in relation to citizenship. However, this imaginary and institutional element cannot answer alone for solidarity in modernity, although it occupies an outstanding position in this regard. Other social relationships must be closely analysed in order to draw a more complete picture of solidarity. Love and family relationships, which have lately been changing quickly, are extremely important as well. While citizenship (particularly insofar as social rights are concerned) to a great extent directs our gaze to the state, these other forms of solidarity are more immediately related to social life, accepting the fact that some of them are of course regulated by state provisions and law in large measure. Moreover, as we have seen, implying the abstract equivalence and interchangeability of persons – for good and for bad – citizenship guarantees that equality, and equal freedom, is to some extent prevalent in the modern world. Where it is not operative, first of all in the capitalist corporate markets of the present, equality does not subsist. Nor does it prosper in other contexts, such as the family and its progressive emancipation from patriarchal control, if equal rights are not recognized (although of themselves they are insufficient to ensure freedom and equality in practice). The same happens with an array of practices of discrimination linked to racism and ethnic issues. Love relationships, in an ever more complicated world, bear also the imprint of equality, although this varies and depends of course upon the people involved; no abstract state law can assert equality to such an extent and so deeply in the social world. The dialectical opposition of freedom was introduced through domination and dogmatism, and that of equality straight through inequality. As to solidarity the opposing pole must be located in exclusion, fragmentation or sheer disarray. The workings of the mechanisms of disembedding and re-embedding may take very distinct and even opposed directions, implying solidarity or its contrary.

While equal freedom became a key issue for the imaginary and the institutions of modernity, the societies bound by this civilization have become more pluralistic.[1] Taking over the ground in the cognitive, moral and expressive dimensions, perhaps in particular in the last domain, difference seems to be everywhere, flying in the face of universalists who looked triumphant until only a couple of decades ago. This entails the need to understand how social pluralism can be, and to what extent has been, dealt with in the integration of society through social solidarity, in an egalitarian way. Sociological theory has been particularly interested in this topic. Political philosophy has been concerned with it too, in particular due to challenges posed by feminist and anti-racist, as well as by multicultural and 'post-colonial', movements. To tackle these problems analytically, a distinction between equality and homogeneity will be very important in my argument. Pluralism is moreover entangled with the broader scope freedom enjoys in modernity. Connected to disembedding mechanisms, modern pluralism is not just fate in an absolute sense, but something with which individuals and collective subjectivities must cope in a highly reflexive and open manner, even though of course they also draw upon social memories. This is tantamount to saying that solidarity must be thought of in an expanded open-ended way and that its concrete contours cannot be taken for granted, as it appears to me much more flexible than it was some decades ago.

Articulated with this, there is a theme of utmost importance. Individualism in modern societies should be analytically understood in two dimensions: as connected to the atomism brought about by the mechanisms of disembedding studied in chapter 1; and as autonomy, which is in part also due to those mechanisms, but implies a more active attitude of the subject. The link of each of these kinds of individualization with collective subjectivity is distinct. The first one is dependent upon, and fosters, 'real abstractions'; the second sort of individualization is closely articulated to the plural character of modern societies, which has become more visible in recent decades, usually implying collective re-embeddings. This is what we have already observed in an oblique way. We do not need to accept totally the view that law is the privileged expression of the shifting forms of solidarity to acknowledge that legal orders and the actual functioning of the judicial system somehow express the dynamic of social life.[2] Our perusal of the contemporary sociology of law has thus indirectly shown that the more homogeneous bourgeois or working-class underpinnings of formal and substantive law are currently being superseded; procedural law is taking their place in many countries, due, we can argue, to an increasingly more plural character of social life, which precipitates momentous changes for solidarity. In this regard, similar to what happened to chapter 1 in relation to chapter 2, the arguments of the present chapter are fundamental to making sense of what was examined in chapter 5.

This compounds what I consider a new phase of modernity, whose aspects – more empirically first, theoretically interpreted afterwards – will come out on the following pages, in tandem therefore with the need for new forms of coordination of social relationships. While liberal modernity and state-organized modernity were both followed by two crises, we have, despite the widespread postmodernist understanding, strode into a new phase of modernity, characterized by overwhelming heterogeneity and a mixed form of articulation of social agents, which makes it at once more flexible and contingent.

I must openly state beforehand that this is not intended to be an exhaustive investigation of solidarity in the contemporary world. I will endeavour only to throw light on its main expressions and social axes. To recall categories developed in the previous chapter, it can be said that the space–time dimension of social life has as its main clusters of relationships and configuration, of life lines and rhythms of development, the imaginary and institutional axes dwelt upon below. To summon a notion of the Theory of Relativity which inspired the conception put forward in chapter 2, the social space and its fourth dimension – time – *bend* and *evince greater density* around the sites of *greater attraction*[3] constituted by love, family, nation, class to some extent, the state – very much changed lately – and the multitude of more particularistic collectivities typical of advanced modernity. They possess strong integrative force and their dynamic underlies – often and even usually today in contradictory ways: family versus class, class versus nation, particularisms versus the state and so on – the complex and tense dynamic of the whole social world, including of course the global level. This attraction is in particular related to the *cathexes*, to the concentrations of *affect*, as psychoanalysis puts it.[4] These underpin the motivation for action and the coming together of people in the conformation of collective subjectivities for common purposes. This means in some measure the opening up of participants to one another, some sort of acknowledgement, as we will see later, of each other's demands, hence of some sort of transcendence of each one's condition towards other people. This may be achieved through the state – and rights, especially social rights, have been central to that – or through intermediate collective subjectivities, a possibility that has become more and more important.

Let us therefore tackle some basic topics related to the notions of differentiation and complexity, from which we will proceed to a discussion of contemporary forms of solidarity. Evolutionary theories are here of paramount importance in both their virtues and flaws. Durkheim and Parsons, as well as Habermas, will be analysed in this context: their theory offers the best approach to differentiation and complexity, without entirely falling prey to systems theory. Armed with these elements I can tackle, in the last chapter of this part 3, the problem of whether we have in fact entered a new phase of modernity in recent decades. I will suggest that the present period is characterized by what may be called 'mixed articulated' modernity.

Differentiation and Solidarity

Social differentiation was from the beginning a crucial topic for sociology. A preliminary analysis and critique of the literature that has tackled it will be necessary here. The discipline took up a main concern of classical political economy at least since Adam Smith. As endogenous processes, differentiation and complexification – which are usually seen as one and the same thing – have been deemed almost a social-natural development, which evolutionarily led from a 'homogeneous aggregation of individuals having like powers and like functions' to a differentiated and integrated whole.[5] However, things are more complicated.

In particular Durkheim's reflections on differentiation consecrated it as a topic of inquiry, although his approach looks out of date today. Durkheim wanted to explain scientifically the transition from 'mechanic' to 'organic solidarity', and how they differ. How individuals were integrated into society in the two opposing different forms of solidarity supply the core of his interpretation. Mechanic solidarity counted on a feeble distinction between the individual and the (constraining) collective conscience, especially since all individuals were very similar to each other, playing the same role in the division of social labour in 'segmentary' societies. Organic solidarity, in contrast, stemmed from the differentiation of social roles, thus fostering the differentiation of the individual conscience from the collective conscience (without ever entirely eliminating segmentary structural features). The material and concomitant moral density of social life imposed the necessity for individuals to have their social functions split into specialized labour, particular personalities and distinct ways of life – the struggle for survival was deflected towards a collaborative undertaking instead of leading to the mutual elimination of rivals in a 'homogeneous' society. Individualization corresponds to a 'regression' of collective conscience.[6]

Durkheim especially targeted Spencer's individualist standpoint which emphasized contract as a means of holding modern societies together, and tried to show that previously to contract a *shared social morality* – which from the start possessed a collective character – was responsible for the rise and maintenance of social solidarity. It is also particularly important to note that Durkheim introduced another crucial topic into his discussion of social differentiation: he put forward the thesis that morality (in religion at first, law, mores, philosophy, etc.) becomes increasingly more abstract in a manner directly proportional to the development of the division of labour; a more complex form of integration ensues from increased abstraction, which simultaneously allows for greater 'individual variation' and social innovation; the hold of tradition dwindles, the orientation to the future becomes overwhelming.[7] Social pluralism was clearly regarded as a positive phenomenon, as an appropriate answer to problems thrown up by the evolution of society. But the perfect integration of society was not absolutely certain, especially if individuals were left to hang too loosely, nor should the division of labour be pushed beyond the necessary limit.[8]

It is interesting to observe that, very much in tune with modern thought in general and French republicanism in particular, Durkheim emphasized 'collective conscience' on the one hand, and individualization on the other. Although some passing remarks were made about professional organizations in his first book, only in the 'Preface to the second edition' did he elaborate more consistent arguments about 'corporations' – that is, intermediate bodies, *particular collective subjectivities* – as a solution for the 'anomie' that beset modernity. The state – that big and rather abstract collective subjectivity liberalism originally fancied as being the only and exclusive one – was excessively distant from individuals; its relations with them were excessively 'external' and 'intermittent' to be effective: it could not penetrate their conscience properly. The *corporation* was therefore instrumental in building a bridge between individuals and society, as represented by the state; it could develop a regional morality (rather abstract and flexible as well), in which solidarity, in a non-coercive way, could be exercised. Anomie would be thereby overcome and the equilibrium of modernity achieved.[9] We must not imagine however that Durkheim reserved a weaker role for the state, his concern with professional groups notwithstanding: he was adamant on how pivotal it was. The state 'thought' and 'decided' for society – it did not work only passively as a receptor; it was rather an 'organizing centre of the sub-groups'. Though 'collective conscience' was broader and more diffuse, it was in the state – the 'very organ of social thinking' – that it became conscious and reflexive.[10] Social differentiation did not exclude, but on the contrary *requested*, that society had a centre so as to achieve integration and rationality.

But the division of labour alone, albeit clear-cut and elegant, was an excessively simple causal–explanatory element for the more sophisticated sociological analysis that developed during the twentieth century. When sociologists returned to the theory of evolution they had to find a more modest place for it in their overall scheme. This is precisely what Parsons did. He characterized the evolution of society as the increasing evolutionary 'adaptation' of society – that is, the capacity of society to cope with its environment. Differentiation was a key process underlying this growth of capacity. Allowing for the specialization of the units of the system, it enhanced the adaptive capacity of society. Increased 'role-pluralism', as Parsons defined it in rigorous theoretical terms, was an outcome of differentiation, whereby the same people become active in distinct collectivities and the stratification system augments its complexity, especially in modernity. The 'regulation of the loyalties, to the community itself and to various other collectivities' becomes therefore 'a major problem of integration for a societal community'.[11]

Parsons was in fact resuming former ideas cast in general theoretical terms and Simmel's view of individuality as a specific 'combination of circles (*Kreise*)', which derived from differentiation,[12] although he lent them a stark functionalist slant. He introduced the 'societal community' as a crucial concept: it would operate the integration of society, vastly altered with those changes. The main function of the 'integrative subsystem' was 'to define the obligations of loyalty to the societal collectivity', both in general and more specific (indeed specialized) terms. 'Organs of government' were typically 'agents of appeal' for mobilization, but the community and its integrative forces are larger than that. Above the integrative function of society, in itself of paramount importance, lies the 'cultural legitimation of a society's normative order'. A differentiated society could be integrated by a broad enough cultural order, although dangers would emerge if pluralism were to produce 'sharply structured cleavages'. Citizenship and national solidarity played a key role in this respect, and Parsons had recourse to Marshall's formulation to argue his point, with one crucial difference, however: he did not mention the tension, decisive for the English author, between citizenship and the class system (a phenomenon Parsons strongly played down).[13]

Hovering over all this are the processes of *inclusion* and value *generalization*. As 'adaptive upgrading' (the greater availability of resources to social units) and, its propelling force, differentiation progress (repeatedly exemplified with recourse to the division of labour: the separation of employment from the household), there arises the necessity of integration of the new units, mechanisms and structures into the normative framework of society. The 'value pattern' of society, responsible for the inclusive cultural order, 'must be couched at a higher level of generality in order to ensure social stability'.[14] From the top–down a process of 'specification' develops, whereby the most general values find concrete and more particularistic – though orientated by that general pattern – normative moorings. This was quite pronounced in the 'American' case; with the inclusion of non-WASPs and even non-Europeans, value generalization was taken further there than was usually the case in Europe.[15] To press the point home: differentiation of previously closed units is what leads in this functionalist account to differences in society, hence to problems of inclusion which are solved through more general, abstract value systems.

It is interesting to note, however, that much of this general discussion was absent from his assessment of the 'Negro' situation in the 1960s. Admittedly, his appraisal of this problem was cast before he elaborated a full account of modernity; all the same, he must have already had at that stage at least the outline of his general theory of evolution. Especially important to observe is that the 'Negroes' were not included in the original North American 'societal community' – they were merely slaves. An 'initial cultural homogeneity' was instrumental for the building of the nation. Following patterns similar in particular to those of Catholics and Jews, and heralding processes that would probably be similar to those undergone by other groups, their later inclusion had nothing to do with differentiation per se; rather, although it partly derived from the inner workings of the very general cultural patterns that were the foundations of the United States, it was social and political struggles that brought the issue to the fore and would bring the 'Negro' to full citizenship, to complete participation in the societal community. Industrialization and urbanization, modernization and differentiation, offered the social conditions for those movements and for 'pluralism' in the sense of liberating people from the ascription of statuses and to share distinct identities and roles in different settings, otherwise the black population could not have overcome its discriminated status. But the causal mechanisms leading to the emergence of the issue were clearly *political* rather than functional; differentiation was patently not, at least simply and directly, the outcome of the progress of the division of labour. The 'Negroes' brought this out, although 'inclusion' and 'assimilation' partook of a functionalist assessment of the status of citizenship that should be ultimately conceived of as the direction in which the movement would go:

> For a long time the status of the Negro was a peculiar Southern problem. Then it became a national problem, but qua Negro. We are now entering a new phase in which it is no longer that, but the problem of eliminating status-inferiority as such, regardless of race, creed, or colour. The Negro, in becoming only a 'special case', even if a very salient one, loses a ground for the special consideration he has enjoyed. At the same time, he has established a position for tapping a much wider basis of support than before. He can become the spokesman for the much broader category of the disadvantaged, those excluded on this egregious ground. The Negro movement, then, can become the American style 'socialist' movement. This is to say that the basic demand is for full inclusion, not for domination or for equality on the basis of separateness.[16]

This does not mean that a link between general cultural pluralism and so-called 'role-pluralism' cannot be crafted, insofar as they can reinforce each other, although, as I will argue below, this is not necessarily the case (as Parsons himself openly recognized[17]). Cultural pluralism was not the result of differentiation; instead in this case it stemmed from forced cross-cultural contact, and implied some de-differentiation. The distinct African ethnic groups were amalgamated into a single (however diversified) *North American* black collectivity, sharing common values among themselves and even with an inclusive social formation. General, 'cultural' pluralism – not 'role-pluralism', a thesis for which it is easier to muster support for Parsons, although he phrased it in an exaggerated and unilateral manner – does not ensue from the functional differentiation of units; nor is value generalization a functional answer to that. Economic, social, political and sexual impositions upon slaves had originally brought pluralism into being, and it transformed itself in the long run; in addition value generalization as well as inclusion within the Western model were also imposed upon 'African-Americans', having little to do directly with the division of labour. Moreover identities, which Parsons saw as tending towards universalism and almost total inclusion in the dominant value system, have become much more fragmented; cultural pluralism is rampant at present in his country, and his theory was ill-equipped to deal with it – which is not to say that we cannot find more or less shared value systems. For Parsons the reflexivity of actors and collectivities is so much subordinated to norms, functionally geared, and the latter curiously to adaptive processes, that there is no room for its specific consideration, or of their relation to what we have studied as disembedding processes.[18]

The argument constructed above should not be taken to mean that the concept of disembedding should simply substitute for that of differentiation:[19] they work in distinct coordinates, performing distinct roles in explaining modernity. It is interesting already to note that this sort of pluralism which is typical of the United States ethnic constitution must be referred to the construction of identities in modernity, especially in Protestantism: as closed and self-sufficient, and sharply delimited from other subjectivities. This is how it was developed for individuals, but also for collectivities, especially when this involved forced labour in the United States (or in South Africa), serving as a model which later inspired other ethnic re-embeddings – in a manner significantly distinct from the Iberian model followed in 'Latin' America, in particular in Brazil.[20] In this subcontinent a broader form of 'hybridization' has been in process, standing in sharp contrast – and often consisting in a problem for nineteenth- and twentieth-century ruling groups – to de-differentiated European nation-states, which were made more homogeneous by power and state action, especially through centralized educational systems. The periphery in fact faced problems that the multicultural societies of Europe and the United States only today are being forced to face again.[21]

One further consideration is crucial here. I have already stated that differentiation (and de-differentiation) is distinct from disembedding mechanisms and processes. The actual course of modernity features them both, yet they must be kept analytically distinct and seen in contingent association. In principle and abstractly, one could think of a society of highly specialized individuals and collectivities, who are not however disembedded and are strongly attached to their positions. These might be said to be 'ascribed', as in so-called 'traditional' societies or in Orwell's *1984* nightmare, a threat that genetic engineering – the ultimate 'rational mastery' of the world – has brought about. It is more difficult perhaps to imagine a society shot through with disembedding processes which would not have in contrast undergone extensive differentiation: at one time disembedded people would necessarily have to resort to usual and more homogeneous ways of doing things and living. As an abstract thought experiment this is well warranted. Modernity has been marked by the association and deepening of these two processes. Its increasing complexity, heterogeneity and pluralism stem from two different sources. They may reinforce each other – differentiation allowing for specialized 'roles' and identities, and disembedding making them contingent and in some measure freely chosen; but they must not be conflated, analytically and historically.

Habermas's position follows closely on that sort of orthodox understanding of the differentiation thesis. Durkheim and Parsons indeed greatly and directly inspire it. He thinks that the life world has become more complex and differentiated (which means the same for him). This has entailed an overburdening of its capacity of coordination through linguistic means, bringing about (though it is not evident whether it implies a necessary development) further flexibility and reflexivity: personality, social norms and the natural world, which were taken as one and the same according to him, are slowly taken apart; in the long run, self-steered systems coordinated by delinguistified means emerge and the life world is allowed to exercise its increasingly plural character in a very long process of development. I will not resume my former analyses of Habermas's theory here; suffice it to note that he is interested also in the pluralization of ever more complex and differentiated societies, in which universalism tends to prevail as well, without his taking enough distance from those traditional theses.[22]

Let me briefly recapitulate some main points. For Durkheim the differentiation of society implied basically the advancement of the division of labour – only secondarily did it embrace the inclusion within solidarity relations of the differentiation of cultural traits pertaining to distinct collectivities; this was a consequence of the increased division of labour. In Parsons's approach the differentiation of society has still much to do with the division of labour and adaptation, but now appears as a broader phenomenon developing throughout society. In Habermas's work things are taken further, since differentiation does arise due to the development of the interchange of society with nature, but refers more generally to the differentiation of the life world as well, without a well-defined relation with the division of labour, or any other causal mechanism, being proposed. This violates the historical record, though. Certainly one can put forth lines of reasoning that show that individualizing and pluralizing processes operate in history which are due to the progress of the division of labour. But unless we look at society as a functionally and culturally integrated system from the start, within the mould of the modern nation-state, this thesis is revealed at best as partially correct. For all we know today, the tendency of sociology to press all social formations within that mould was a misstep, since it implies clear-cut and watertight boundaries, not to mention homogeneity.[23] This is hardly the case for most historical formations: therein we find cultures lumped together which exist side by side and only partly communicating, although they sometimes interpenetrate, and whose coexistence and 'differentiation' has nothing to do with the division of labour. In addition differentiation and disembedding processes rub shoulders in modernity, but must not be conflated, and 'culture' must not be treated as a mere dependent variable of economic processes or of the 'adaptation' of society to the environment.

Astonishingly this is what happens in Parsons's theory of evolution when he lends such a prominent place to 'adaptation', despite his supposed culturalist bias and the enhanced status of differentiation for his theory. This is also what causes trouble for Habermas's thesis about the 'uncoupling' of (economic and political) systems from the life world and the latter's opening up for reflexivity and pluralization, in spite of his attempt at discovering two distinct and independent logics of rationalization, respectively moral and cognitive. 'Differentiation' that is aloof to the division of labour occurs everywhere in the evolutionary process, standing out in the expansion, through conquest, of high, imperial civilizations. In other words differentiation may be brought about by integration, which may imply, in the same movement, processes of de-differentiation as well. In the early period of modernity, especially in core countries, nation-states were able to suppress much of their internal 'multicultural' differentiation, in terms of both ethnic cultures and lifestyles, a process that was central for the very existence of that political–cultural formation. Much later state-organized modernity was particularly powerful in this respect, providing for a sort of normatization that went a long way in the direction of social homogeneity, however important class divisions and suppressed ethnic and sexual differences lurked steadily in the background (being usually seen as 'deviance'). For various reasons, which will be more thoroughly analysed below, this has been (albeit by no means absolutely), partly on the wane in more recent years, due to the intensification of globalization and changes in the structure of nation-states, including renewed and far-reaching processes of disembedding, as well as the second crisis of modernity.[24]

This is not to say that processes more typical of the development of the division of labour do not continue. Nevertheless, this is not simple. I have argued elsewhere that sociology too often confuses complexity and differentiation.[25] Both concepts should be carefully distinguished: the former describes an increasingly differentiated and plural social life which comes about either through processes of differentiation or through the integration of distinct collectivities or even civilizations within a broader, often loosely held together, whole, in which also processes of *de-differentiation* develop. The status of citizenship, with its abstract and universalist character, is a prime example of such de-differentiating processes. These may have nothing directly to do, as is manifest in this case, with the division of labour, unless we want once again to press it into becoming a dependent variable of processes of adaptation.

In moral terms that is what must be taken as a crucial concern. Contemporary societies are complex and plural and there is no way we can think of them as unitary value systems, although, as Parsons pointed out, some basic 'values' and 'norms' (although the latter must not be seen as always a specification of the former, the other way round may be true instead) are likely to be shared as a common framework; otherwise it is unlikely that society would be held together. In the end it would degenerate into a continuous struggle among individuals and collectivities, backed by force alone. There is no reason to mourn the loss of a supposed basic unity, contrary to what some Aristotelian authors are prone to argue. 'Disorder' and the mere 'simulacra of morality' are not exactly what we have today, even though our world is in many aspects a dismal one; it is unlikely also that all we have in our moral arguments are fragments from discourses which previously formed 'totalities'. Individualism and the development of ideas in relation to one's desires and needs – 'emotivism' as MacIntyre would have it – may really be a problem[26] (although in the Greek polis that may have well happened, one may guess, among lay people, who lacked the training and metaphysical ambitions of professional philosophers). Surely it is the case that contemporary culture is quite self-indulgent; but that does not disqualify the idea of pluralism *tout court*. In fact maybe we have the opposite problem: we are not plural enough, especially insofar as the main values and norms of social life are concerned, since dominant codes are still very much a feature of our national and world societies, especially regarding the functioning of political and economic systems, in which domination rather than freedom is the salient element.

Habermas's account is in this regard more adequate. Although his view of processes of differentiation is quite restricted and traditional, for the reasons presented above, and however absent from his work a concept of collective subjectivity may be, the normative consequences he takes from that, especially in his discourse ethics and its derivations, do justice to the pluralistic character of contemporary society. There is no a priori normative framework in his work, irrespective of the procedural democratic and undistorted processes of communication he has in mind being deeply embedded in Western culture, a point he tries to eschew by lending those two elements greater universality, despite what may be regarded as the weakness of his arguments. He proposes a conception of the creation of norms through communicative action in which concrete agents, with concrete interests, come together and, without pretending neutrality or an abstract interest in the interaction, may be able to achieve a higher moral standpoint which sublates the original positions. Thereby he intends to meet Hegel's objections to abstract Kantian ethics. In plural social formations this is the only way to deal with values, norms, public opinion, etc.[27] However, Habermas's normative expectations were excessively strong (and at bottom they remain so), since he saw only actual 'understanding' as embodying an adequate outcome for communicative action and discourse ethics, disdaining and excluding compromises and negotiations from such a framework – only more recently and partially has he admitted them as positive.[28] Moreover collectivities as much as individuals must nevertheless be considered in order to grasp this process properly. Pluralism in modernity does not refer to individuals alone but also, and always, to collective subjectivities (the former are interwoven with, and are the stuff of, the latter, and vice versa). This will be laid bare when I analyse more substantive elements of the matter.

I referred above to the main axes of social solidarity that concentrate emotional investments. When we link this to the increased complexification of social life, we may suggest that the number of points of concentration of emotional investment multiply, something targeted by Simmel's pluralization social circles and Parsons's role-pluralism. This multiplication happens in actual and virtual terms.

There is on one side a dispersion of energy in distinct focuses of investment, due to a pluralization of identities and social relations that affects the identities and relations of individuals and collectivities. This is another facet of complexity and differentiation (and of de-differentiation in some part, insofar as this allows for a reconfiguration of those axes). On the other side there is a growth in the possibilities of investment, a virtual pluralization, since the range of 'choice' (that is, of freedom) of identities and social relations also multiplies. We will see this substantively in the next chapter.

A synthetic definition of solidarity must be derived from the above discussion. Solidarity refers here to specific social processes whereby individuals and collectivities are socially recognized in their right and rightful duties towards other individuals and collectivities; that is, it defines, in extremely variable ways, the belonging of such individuals and collectivities to a more inclusive whole. Solidarity may be achieved by different means, and has both imaginary and institutional aspects, which are likely to reinforce but may be at odds with one another too. Along the distinct stages of modernity, to be examined in chapter 8, the ways in which solidarity has been thought out and practised have changed a lot and have been embedded in successive overall frames: from the definition of social roles covered by universal rights which rest on 'real abstractions' to the intervention of the state through social rights in order to further incorporate people, to a more complicated situation today, which has required subtler and more complex forms of coordination and imagination so as to ensure that social solidarity is actually established. This is due precisely to the complexity of social life, to its increasingly pluralistic character.

Solidarity rather than order is at stake here. The articulation of individual actors and collectivities has often been conceived of – especially inasmuch as people start with individualist standpoints or even in direct dialogue with them – as what Parsons christened the 'problem of order',[29] which provides much of what is central to his theory of evolution. Although I do not want to deal with such a delicate issue here, it is worth noting that, as an empirical problem, order is something almost given in social life, regardless of how much tension, struggle or even warfare one may find in a social formation. 'Deviation' or 'anomie' are not a problem either, contrary to Durkheimian, Parsonian, or whichever functionalist perspectives. In this case, despite overall social values and norms being flaunted openly or surreptitiously, order in an empirical sense is still and always will be there to be found, pointing to ongoing processes and (contingent and shifting) patterns. Normatively, however, we stand in a different position: whether society willingly holds together and includes people in its dynamic is already something else. But then we should speak of greater or lesser social *solidarity* instead of 'order'. For whether people recognize themselves as part of a commonly shared social world or see themselves as living on its fringes or perhaps entirely excluded from it does not summon 'order' as a social construct, unless we expect authoritarian reverberations to be felt. Social values and norms which are upheld and include people provide for social ties of belonging which imply the acknowledgement of rights and duties by the members of that social whole beyond the mere integrated or 'normal' 'functioning' of society, and must be as such accepted, even if in a rather passive way – which is indeed one of the salient features of citizenship, as seen in chapter 2 and theorized through the concept of 'real abstractions'. This book focuses therefore on solidarity in this specific sense, not merely as a process that varies according to the development of the 'division of labour', but one which does not rest content with a definition of 'feelings' or imaginary constructions either, since it must find also an institutional embodiment to become effective. It must be added that solidarity rests on mechanisms of coordination as well as on hermeneutic (that is, cognitive, normative and expressive) patterns which are more or less extensively and commonly shared.

To put the matter differently, we could also speak of *social integration* in a technical sense. That is, we are talking about the different ways and in particular mechanisms that hold people together and articulate their interaction. In recent years, resuming Lockwood's contribution, especially in Giddens's and Habermas's works, this issue has been placed at the forefront of theoretical thinking in sociology. Lockwood tried to bring collective actors and social systems together, under the influence of Marxism and Parsonianism (utilizing basically the latter's wording), but attributing different expressions to processes of collective action as social integration and to processes of functional articulation as system integration. Giddens changed that to describe different sorts of interaction in terms of their distancing in space or as face-to-face interaction; Habermas separated them out to describe domains of communicative action – in the life world – and purposive action – in self-steered systems. Without going into detail here, it is worth noting that such a separation is unnecessary. insofar as we do not embrace functionalism and oppose it to action, Lockwood's proposal is not useful; if we refuse Habermas's problematic distinction between life world and systems, his rephrasing of the issue hardly makes sense; and once we do not shy away and recognize the role of collective subjectivities in social life Giddens's own use of the two expressions loses its *raison d'être*. Instead of these, in my view, flawed approaches I will therefore speak of solidarity as equivalent to social or system integration without any particular distinction, including in it the relations between both individuals and collectivities and as pertaining to all domains of social life. But it must not be by any means confused with efficacy or efficiency, something Habermas seems to have in mind when he speaks of systemic integration above all qua the coordination of action aiming at greater adequacy of means to ends. These are two distinct questions, although the mechanisms capable of weaving social solidarity need to be themselves efficient, without the opposite being necessarily true, that is, efficiency, instrumental rationalization, does not imply per se integration, solidarity.[30] Solidarity or social or system integration therefore is based on some specific principles of organization and mechanisms of coordination that will be introduced below. Nevertheless, it must also be referred to in the hermeneutic dimension of social systems, to the way people understand themselves and others, in other words to something in the vicinity of Durkheim's 'collective conscience', a shared moral framework – although I do not accept either his homogeneous view of that entity or the idea that it would be previous to actual social interactions. A more dynamic and heterogeneous view of 'culture' – that is, of the hermeneutic dimension of social systems – is supposed here. Finally let me stress that there is no simple, let alone automatic, solution for problems of social integration, especially when they are brought about by evolutionary developments. Complexity may produce impasses that are hard to solve and societal solutions may not meet their challenge.[31] The penal alternative, briefly pointed out in chapter 2, typical of the United States and Brazil, but, in milder forms, widespread, works for instance as a partial solution only, excluding rather than integrating individuals and collectivities, undermining instead of strengthening social solidarity.

Solidarity is present in several concrete dimensions of social life: in family and generational ties, in citizenship and social policy, in nation and class as well as in culturally plural identities and practices, in state and economic relationships. I will examine them at some length below. This will show us, I hope, how solidarity in the sense defined above has evolved. Originally, in the early hours of modernity, solidarity was seen simply as the third term of the trinity that synthetically expressed the ideals of the French Revolution – 'liberty, equality, *fraternity*'. In fact this piece of patriarchal imagination has by no means disappeared from social life, regardless of changes having obviously got very much under way. However, while crucial for the definition of the modern contractarian state and citizenship – in which two elements were pivotal: the dethroning of the powerful father by equally powerful rights-sharing males and the abandonment of the kinship tie as the basis for social bonds[32] – it has never of course actually exhausted the scope of solidarity in modernity. This has not only been due to the role of women, which has certainly been overwhelming. Other dimensions must be brought into the frame in order that a proper understanding of its reach can be achieved.

7 • The Fundamental Forms of Contemporary Solidarity

Proximate Relationships and Solidarity

In general theoretical terms we can verify in sociological literature a shared understanding of modernity, and the evolutionary processes underlying it, which stresses the growing complexity of social institutions and relationships. The identified problem was the reduction of this process to 'adaptive upgrading' and, for what interests us directly here, the immediate identification of differentiation and complexification, against which I have argued. We can also perceive in concrete terms, when we view contemporary modernity, precisely those processes of complexification which make these social formations more pluralistic, entailing new forms of coordination and social solidarity – both in Durkheim's sense, that is, as to what refers to social integration in general, and with regard to social policy in particular. This section is dedicated to key features of social structuring in advanced modernity, featuring love relationships and the decentring of the family. I then tackle nationalism and the decreased importance of class as identity-endowing, as well as the growth of plural identities, epitomized especially by multicultural movements. Finally I deal with the topic of social policy and the welfare state. I note the development of an intense social pluralization and the exponential growth of social complexity in substantive terms. This analysis is important in itself but especially with respect to the thesis I present in the next chapter, according to which we have now entered a new phase of modernity. The understanding of the fundamental forms of social solidarity, that is, the ones listed above and discussed below, provides the groundwork for the development of that thesis. I must stress, however, that my intention is not to carry out an exhaustive analysis of such problems, but to build the basis for the theoretical discussion that will follow later on.

The basic cell of social solidarity today, as in most societies, is still the family. That is not because the family played a functionally – for children, socializing, for adults, stabilizing – integrative role in the shaping and maintenance of the personality, according to the Parsonian perspective, for which the 'normal' case was the typically 'isolated' nuclear family.[1] There was something quite ideological in this, since it provided a model for behaviour, disregarding the links for material, social and affective support nuclear families often entertain with other units (parents mainly) in the upper, middle and working classes (something conditioned by resources for geographical mobility). The family is at present a basic form of mutual aid and material and emotional support, a place for the nurturing and upbringing of future generations; the relationships with other cells are woven through a more or less open 'choice'.[2] The love couple is very much at its centre; little has changed in this regard from some generations ago. Nonetheless, a de-centring of the family as a collective subjectivity has come about, which has to do with individualizing processes and the wider scope of freedom in this domain as well as with the emancipation of women. Two topics stand out here: the evolution of the basic dyadic relationship and the new ways of family structuring. The centrality of the family can be in addition contrasted with the lateral role played by other relationships that assume a personal form, especially with friendship. Deemed by philosophers of the past as lying at the core of the social community, and undergoing a recent upsurge of interest, friends have by no means, and have not as yet today in any case, ever occupied the same place family relationships have had throughout modernity, which does not mean that there would not be food for thought in renewed approaches to this topic. Nor should this be taken to mean that friends are unimportant for emotional well-being or for practical matters.

The history of marriage and the family can be told to some extent as a 'brutal' one. Refraining from a full exploration of the theme and remaining within the bounds of modernity, we can note that the social contract which imaginarily has been seen as giving birth to civil society and freedom had as its counterpart a sexual contract, which both included women in social life – via the private sphere – and excluded them from the public sphere: '[c]ivil freedom depends on patriarchal right'. Husbands – who until fairly recently in most countries still held at least some special powers – thus became masters of the household and patriarchy. This included the power over the offspring and found a secure modern basis through the sexual contract, rather than due merely to paternity. A hierarchical relationship was established by contract – a modern device, not the remnant of feudalism or any other social form, to be used by free individuals, whereby one of them can give up her freedom, as women traditionally in marriage and workers in the capitalist economy. Women's subordination and exploitation stem from its enactment. The figure of the individual in civil society, the citizen – our already familiar basic 'real abstraction' – hides such sleight of hand of contract theories, the imaginary and ideological underpinnings of the modern state, desexualizing people in the public sphere and blotting out the political character of the private sphere.[3] However, despite the effective permanence of some legal devices that warrant women's legal subordination in marriage and the gender inequalities that obviously are a facet of contemporary modern social life, much has changed during the last century. This has implied changes in the relationships of couples and in the evolving definition of love, the same mutation occurring in the way families are structured.

The basic dyad which is the kernel of the family in modernity has been associated, the 'brutal' character of women's subordination notwithstanding, with romantic love. Children are part and parcel of the family project, but are usually considered a completion of that special tie, although of course specific longings of people do not necessarily conform to ideas as general as these; which means that economic survival, having children or other motivations may offer the actual drive for entering relationships in many cases. Moreover the family, even in countries where the nuclear model has prevailed, must not be reduced to parents and children. Other relatives also play an important role. This is especially the case of the relationship between grandparents and their grandchildren. Depending on the context such relationships may lie more on personal disclosure or on more formal ties of companionship. But they are quite relevant and evince personal preferences that are present in the more central relationships that feature in the nuclear family, in material as well as in affective terms.[4] In addition generational ties, in age-homogeneous groups – of which the youth but also Third Age ones are especially important – perform an independent part in this process of solidarity building – which strongly contrasts with the age-heterogeneous character of the family, whether its decentring has come about or not. These collectivities cannot be grasped as really altogether homogeneous in their total extent, in terms of 'styles of thought', 'habitus', social inclinations, ideas and projects. This is more likely to be true regarding smaller age-groups than the broad collective subjectivities which, in a more or less decentred and internally heterogeneous manner, in themselves and their sub-units or due to their entanglement with other social systems, are also relevant for the establishment of social solidarity and social coordination. This happens of course especially where identity has become an open process.[5]

The idea of romantic love has surrounded marriage and the constitution of family units, although once again changes in contemporary modernity have in some part lent a different shape to such units. For most writers romantic love connects to leisure culture, the invention of motherhood and similar factors typical of modernity. From 'passionate love' to 'romantic love', and unstable attempts to find other ways out of contradictions between erotic arousal, friendship, stability and absolute fusion,[6] in the history of the West love between two people became a form of transcendence in this world as the opening to the other which, although increasingly linked to freedom, has not solved its own problems in this regard either, since 'the romantic dream of an erotic bonding to an idealized and unique beloved is understood to serve as a substitute for outmoded loci for identity, offering an experience of self-transformation, personal choice, a meaningful future and sensual expansion'. At the same time it 'buttresses some of the central premises of modern culture, including individualism, autonomy, and the hope of personal salvation through the "meeting of souls"'.[7]

Conceptually, romantic love must be comprehended more as an act of imagination, carried out regardless of the other's real qualities. It has deep roots in Western culture, including especially the Christian notion of 'God's unconditional, unreserved and undeserved love for humanity (*agape*)'.[8] For Giddens passionate love, implying sexual attachment as well as the disruption of routine and the total involvement with the other, is present in many cultures, romantic love being culturally specific, implying an association with freedom and self-realization. Lindholm, in turn, thinks that romantic love is found in other cultures as an attempt to attain transcendence and escape contradictions and social tensions, being akin to the experience of religious ecstasy.[9] Either way, although a critical angle vis-à-vis its commitment to familist ideology must be maintained, romantic love can in a certain measure be evaluated positively, insofar as it stands as a possibility of openness to the other, however limited by its projective character. It may appear as something highly problematic and almost perverse too, representing a sort of addiction in which love substitutes for God, in a fundamentalist manner, frequently generating possessiveness and anti-reflexive patterns of relationship, let alone the normal fact that ending relationships is always painful, effects lingering on in people's minds and in shared parenthood long after formal marriage break-ups.[10] Moreover for Giddens the time of romantic love is past: according to him we live now in a period in which 'pure relationships' and what he calls 'confluent love' predominate. Pure relationships would be: 'free-floating', that is, not anchored in 'external conditions'; sought after only for what they can bring to the participants; reflexively organized; focused on intimacy; dependent upon mutual trust; and a focus for the development of self-identity, appearing primarily in the fields of marriage, sexuality and friendship. The relationship between children and parents on the other hand, although suffering the influence of such schemes, cannot be really articulated this way since it is unbalanced in terms of power and central for socialization.[11] Romantic love was heavily marked by projective identity; its substitute, for which it has itself laid the bed, namely confluent love, is instead active, contingent love, no longer seen as eternal and totalizing, nor necessarily monogamous or heterosexual.[12] In any case it still furnishes the basis of the family, though, as discussed below, in quite a distinct way.

This is nonetheless a problematic thesis, irrespective of how much novelty it is able to anticipate. Most people do not actually devise marriage as eternal, but the ideology of romantic love and fidelity, according to all research data, is very strong. We are far from Russell's hopes when he imagined that jealousy, a means of controlling women in patriarchy, would be eventually rejected by them, who would prefer freedom for both sexes rather than to impose upon men the restrictions originally devised for the maintenance of an unsullied offspring.[13] The relationship of love with freedom is thus even today a tense one – greater with respect to divorce and marriage, smaller as to ongoing relationships, sexually and in other aspects. 'Serial monogamy' and the absolute centrality of marriage[14] make this sort of basic dyadic relationship the locus of social solidarity in which the tensions of modernity concerning freedom and domination, freedom and 'tradition', are highly visible. Moreover we must take into account that, since women have entered massively into the labour market this has become central for everyone's biography, representing strong restrictions to freedom as to love and relationships – insofar as it yields constraints and uncountable tensions[15] – although on the other hand liberating both partners to choose to remain within them or quit.

Let us now turn our gaze to the development of the family. Divorce and remarriage have been decisive for changes in this domain. While the ideology of romantic love and what Giddens has called confluent love seem to at least coexist in a tense relationship, and the ideologies about the family only slowly change, possibly and sometimes away from a demand of exclusivity, in practice the *decentring* of the family as a *collective subjectivity* has gone far indeed by this stage. Originally the *modern* family was very simple in its pure form, predominant among even the working classes of Europe and the United States, although countries such as Brazil or regions such as Southern Italy were also influenced by other patterns. The patriarch was its head and its absolute decision-making centre; tasks were well defined and the nuclear unit was segmentarily isolated from other similar units, including the father, the mother and legitimate children. This had nothing to do with 'feudalism', although hierarchy was writ large as a mechanism of power and co-ordination, precisely as in other spheres of modernity. The emancipation of women, implying democratization and the decline of hierarchical relations within the family, at least with respect to the loving couple, and the inclusion of children from other marriages within new ones, have made the picture more complicated, since who is who, who plays which role, who cares for whom has become in principle open to a contingent definition. Opportunities and problems lie in such a transformed situation. 'Step families' are a consequence of divorce and remarriage. They consist in a widespread phenomenon – implying a mixture of siblings, parents, new spouses, along with 'other complex kin connections'.[16]

This probably changes also the patterns of emotional investment and the love and hatred ambivalence, as well as the child–parents identification typical of the nuclear family, in which only the two sexually specialized adults had a deeper involvement with the off-spring and were taken as models for the child's development. In more decentred and extended families emotional involvement and models of identification are likely to be found between more numerous adults and children who are not biologically directly related, a move away from the bourgeois family structure which may be of great consequence, not necessarily deleterious as some might imagine.[17] The singular cells of extensive families cannot consist today in the sole centre of main primary solidarity (and ambivalence), concentrating emotional investment as black holes that attract everything around them. Doubtless the family is still very important yet it is composed, in its decentring, of constellations rather than of single stars: the space–time of solidarity has become more dispersed and heterogeneous in this respect.

Anxiety and confusion are almost inevitable in this process of speedy change. There are opportunities insofar as people are able to work out arrangements that allow for a network (broadly speaking but especially in the particular technical sense I will introduce in the next chapter) by means of which children are collaboratively, voluntarily taken care of. The boundaries of the family have been corroded and it is not at all unequivocal where one unit starts and the other ends, let alone the dispersion of power in the hands of different women and men vis-à-vis different children. Identity has also become more fluid: no roles and or boundaries can be set as though they were not problematic and not to be reflexively organized. *The decentring of the family has entailed a greater diversity of social arrangements and, as a direct consequence, increased complexity at the core of social life, in its main site of solidarity* (including the continued existence of families organized as nuclear ones). The decentred family – or often its nuclear counterpart, since women have become more powerful also therein – cannot be coordinated simply by the hierarchical power of its male head, who reigned in that small, emotionally self-sufficient and closed universe: negotiations, flexibility, a sharing of power within and among units is to be expected. Whether people acknowledge this or not is an open question. Unfortunately this is as yet unlikely to be the case in all situations, and therefore is bound to bring about misunderstanding and suffering. Old expectations, which are clearly reflected in our lack of vocabulary for narrating new family structures, may mar an easier realization of tasks and the expression and sharing of emotions and affect. In particular conservative projects – which bring together neoliberal economics and political authoritarianism with proposals to turn the clock back in terms of lifestyles – are enthusiastic about traditionally modern – that is, nuclear and closed – models of family achieving a reasonable degree of success. They are not by any means able to stop or reduce the pace of change,[18] but even those who celebrated such changes just a moment ago may fall prey to more conservative views.[19]

A quick contrast with friendship suffices to stress the continuing centrality of the family for social solidarity. The general and theoretical consequences of such altered circumstances will be analysed in the next chapter.

In contrast to marriage and family, which imply strong ties, friendship pertains to the sphere of 'weak ties'.[20] It is not necessarily unimportant or lacking in impact for this reason. It plays a different role in social life though, compared both with marriage and family and with its position in other societies. It stood out especially in Greek conceptions of society and ethics, or at least the Aristotelian version of Athenian life and ethics. Friendship provided the basis of the polis and its overall moral framework, underpinning the very notion of justice. It involved affection, but was not based mainly on it, according to Aristotle.[21] Friendship today has become much more selective, partial and discrete, involving variable degrees of emotional intensity, although, as a 'pure relationship', it can be the site of disclosure and personal expression, hence a moment of transcendence and openness to other people.[22] However, despite efforts to politicize it and find it a more prominent place in social solidarity,[23] so as to challenge the privatization of contemporary life, it is not at all clear how this could be achieved, both culturally and institutionally. These ties are neither strong nor close-knit enough to allow for a reorganization of social tasks, whether emotional or practical, *pace* the possibilities perhaps present in new ways of thinking and organizing life around relations between friends and ensuing extended networks. New forms of *responsibility*, stretching further than those provided by marriage and family, maybe stronger also than merely generational ones, could be thereby accomplished. But this must still be developed.

Nation and Class: Rise and Retraction

At a more encompassing level two sorts of collective subjectivity played a prominent role during most of modernity. Their importance has declined in recent decades, which is not to say that they have vanished into thin air. On the contrary, their influence may be strong on many occasions. The nation initially, and classes later on, furnished core categories for the construction of social identities and the exercise of solidarity. Both of them had imaginary elements, providing for 'imagined communities'; but they had their roots in deeper social realities that such a notion may conceal. For different reasons they cannot solve today all the problems they once almost did, but they retain variable importance. All in all we are dealing with the politics of identity – referred either to nation and class or to more pluralized collectivities – which, although undergoing important changes, is not new. In fact it is as old as modernity[24] and the emergence of disembedding mechanisms, implying a number of common elements and strategies. It may work through different and shifting identities or encourage essentialism, as though one given identity exhausted an unchanging (and unchangeable) reality for individuals and collectivities, in any case consisting 'quintessentially' in objects of public address.[25]

All human collectivities are to some extent imagined, although they have roots in practical realities, in social relationships that correspond more or less to what is imaginarily constructed. The nation, due to its encompassing character, demanded important steps in this direction, entailing nonetheless some limitation since it is distinguished vis-à-vis other nations; as being sovereign, a concept developed during the Enlightenment and against dynastic legitimacy; and as a community, inasmuch as, irrespective of obvious inequalities and exploitation, it purportedly conformed a 'deep, horizontal comradeship' – an all-embracing fraternity.[26] It produced a special kind of solidarity upon which the concept of citizenship was built, as will be seen below, and which Durkheim took as a framework, as noted above, for his concept of 'organic solidarity'. Language, intellectual offensives and general educational systems, although not all with the same range or strength, were prime vehicles for the constitution of national identities, alongside citizenship rights, as examined in part 2. Moreover the tough realities of the unification of national capitalist markets in Europe and the Americas were also decisive for the rise of national consciousness and the solidary links that were important for the making of the nation as a paramount modern reality. Common memories as well as the mutual forgetting of at least awkward and frequently violent and murderous moments were the product and a pre-condition of national identities, as Renan once realized.[27] The *homogeneity* of the nation was a pillar of its existence and internal solidarity, for which men were willing to pay with their own lives if necessary. However, this was possible only due to the emergence of a new political reality: the modern nation-state, with increased powers of surveillance and border control, imposing a common language and education to a considerable degree, and providing for a unified capitalist market through general taxation, an enforced and exclusive monetary system and a centralized legal order, especially as to contracts.[28]

While social pluralism has its source in processes of pluralization partly based on Parsons's 'role-pluralism', other processes are connected to the aggregation of complexity by means of exogenous inputs. These, in the case of the nation-state, have made its borders less and less tight, hence untenable in its original form with regard to identities and 'culture'. Immigration and external influences have moulded the locally and nationally informed contexts with inputs from afar.[29]

Globalization brings about a tendency towards a homogeneous world culture, to a great extent based on commodity production and commodified mass media, but it also generates an increased plurality of cultural patterns and the reinforcement of localized patterns and identities, not consisting by any means in a Western project *tout court*, although it originated in that region: a complex mix between particularization and universalization, what some have named 'glocalization', is under way.

Internal and external diversity is an outcome of globalization as much as the spread of world culture.[30] Homogeneous national cultures – which were never that homogeneous anyway, since ethnic and regional differences have never ceased to exist even in cases of highly successful state and nation-building, for instance in Argentine, Brazil, France or Britain – have become more difficult to reproduce. However, differences still exist between countries in the periphery and in the centre of the global system. People in the centre can sometimes eschew the consequences of cross-cultural contact – take for example the entrepreneurial subculture that has developed internationally and is highly Westernized. On the other hand, while the periphery had in the past – due for instance to slavery – to deal with multicultural arrangements, the centre faces immigration on a large scale today and confronts that sort of problem belatedly. Media influences and cultural subordination, due to a neo-colonial mentality, feature as a much heavier burden in the 'South' than in the 'North', regardless of the impact of the criss-crossing of cultural influences over the whole world.[31]

Pluralism comes about therefore as a consequence of cultural complexification, which imparts national frontiers and ethnically and nationally bounded 'roles' and identities, but at the same time yields, and is heightened by, a feedback process. Disembeddings and re-embeddings become ever more usual and an intense demand. People have become freer and simultaneously have to exercise creativity in order to reshape their identities at the individual and the collective levels, although also here we can find 'fundamentalist' pressures – derived from processes discussed in chapter 2 as an answer to the anguish brought about by disembedding mechanisms – in the direction of foreclosed and stiff culturally and ethnically bound identities. In other words: individualizing processes, which turn identities into something to be built differentially by individuals and collectivities, may combine productively with the emergence of plural ethnic or national, gender, race, sex, etc., patterns, signifying a growth of heterogeneity in social life; nonetheless, those processes may be opposed or even blocked by a fixation on pseudo-traditionalist ways of life and hermeneutic patterns which tend to homogenize the collective subjectivities to which they are attached, through a potentially anti-reflexive exercise of reflexivity.

In addition, in part stemming from such a conundrum engendered by globalization, and in contrast to homogeneous constructions of nation and state, pluralism in the form of multiculturalism, in a highly political way, has recently moved to the fore. It is important to stress also that, in a more active way and in relation to another type of issue, 'collective rights' achieved paramount visibility, evincing as usual a problematic relationship with the basic, traditionally individualistic framework of citizenship as well as with abstract universalism. Whereas globalization represents an external pressure, the internal tensions of nation-states (likewise radical individualizing processes) work from within, although of course such distinctions have become harder to sustain. The next sections will explore this dimension in greater detail, but it is worth mentioning the problem here. Take for instance the debate between Habermas and Taylor. Having as a background acute cultural questions in Canada, in virtue of the country's division into groups of distinct ethnic heritage, the latter demands recognition of the rights of specific collectivities within more inclusive ones. Although much more manifestly committed to a Romantic standpoint which has *authenticity* as a background notion, Taylor moves along lines similar to those espoused by Kymlika, who provides a liberal standpoint on the topic while introducing 'collective rights' as a crucial theme.[32] None of them have however really elaborated the issue in conceptual terms which would require an in-depth investigation of the very modern notion of rights and perhaps a challenge to it.

Habermas is in turn adamant in his refusal of collective rights, resolutely harking back to a more traditional view of citizenship. For him, what matters is the free flow of arguments in the public sphere, drawing attention to the disadvantaged situation of specific groups within society that would be followed by legislation intended to equalize the position of all individuals. Those policies – for instance, positive discrimination – aim at overcoming that position of inferiority and are for this reason alone legitimate. Thereby the rights of each person, not of groups as such, could be equally enjoyed.[33] We are left with a question mark hanging over the definition of what citizenship rights actually refer to, even after natural law has to a great extent waned, as seen when we discussed Habermas's conception of law in chapter 5. It becomes more complicated to define equality, the core of original citizenship rights, since (the right to) *difference* is now explicitly added. This is everywhere a relevant issue, but in countries such as Brazil, where there has been no clear-cut division between ethnic or cultural groups, despite racism and discrimination being rampant, a solution based on multiculturalism appears to be more complicated, although collective rights – especially through positive discrimination – cannot and should not be ruled out in principle. However, a broader conception of pluralism, which encompasses multiple identity constructions in its kernel rather than sharply defined and bounded collective subjectivities (as is usually the case in multicultural approaches in Canada or the United States) seems to be required in order both to accommodate anti-discrimination policies as well as collective identity constructions and a more extensive pluralization of identities and lifestyles.[34] This might answer also concerns of North American, and increasingly German, 'communitarian' liberals, since they do not usually stress so much the exclusivity of group belonging, being more concerned with community action within the bounds of a commonly shared cultural tissue.[35] In any case, it is more interesting to think of multiculturalism in a less essentialist and excluding basis, making room for a more encompassing view of social pluralism than that provided by the aforementioned models.

Either way, it should be clear – and this links up with discussions enacted in previous chapters and above in the present one, about the relationship between heterogeneity and inequality on the one hand, and homogeneity and equality on the other – that 'cultural differences can be freely elaborated and democratically mediated only on the basis of social equality'.[36] Otherwise the heterogeneity of society can be sustained only in terms of the social hierarchization and the differential use of resources available to distinct collectivities, as though no class divisions were significant or could be simply disregarded. The politics of recognition and the politics of redistribution should not be seen as antagonistic; on the contrary, they stand not only on a par with one another but are likely to be complementary if they take a democratic, universalizing direction. In addition to this normative standpoint, which brings citizenship to the fore, as will be seen below, we need to grasp the relationship of the politics of difference, as one aspect of the multiculturalism debate, with the changes in class politics in the last decades: with the apparent decrease of class importance and the obvious loss of impact of class-based movements, diverse social movements mobilize across the multiple dimensions of 'difference'.[37] In addition religious movements have gained strength again. This does not mean that 'secularization', the loss of sway of religion over the whole of social life, has been reversed, especially with respect to the state. But it probably means that some sort of 're-enchantment' of the world has come about, in a highly pluralistic and shifting way, once individuals can move from religion to religion freely, since there is precisely greater room for freedom also in this domain and religions become more and more reflexively reconstructed and optional.[38]

Class is by no means socially less relevant overall than it was a couple of decades ago, in spite of changes in some of its aspects and in identity construction and social struggles. Recent studies in advanced capitalist countries have shown – alongside some variation especially in the size of the petty bourgeoisie, which is particularly large in Japan – that the capitalist class proper, defined as self-employed people who hire ten or more employees, comprises no more than 2 per cent of the labour force in most of those countries (namely the United States, the United Kingdom, Canada and Japan), and sometimes even less than 1 per cent (in Sweden and Norway). On the other hand all those countries have an extended working class (excluding experts and managers) ranking around 71–2 per cent of the labour force, arising to 79.2 per cent in the case of Sweden. In Brazil a capitalist class has been found comprising merely 0.5 to 0.7 per cent of class positions, while the working class proper comprises almost 50 per cent of the population, with a great amount of intermediate categories (small businessmen, the petty bourgeoisie, the middle classes, self-employed workers, etc.), much bigger than in the core capitalist countries.[39] Does this represent anything more directly in terms of class identity and struggle? For Marx and Engels it certainly did. According to them there was a sharp tendency towards the simplification of the class structure, leading to a polarization between workers (increasingly homogeneous) and the bourgeoisie – despite Marx's partial and late acknowledgement of the importance of the middle classes. To this we must add the passage from local and economic coalitions to a political and national, eventually, international level, entailing a transition from the 'class in-itself' to the 'class for-itself'. The full development of the working class would lead to organization and consciousness, that is, to a *highly centred collective subjectivity*, thus to revolution and socialism.[40]

Instead of national solidarity, based on ethnic or political principles, class would introduce a new form of solidarity rooted in cleavages of wealth and power, in the control of the 'means of production', first fostering ties between those who were deprived of property and later of society as a whole, in socialism and in communism, beyond class divisions and struggles. Very few people would sustain this perspective today as plausible, even though more careful approaches relative to a heterogeneous but still developing, numerically and politically, working class can be found and are not entirely out of touch with reality. A more sober view would not however hypothesize that the existence of an extended working class directly leads to class solidarity – indeed it often recognizes the opposite, due to a heterogeneity of work and labour which strongly benefits 'capital'.[41]

Bauman, on the contrary, has claimed that 'industrial workers' are now a rapidly shrinking part of the population. Besides, workers' militancy is everywhere on the defensive, displacing particularistic, authoritarian traits. They were also totally captured by the entertainment industry.[42] Other authors who actually believe in a decline of the working class in numbers and as regards political significance would be more careful in accepting such an extreme formulation. Offe affirmed that labour had become heterogeneous – contrary to the view of Marx and Engels – and lost significance for political interests and attitudes, entailing therefore '[t]he decentring of work relative to other spheres of life, its confinement to the margins of biography' and the disintegration of a proletarian way of life.[43] But he never simply stated the loss of importance of work and the working class in capitalist contemporary societies. Lash and Urry originally pointed to the decline of industry and the working class, without deriving from this a corresponding decrease in class struggle, although this might be couched in a 'radical-democratic' rather than in a class vocabulary. Furthermore, the strategies of organized labour were crucial for class significance in the encompassing society.[44]

In any case cultural fragmentation and pluralism have come to the fore. This throws up new social movements of different sorts, frequently centred around identity building or unconventional issues; it yields more circumscribed, aesthetically dominated, collective identities too, something like modern 'tribes'.[45] Neocorporatism – the typical form of class relations, mediated by the state, assumed during state-organized modernity – has either disappeared or suffered a severe blow, dealt by changes in economics and politics.[46] Moreover, in new social movements hierarchy as a principle of coordination has lost the importance it had in previous social mobilizations and organizations: they often evince a 'segmented, reticular, multi-faceted structure', consisting of 'diversified and autonomous units which devote a large part of their available resources to the construction and maintenance of internal solidarity', counting on a 'communication and exchange network' to keep dispersed 'cells' in contact.[47] Nonetheless, we must not forget that this sort of assessment tends to underrate social hierarchies of class and power as well as renewed struggles all over the world for redistributive goals.[48] Although class receded in both political and sociological discourse, movements against poverty and 'exclusion' have been resumed in many countries, characterizing much of present-day social critique and being also inclined towards a network form of organization and self-definition.[49]

A more credible and shrewd, but also problematic, view of the declining importance of class politics, which would give way to an individually based pluralism, is put forward by Beck. He is eager to suggest that risk distribution rather than wealth has become the new principle of stratification of contemporary society.[50] More interesting than such a banal and, in my opinion, patently absurd idea is his hypothesis that individualization has corroded the importance of class, since people are '*set free* from the social forms of industrial society – class, stratification, family, gender status of men and women'. This implies what he calls 'detraditionalization', while relations of inequality remain stable to the extent that, in an affluent society, planning *individual* labour market biographies becomes crucial, leading to hierarchies of income, beyond structural definitions of class-based status and lifestyles. As a consequence class solidarity tends also to vanish.[51]

However undeniably insightful Beck's hypothesis, not only is the idea of detraditionalization deeply flawed, but there is too much exaggeration in his characterization of individualism as necessarily inimical to class identity. This can be observed in contemporary societies to some extent, being however only partially borne out by data such as on unionization across the world, which has not everywhere varied so much in the last decades of the twentieth century, regardless of the economic difficulties and political offensives launched against working-class politics from the right.[52] That said, there is more than a grain of truth in Beck's analyses. He clearly perceives the growing importance of multiple, plural identities in advanced modern societies. It is in the coupling of class as a source of social identity and those other plural forms of identification that individuals and collectivities craft conceptions of themselves and of the world.

A brief remark before going further: such discussions are valid mainly for the working, popular classes. Not much shrewdness is needed to note that, notwithstanding the relative scarcity of studies about the theme, ruling classes keep thriving, guaranteeing their solidarity partly with recourse to the state, in the midst of the simultaneous competition that develops among them, as Marx and Engels long ago pointed out, and by means of powerful organizations, such as the International Monetary Fund and the World Bank, with their typical economic policies, some even far-fetchedly speaking of a single global capitalist class.[53] There is no diminishing importance of class contemporarily in this regard. Moreover, it has been found out that the bases for the so-called 'new' social movements are the middle classes of contemporary European societies.[54] Even where they appear absent, the social salience of classes is reaffirmed today.

Citizenship, Welfare and the State

As already mentioned in chapter 3, alongside a political principle of democracy and the juridical status of legal personhood, citizenship consists in a 'form of membership' affording a 'special tie', a 'social status' and a potentially crucial 'pole of identification' which therefore generates a focus of solidarity.[55] This seemed rather simple in culturally homogeneous societies. Nevertheless, the pluralization of lifestyles that has become a key element in the last decades has enormously complicated the situation, already more complex in those countries which had original native populations and the forced transportation especially of Africans as a founding movement. In addition, in many countries all over the world immigration has further compounded the present pluralistic puzzle, which neither abstract liberalism nor abstract republicanism seem to be capable of coping with properly. Surely the confines of lifestyle diversity are set by reification and the limits to freedom contemporarily, but it has not been absolute. Rejection of plurality has been widespread as well. Once again it cannot do away with its enemy. It is thus exactly the imaginary of solidarity and pluralism, exclusion and inclusion, that will occupy us now, returning to questions related to processes of disembedding and 'real abstractions'. They underpin social pluralism and, not at all functionally perfect, solidarity.

Regardless of the projects of the 'elites' for its construction,[56] and however authoritarian the regulations put forward and handed from the top–down by state bureaucracy to individuals (and collectivities), the struggles of a relatively homogeneous working class for social rights were crucial for and constitutive of the emergence of the welfare state. Its outcomes, nevertheless, not merely in the sense of their legal phrasing but also substantively, appear in a great measure as something taken away from those who fought for them. Some years ago the strength of social democracy seemed to depend on the expansion of the universalism of its citizenship model, in contrast to liberal and even merit-based versions. This implied the eradication of means-tested benefits, individualistic schemes, principles of self-help and similar deviations from the citizenship model – reforms should be, or should have been, we can say now, geared towards avoiding situations of discontent of both those who, respectively and not always being the same people, pay taxes and receive benefits. The continuing relevance of the post-war compromise seemingly demanded only to be reinforced.[57]

Later on this sort of optimism sharply decreased. The crisis of the Keynesian welfare state gave way, especially due to the shrinking of the working class, to processes of globalization which made the national state less capable of administering taxation and welfare, as well as the dismal fact that universalist policies did not prevent the rich from looking for services in the private market.[58] This is really a complicated debate, since although some hold fast to the traditional model – offering good arguments in its support, especially pointing out the continuous backing of even the middle classes for the welfare state and refusing the 'public choice' notion of fiscal irresponsibility[59] – others, more numerous, have stressed its crisis and tried to outline ways out of it.

Globalization has altered not only the basis of the welfare state: it has placed citizenship on the agenda in a different way. Cosmopolitanism came to the fore and the issues connected to citizenship have the object of attempts at reformulation. In particular its juridical dimension can be seen as potentially universalizing, elastic and inclusive, and not necessarily tied to a particular status, collective identity, or membership in a demos. It became therefore amenable to a 'global positivization of human rights', an actual and contemporary, albeit still limited, trend. This convinces Cohen to argue for the dissolution of the 'classical synthesis' and for a 'postmodern' one, since the same is not true with respect to the two other aspects of citizenship she has listed (political participation and solidarity). Marshall's 'happy consciousness' could still identify all three aspects within a national community, but this is no longer the case; even Habermas's proposals for citizenship are beleaguered by this nation-state-orientated shortcoming.[60] Human rights as such have come to occupy a significant place in discourse and international practices, especially concerning international courts, and legal rights of 'non-residents' have been steadily expanding in the last decades, entailing the 'dissociation of the status of legal personhood' from citizenship. There is no reason to expect that a capable global government would once again synthesize the three modern components of citizenship.[61] The key issue is thus 'to distinguish between the set of rights that should belong to citizens as members of a discrete polity, the rights associated with residence and the set of rights that should belong to everyone'.[62] Tensions do not thereby simply go away, but new possibilities are opened by this 'postmodern' model. Whatever the meaning she attaches to the word 'postmodern', it is clear that Cohen's model is extremely modern in its underlying conception of who should be the 'subject of law': the *abstract individual* features prominently, as a 'human being', in her framework – an even greater extension of *real abstractions* should therefore be expected.

As I have already mentioned, the welfare state has assumed varied forms since its inception. A general trait however emerged which gave full expression to a specific phrasing of solidarity. An analysis of the radically universalist, rather abstract and state-centred conception of republicanism in France, and of its critique, will allow for a deeper understanding of some general aspects of solidarity in modernity. Although Castel's work was in fact a reaction to those criticisms, adopting a more traditionalist position, I will start my analysis through his ideas, since they display precisely that republican bias; only then will I move to Rosanvallon's heterodox, critical approach.

The debate about the future of labour has been raging for a number of years. Castel starts there in order to tackle what he names the 'social state'. He considers work not so much as a technical relation of production, but as the 'privileged support for inscription in the social structure'. Work and social protection have been closely associated in mature modernity; this is what buttresses the social integration of individuals. The contemporary appearance of 'mass vulnerability' has close connections with the crisis of wage society. Castel refuses the idea of exclusion, claiming that the situations people face are differentiated; accordingly he speaks instead of 'disaffiliation' from the labour market, which generates a sort of 'negative individualism' characterized by the loss of social ties and of social relevance on the civic and political planes.[63]

Against the Middle Ages' protection of those unfit for work by the locally powerful, liberalism, with its individualistic presuppositions, was convinced that free work was the remedy for the evils of poverty that mounted on the fringes of a society populated by ever-growing numbers of displaced people. Freedom to offer one's labour in the market did not solve the problem, though – pauperism emerged then as a threat to liberal wisdom. A policy of tutelage, delegated to philanthropy, often under the control of the captains of industry, was the initial liberal answer to the shortcomings of the new society, without recourse to the state and lacking a notion of rights.[64] The members of the 'inferior classes' were incapable of moral direction and were to be guided by the upper layers of society. This solution proved untenable and the emergence of class struggle demanded a new route, found with the 'social state'. Polemicizing with a view that, in France, tends to understand the welfare state as the 'Providence State', Castel argues that there is nothing generous in its strategies.[65] With the advent of 'social property' solidarity ended up centred on the state through insurance, initially for retirement or invalidity. There was no questioning about the bourgeois property remaining sacred and protected. The class character of society was left untouched. But a new form was introduced in order to shield people from the disgraces that could befall them. The state operated the transfer of what could be deemed a property that could be attributed to each person, which was not private however, and could be used only under specific conditions: disease, retirement, etc. The development of wage society led to an expansion of this model. *Integration* was the goal of state-based policy, aiming at producing *equilibrium* and *homogeneity*. Recent attempts at remedying those problems target specific groups and look merely for 'insertion', which is difficult to achieve insofar as those groups remain outside the labour market, suffering from especially deep difficulties. Only inclusion, the affiliation of all in a renewed wage society, appears feasible to Castel, if we do not want to retreat to an unequal, divided and fragmented society.[66]

It is not easy to dismiss Castel's worries, although his solution seems old-fashioned and hardly satisfactory. After all how can solidarity let people off the hook in such extreme situations if even the basic rights of citizenship, such as described by Marshall, are placed beyond their reach? Social policies must indeed maintain a universalizing aspect.

But we must investigate the other side of the matter, which shows us that state-centred solidarity has become increasingly incompatible with individualization and social pluralism. They must be accounted for if an effective social policy is to be devised.

Rosanvallon has been especially interested in this sort of problematic, although his position has changed over time. He was one of the first to spot some thorny problems in the functioning of the welfare state, related to escalating taxes and demands, but due above all to an 'excessively statist conception of solidarity'. The purported fiscal crisis of the 'Providence State' could not be taken at face value. However, this was not his main focus. For him there is not exactly continuity between the modern state, which from Hobbes and Locke on was associated with individualism, and the 'Providence State', but rather a 'radicalization' of the 'classical' role of the state in offering protection and the reduction of uncertainty. The new lay state substitutes for the religiously based providence. This role is difficult to sustain today.[67] He claimed also that the debate that links privatization with 'statization' misses the point: what should really be at stake is the question of 'what is a collective service' rather than who pays for it. One should think of the decentralization and autonomization of services, diminishing bureaucracy and increasing rationalization, making them more sensitive to local aspirations; he deemed their transfer to non-public collectivities particularly interesting. Thereby the polarization between individualism and statism could be surpassed, with the recreation of sociability and solidarity, against a social form in which the state was the sole expression of 'collective life' and counterpoint to atomized individuals. To that he opposed a new way of organizing state and society as well as their interfaces and relationships, wherein 'positive alternatives to the Providence State' supposed that the 'segments of civil society' could be recognized as 'subjects of law and as productive instances of an autonomous law (*droit*) in relation to a law (*loi*) of state essence'.[68]

To draw upon a concept I have myself crafted and utilized in other passages already in this book, collective subjectivities would have a pivotal part to play in this new arrangement: neither individuals alone nor the state as the all-too-inclusive and general representative of society would have to answer for individual and social welfare. Rosanvallon did not hold illusions that this might be an easy move, since the yearning of individuals for autonomy is strong and the need to re-organize social institutions (including a different relationship with work and free time) to accommodate those new tasks would be necessary; he did not propose a return to a nostalgically imagined community, nor did he envision a mere revitalization of civil society – it is a whole new way of getting things done and a new set of institutions that comes into view. The state would remain an important partner, without henceforth obfuscating society; greater social visibility would be achieved and social conflicts as well as identities would be unblocked; frozen social spaces would thaw and democracy would be allowed to flourish. Self-management, once though not at present his socialist alternative, might moreover afford a new social democratic compromise.[69]

Later Rosanvallon gave a radical turn to his criticism of the welfare state, decisively altering his standpoint in an individualistic direction. Supposing now that the crisis of the 1970s had been due to funding problems, he affirmed that it had become deeper. It was linked to the 'organizing principles of solidarity' and the very conception of social rights. At this stage of transformation of modernity and increasing unemployment, whose financial pressure could not be sustained by the state, social rights had to be rethought. Social insurance aimed at controlling risk as accidental; having become permanent, unemployment challenged this formula; on the other hand risk was connected to catastrophes. Precarious situations, caused by vulnerability rather than of risk, are the core of the social question. Individual responsibility comes to the fore again.[70] Apart from specific problems, it is with a specious (and absurdly concrete) interpretation of Rawls's central argument that Rosanvallon tries to justify changes in the welfare state. The supple information available about the conditions of life of each person prevents us from supposing a 'veil of ignorance'. Therefore taxes and services find trouble being legitimated; conflicts multiply.[71] Everywhere the selectivity of assistance is established. The 'Providence State' watched over the well-being of homogeneous populations; the heterogenization of social life wreaks havoc in that pattern of policy, demanding that autonomous individuals must administer their lives and social resources. There are no groups, classes or communities that can be collectively mobilized; social policy must become individualizing and no longer statistical. The 'Providence State' should be turned into a 'service state' whose goal would be to give to each one the means to change a life-course, overcome a rupture or anticipate a breakdown. This engenders the risk that the state might achieve deeper control over individuals, juridifying life-courses, insofar as it must decide when borderline situations appear in someone's life. People should be therefore enabled to contest such decisions. This new web of regulations would allow for a 'complex form of freedom'.[72]

Although Rosanvallon touches upon extremely relevant issues, his solution is to me as unsatisfactory as Castel's. He is undoubtedly right to emphasize the enhanced pluralism of Western societies; but his withdrawal of support for both a more universalist approach and intermediate collective agencies implies a way of dealing with social solidarity that makes it far too weak and fuzzy. If Castel's proposals are excessively traditionalist and state-centred, Rosanvallon gives in to traditional individualism. Collective subjectivities vanish from their approaches, both incapable of dealing with a main trend of the build-up of the state and therefore of citizenship, as we saw in the analysis of contemporary legal and juridical trends: a closer connection between state and society has emerged, and in social policy this is probably at stake as well, although we should be wary of resurrecting philanthropy as a reasonable alternative or even of the role of a badly defined and arbitrarily behaving 'third-sector'. The universality, abstract as it may be, of citizenship rights as a crucial feature of social solidarity must be upheld. How to tackle this in altered conditions, taking advantage of the opportunities opened by them, will occupy us in the next chapter and in part 4.

8 • Complexity and Mixed Articulation

Stages of Modernity

We have seen that the complexification of social relationships has been taken further by modernity, especially in its contemporary phase. An intensified social pluralization, hence greater opening of identities, sets in, making moreover less foreseeable the problem of social interaction. The contingency of social relations has greatly increased. This means more fluid and indeterminate normative and expressive patterns, as well as more social opacity cognitively. It is more difficult to tell a priori the characteristics of the numerous subjects, their inclinations, which interactive patterns and directions tend to be established. For both participants and observers the situation is shown as more complex per se and problems of understanding as well as the very answers of subjects become less evident in this context of further complexification.

This is particularly clear when we consider the reduction of the 'steering' capacity of the state in this context, which stems from the pluralization brought about by complexity, and the (relative) decline of organized collective action channelled by bodies such as unions, business associations and similar organizations; pluralism has brought up more diffuse and disperse themes and forms of action which, due to the lack of 'organized collective actors', make the connection between state and society more tenuous and problematic.[1] This means that social coordination driven via hierarchies, which work from the top–down, is not capable of attaining an optimal level, irrespective of how much input those hierarchies can accept from the centre – as noted in chapter 5 vis-à-vis the evolution of legal and juridical systems in modernity, which was divided in three stages. We must now broaden our focus and put forward a wider hypothesis, which will divide modernity in its multiple dimensions in three phases.

A brief review of a literature which was rather important just a while ago, but whose developments were inconclusive, helps to show the cases in point. Partly inspired by some views of Hilferding (the Austrian socialist economist in the beginning of the last century) Offe was one of the first to speak about organized modernity, in which the welfare state and Keynesian economics performed a crucial part. He was also one of the first to point to its crisis. He was followed by others, such as Lash and Urry, who spoke of the end of 'organized capitalism' (though now they have leapt to a view of the contemporary world as 'postmodernity', a standpoint which simply obscures the questions to be debated rather than proposing a cogent explanation for them). Wagner took the issue further, proposing a thesis about two phases of modernity – one which was liberal and displayed great room for contingency, the other state-directed and searching for order against freedom; they both had been followed by crisis. At the time he published his interesting piece – which however mistakenly conflates order with the state, while in my understanding the market should be seen as an instrument for achieving the same goal – we seemed still to be going through that second crisis. I think we are now past this: we have entered a new phase of modernity, characterized by greater complexity, partly analysed above, and a more flexible form of coordination, due to the need for *attaining instrumental efficiency* but also for *crafting new forms of social solidarity* in this advanced phase. In this regard Boltanski and Chiapello's interpretation of the new phase of capitalism will be decisive when I resume the issue in chapter 10, although I must critically say right away that they tend onesidedly to consider networks as the single articulating element in the new social order.[2]

Before taking the issue further let me just recall some analytical issues I have elaborated upon elsewhere. The market – the typical element of coordination of liberal modernity – is to be perceived as articulated by the 'free exchange' of commodities. In that first phase it was seconded by the state, which played a relatively circumscribed role (at least ideally), maintaining basic rights and the observance of the contracts privately enacted. As seen in chapter 2, the formal rationalization of law corresponded to this. The state is characterized mainly by the functioning of 'hierarchies' as coordinating devices, for which 'command' is decisive (and the substantive rationalization of law was concomitant and part and parcel of the increased importance of the state in the second phase of modernity). Today another principle, which has neither been impotent nor become dominant or exclusive, has in any case acquired outstanding relevance for the coordination of social life and the establishment of social solidarity. In a pluralistic and rather decentred social formation its flexibility has lent it a prominent position: the state is excessively large and clumsy to interfere and deal with fine problems of coordination (a point Durkheim had already spotted in the beginning of the last century); on the other hand, the typical competition of markets cannot work as a means of weaving solidarity between its members, however much more complex and dependent upon stable relations markets indeed are, contrary to the neo-classical, neoliberal view (astonishingly enough, shared by a great number of left-wing authors such as Habermas).[3] My argument is thus that we have entered a third phase of modernity, in which a complex combination, in many or even in almost all domains of the social world, between those three principles of coordination has become responsible for both efficiency and the elusive solidarity of contemporary social life. The table synthesizes those principles and their underlying mechanisms (Table 1).

Table 1 The third phase of modernity

Principles of organization	Mechanisms of coordination
Market	Voluntary exchange
Hierarchy	Command
Network	Voluntary collaboration

In virtue of its specific characteristics, and the novelty I hope it offers, the previous chapter was much more concerned with empirical elements of contemporary society than the prior ones. At this point a clear theoretical approach will be taken. My goal here, which stems from issues partly identified in my discussion of contemporary law, is to provide a new view of the relationship between solidarity and social coordination and contemporary modernity. Let me briefly recapitulate. I have examined mainly the family: its transformation from a segmented and hierarchical cell, homogeneous throughout society, to a decentred one, stretching out in many connections and an increasingly horizontal network of couples, single (that is, divorced) people and children; plus the nation, with its lesser but not to be underestimated importance; and social classes, today much more heterogeneous and decentred, yet maintaining variable relevance. In contrast to nations and classes, multi-culturalism, globalizing and across-the-boundary influences as well as a multiplication of lifestyle differences were identified. Also the state, overall and in particular in what concerns social policy, has evinced a much more fluid and power-sharing structure, although differentials of power can bring about very particularistic and hierarchical bonds rather than horizontal ones for political relationships. Business groups have been especially favoured in the course of these changes. Here I need to complete my depiction with at least one more element, directly rooted in economic life. This was in fact the crux of the (to a great extent neo-Marxist) argument of those who originally spoke of 'organized capitalism', despite the role performed by the state in their view – although in Wagner's case the lens had already been broadened, indeed in a linguistically and culturally orientated manner. That is not what will be pursued here in any case, since it is the relationships and forms of solidarity in the whole of social life, that is, in a multidimensional perspective, that matter for my argument. This does not however make the economy a less pivotal domain for my analysis.

Nor do I by any means want to imply that networks have become the main form of coordination in economic relationships under capitalism. But, from what we have learned, it is undeniable that in many areas of paramount economic and technological activity they have, if not taken over, at least pervaded social processes. Markets and hierarchies, in other words monetary exchange and command, still by and large organize most of the economy all over societies and globally. Voluntary collaboration has nonetheless assumed a more prominent place. The Silicon Valley, the main high-tech area in the United States, featuring the association between state funding, small and quickly surpassed firms, continuously created anew, as well as university research and labour formation; Third Italy, with its mix of small business, international subcontracting, state support, strong social ties and shared knowledge; and Mondragón, the Basque area of burgeoning cooperatives: these are only some egregious examples of such a transformed way of producing material and today almost immaterial goods. Other, less visible, but nonetheless equally important, network links across the economy, between private firms, the state and sometimes research centres, can also be found and have been in the forefront of economic development and innovation.[4] Network alliances between government, research centres and business firms are presently absolutely central for scientific and technological breakthroughs. In fact at a certain stage it implied a revision of legislation in the United States in order to set them apart from anti-trust legislation, which tended to prevent joint research by firms, with something similar happening in the European Community, although for instance in Japan this has always been an important factor in the search for modernization.[5]

Here too the concepts of either liberal or state-organized modernity are not sharp and up to date enough to account for the mixed articulation of economic activities, which is more influenced by networks – which incidentally are not of course entirely new, having been found in previous periods as well, their lesser centrality notwithstanding. Let me just sound warning bells about a common mistake: many instances of supposed network relationships, often stemming from outsourcing, are merely disguised forms of highly hierarchical economic connections and dependencies which sell themselves as collaborative enterprises of egalitarian partners, the reality being entirely different.

This does not diminish the importance of truly network processes of coordination, in the economy or wherever. In fact it is not by chance that networks have been in evidence lately.[6] There is much ideology in a traditional sense behind it; there is a lot of smokescreen too, as if we lived in a world which is no longer capitalist proper – that is, in which collaboration were widespread, substituting for competition and exploitation; there is a good deal of misunderstanding also concerning the sense of the term 'network', which, similar to all notions that can be found in daily vocabulary and communication, necessarily possesses a multiplicity of meanings; one crucial task of social scientists consists in defining such concepts in a much more precise form when they choose to operate with them, which I have tried to do in this case above and elsewhere. For some, 'network' is just an extended row of relationships, without any precise meaning being attached to the way they are brought together – the major emphasis in this case might for instance be on how the properties of networks influence their units and how they are able to mobilize resources to influence actors outside;[7] for others it entails some sort of cooperative disposition, which is not usually well-defined or contrasted with other forms of coordination.

In Castells, an author who more than anyone else has lent visibility to the theme, this sort of confusion is writ large. According to his more explicit conceptualization, making use otherwise of that type of broader definition, '[a] network is a set of interconnected nodes' – each of which is a 'point at which a curve intersects itself'. He gets closer to a proper theoretical view on the other hand when writing that

> [t]he morphology of the network seems well adapted to increasing complexity of interaction and to unpredictable patterns of development arising from the creative power of such interaction. This topological

configuration, the network, can now be materially implemented, in all kinds of processes and organizations, by newly available information technologies.[8]

The widespread use of the term signals its importance in social life: we often talk about things we fuzzily recognize, make use of loose notions to refer to them and an index of the importance of a given phenomenon in social life is how much it draws attention – although sometimes the opposite may be true, since sectional and thus ideologically vested interests may be threatened by excessive social awareness. Networks have attracted a lot of attention and the social sciences have actively and speedily striven to make sense of them, crafting analytical concepts. One conceptual, analytical version was proposed above to cope with this highly visible feature of contemporary modernity in what I see as a more precise manner.

We can summarize the development of modernity in its three phases and intermediate crises as the accumulation, the 'piling up', with concomitant substantive changes and shifting balances, of social relations structured according to different principles of organization, namely market, hierarchy and network. One has not displaced the other, although they may have assumed greater importance or taken prominence at different stages. In a synthetic way therefore the development of modernity could be described as follows.

At first liberal modernity had the nuclear – exclusive, patriarchal and highly hierarchical – family at the core of social solidarity. In the broader society market relationships implied strong competition and the system of liberal rights and state power – along with institutions which projected a national ethos and common culture – guaranteed overall social solidarity, that is, through hierarchical relations to some extent. State-organized modernity had preserved all these institutions but decreased the importance of some of them – especially the market – and was at the same time witness to and based itself on stronger and further-reaching state action, while (in a society in principle relatively homogeneous) societal cohesion overall had social rights as a prime vehicle of social solidarity. The third phase of modernity, whose unfolding is now under way, has redrawn the boundaries and functions between state and society, which have both become more fluid and plural, as well as being witness to changing patterns of family life, which has become decentred, and new forms of identity and more particularistic ties of solidarity. Much of what was operative before remains in being: state and firm hierarchies, exchange in the market and many elements of patriarchy. But greater complexity and variability have given centrality to a principle of coordination – network – which has become more necessary to articulate more fluid and flexible processes, which cannot be understood and projected a priori, due to increased social variability. Law has also assumed a procedural, society-orientated guise, specifically in order to cope with this elusive social tissue. The successive waves of modernization and differing societal configurations have yielded a rather complex imaginary and institutional stage of modernity. The expression 'mixed articulated modernity' aims precisely at making this clear.[9]

Complexity and Contemporary Modernity

Bearing this in mind and eschewing the functionalist idea underpinning the notions of differentiation, complexity and integration in Durkheim, Parsons and Habermas, a thesis emerges: *an increase in the complexity of social life, which derives from a manifold social process in which differentiation and de-differentiation feature alongside each other, has demanded a growth in complexity in the form of solidarity in contemporary modernity*. This means that *a more complex mix and the joint operation of distinct principles of coordination – market, hierarchy and network – is imposed upon our dealings with nature and with one another*. Contemporary modernity has left its pristine days, its moments of inception, far behind, when supposedly the market alone, seconded by a weak and self-restrained state and resting on a centred, autonomous and authoritarian family structure, could meet all the necessities human beings might display. Neoliberals still believe in that, but this is clearly a backward-looking utopia, which has nothing to do with the actual, present course of the world. In a highly heterogeneous and complex society, the a posteriori coordination of individuals and collective subjectivities, in the market or elsewhere, as well as their mere framing through civil rights and repressive (command) law – which, albeit previously defined, is often operative only in the aftermath of events – is patently and absolutely insufficient and inadequate. This does not mean that state-hierarchical action is to no avail, yet it requires indeed a new angle, distinct from state socialism, but also from the social democratic welfare state and its 'Latin' American corporatist and developmentalist version.[10]

As seen in chapter 6, Durkheim underscored the distance of the state from the basis of society, hence its incapacity to contribute more finely to the development of social solidarity. Today this has become even more dramatic: overwhelming complexity has turned society into a more opaque object for the state, while simultaneously demanding mechanisms of coordination, principles of organization that bring individuals and collectivities together previous to the enactment of events in social life. In other words, a demand for a priori coordination has set in. It must nonetheless be context-sensitive and respect the heterogeneity and increasing particularity of social situations, thus eschewing rigid a priori patterns, whether legally defined or not. Network mechanisms, which neither necessarily nor always exclude hierarchy and market in specific social settings, have become crucial to connect agents and coordinate their action either positively – in order to advance common projects – or negatively – so as to avoid confrontations and unnecessary social conflicts and sometimes warfare. My investigation of the recent literature on procedural law has already evinced this; the broader compass of this chapter, where solidarity, difference and heterogeneity receive pride of place, makes the point more salient and substantive. Sustaining a functionalist argument is out of the question, but it is important to acknowledge, vis-à-vis the developments I have analysed, that diverse actors and collectivities have pursued several solutions to the problems they throw up.

Many social domains are extremely reified, according to many authors analysed in chapter 1, meaning that freedom has been expelled from modernity. This is in fact true in many domains, although never in a way as extreme as Lukács or Adorno and Horkheimer believed. The economy has for instance been characterized by great rigidity, especially concerning the relationships of subordination and exploitation between capital and labour, a fact deepened recently by neoliberal strategies and economic restructuring. However, not only has this not been absolute, but the struggles carried out by 'labour' – irrespective of the relative decline of importance of class identities and problems of organization for the working classes – have evinced too that people individually and collectively are never merely patients to superior forces (in this case, capital), always retaining the capacity for agency. Also the economic changes of recent times have opened room, due to the increased pace of technological innovation, for flexible strategies of small firms or projects based on connections between distinct and collaborative collective subjectivities, which freely come into network relationships aiming at enhancing their power vis-à-vis big, sometimes almost monopolistic, firms (which undoubtedly remain the major players of capitalist global markets).

In politics, again, this is probably more complicated even if we accept the ideas (cf. the following chapter) of authors who stress the broadening of the 'public sphere' and 'civil society'. Political parties and state bureaucracies are closed to participation; present social movements seem unable to challenge them. But, as already seen, these social movements tend themselves to be much less hierarchical, depending much more on grass-roots mobilization. Moreover, the state as such has become the site of political struggles, not merely an agency of mediation between interests. In the new configuration 'the state is a divided and fractured political relationship, open to competition between agents of political subcontracting, with alternative conceptions of common goods and public goods' – hence becoming 'a field of political struggle much less codified and regulated than conventional political struggles'. 'Societal fascism' has despotically tried to turn the state into a part of its private sphere; democratic struggles will have to offer alternative standpoints and institutional arrangements.[11] An alternative form of popular representation and participation, especially in 'Latin' America, may become what some have called 'associative networks', which link up with a dispersed state decision-making centre.[12] Internationally too, the development of networks between non-governmental organizations has been seen as a novel element in the constitution of a global order, however problematic they may be as agents; the same is true concerning social movements, which have set up loose networks or accomplished more stable forms of transnational mobilization.[13] This is further reinforced if we do not overlook the previously examined changes in the state, which, despite giving occasion for concern and even anxiety, show that increased flexibility may generate spaces for intervention and political struggle that were unavailable a short while ago, perhaps even including the global dimension, although thorny problems arise which I will address in chapter 11.

Neoliberalism, its ideological and anti-working-class and anti-socialist core notwithstanding, possessed some understanding of the stalemates the new situation presented to the state, and proposed the market in its purest form as the solution for them. The steering capacity of the state should be relieved by means of a dislocation of the principle of coordination from those hierarchies to a disperse relationship between agents. Hayek's argument about the incapacity of planning to answer social needs and dynamic, insofar as planners had no knowledge of what really went on in social life, as well as Luhmann's notion of a decentring of social dynamic away from (a blind) state action, both recognize the complexity of modern, especially advanced modern, social life and the need to find a substitute for a state incapable of doing all it is asked to;[14] however, they are both excessively conservative about how that new form of coordination should be achieved, with the market being seen as absolute (particularly for Hayek) and simple. No renewed form of articulation is proposed or perceived. Here, after a more detailed perusal of the complexity of contemporary modernity, we meet the theme of organizational hierarchy but also social solidarity in its broadest theoretical form. While my analysis of law revealed the problems underlying the actual functioning of the principle of equality today, expressed mainly through the notion and the institutions of citizenship, the effort of the present chapter has brought to the fore the social trends which refashion social solidarity – that is, social integration broadly understood – and the principles of coordination connected with it.

Overall, therefore, even in some areas of economic systems and perhaps in social movements themselves as well as in dimensions of state action and structure, freedom has to a variable extent been expanded. This derives in large measure from the impact of disembedding mechanisms, although countervailing mechanisms have entailed other types of constraint. In many social relations and loci of solidarity – in domains Habermas would classify as pertaining to the life world – this is of course pretty obvious: family, love ties, identity building and social movement organization are just the outstanding expressions of such a changed reality. It is not always easy to enjoy this freedom. *Above all it is not a simple matter to prevent current changes leading towards domination rather than freedom*, a threat that obviously lurks in the contemporary situation *as the apotheosis of rational mastery* directed by irrational, particularistic values of powerful agents, which cannot be universalized beyond very shallow ideologies. Moreover abstract universalism has not really been able to provide an umbrella for all individuals and collectivities. Particularism is rampant and demands that we begin with it in some measure, so as to arrive at universal standards and patterns. 'Value generalization', to use Parsons's phrase, can no longer be taken as merely the specification, from the top–down, of values, patterns and norms orientated to universal standards. The pluralization of social life means that, in order to achieve universalism, we must begin with the concrete, specific, particular interests of individuals and collectivities – as Habermas has in great measure correctly perceived and addressed in his discourse ethics against traditional republicanism and Kantianism – although an encompassing universalist ethics must be supposed in order that we can even establish that procedure. However, in order that this does not degenerate into mere individualism and particularism, the 'communicative action' Habermas envisages is not enough. We need more specifically social processes that bond people together in neither a competitive, as is the case of markets, nor a hierarchical way, as within state and business bureaucratic structures.

It is thus to network as a form of coordination, as a principle of organization that we must turn, in both empirical and normative terms: the solidarity of particular collective subjectivities – within and between themselves – and of 'society' (sometimes even on the global plane) is likely to be fostered in such complex a social world precisely by this sort of collaborative social relationship. That said, let me stress that 'real abstractions' must not now be seen as superfluous. Universal rights cannot be disconnected from them and social solidarity leans therefore upon this overarching phrasing of the belonging to a social formation. They are however less robust with respect to that cohesive role in this changed configuration. Each of the sites and axes of solidarity examined here operate as nodal foci of the social space–time. They concentrate energy, affects, investments and attract individuals and collectivities. These see in them the cognitive, normative and expressive concrete means whereby social life is organized, insofar as emotionally charged identities are crafted, and actions and movements enacted with recourse to those sorts of relationship. Who people are, what they can and should do, as well as know, and how they express themselves as human beings and collectivities hinge today mainly on their identification with some sort of love and family ideal and reality, with their belonging to a nation or class or in a specific, particular group dedicated to some cultural or religious activity and on how citizenship is defined and work. Other areas of the social space–time are much thinner than those mentioned above and probably have, at least most of them, their structuring and dynamic somehow and in a variable degree conditioned by those principal sites and axes, even though these are themselves much more decentred and usually heterogeneous today than they probably were in the past.

Let me resume now a point made in chapter 6: the space–time configuration of advanced modernity appears as much more flexible and cut across in modernity by increasingly contradictory rhythms. It is more difficult to be framed simply by the abstract, Newtonian and Hobbesian, conception of time and space, expecting the lingering influence enjoyed by free marketeers and methodological individualism in politics and in social thought. This derives from its highly plural character and localized as well as specific structurings and dynamics. Networks are especially well suited, though by no means operating alone, to offer the means by which to coordinate this complex space–time configuration wherein affects and investments are much more disperse and unevenly distributed, and cannot be taken for granted any longer, that is, in an a priori manner. Motivations for action, which become more differentiated and concretely defined, may take shape in a more harmonious and complementary way (not necessarily excluding conflict and struggle against inequalities and domination) rather than wreak havoc when turned into purely destructive drives and blind conflicts. These can instead, being inherent to social life, be put to productive use within collaborative frameworks. And for such a renewal of social solidarity the traditional faith of the left in the state is somewhat outdated. It cannot ensure actual overall social solidarity to such an extent and with such intensity, either through the definition of rights as institutional and moral norms that establish a common belonging and thus a 'collective conscience' or as the encompassing hierarchical organizer of the nation. This does not mean that the state is superfluous or that its influence and power are waning, as some are prone to claim, but it does not enjoy the centrality it did in the heyday of both liberal and state-organized modernity.

I have throughout part 3 pointed to the increasing heterogeneity of social life in the third phase of modernity. We must reckon with that now in another sense, which does not, however, imply any discontinuity with previous phases of modernity that have always been heterogeneous at a global level. The extent of the growing importance of networks as well as the particular form and content in which they appear entwined with market and hierarchies varies enormously across the globe. We can resume Trotsky's notion of 'uneven and combined' development of capitalism to stress this issue, if we get rid of the reductionist materialist slant he strongly embraced.[15] We could therefore speak of the uneven and combined development of modernity in its third phase at the global level, paying attention also to the fact that those entwinements and specific contents are dependent in large measure upon collective awareness and reflexivity, choice and its unintended consequences. Of course some areas – especially the core countries of the system – play a key and dominant role in the dynamic of the whole system.

Freedom, Equality and Solidarity

Freedom, particularism and solidarity, tending towards the universalization of values, norms and patterns of behaviour, would thereby possibly join forces in our extremely complex social formations. This happens in many domains and in variable measure everywhere today, in spite of counter-tendencies connected to domination, exclusion and mere rational mastery. Law has been particularly effective when it is capable of recognizing this sort of problem and answering it creatively. Social solidarity would thus have found an appropriate mechanism, which does not rest on previous norms and a culturally and socially homogeneous sort of 'collective consciousness', but hinges on the acknowledgement of particular collective subjectivities, of distinct desires and perspectives. It must be daily refashioned in an active, voluntary and responsible way by individuals and collectivities. Law as such, instead of figuring as a mere expression of underlying social processes, can support the development of social solidarity insofar as it is crafted to produce voluntary collaboration between agents, including in many cases the state, through either the juridical system proper or counting on other of its manifold branches.

The unfolding of contemporary modernity in a democratic and integrated direction may depend on such a move. Otherwise it is not unlikely that it will fall into a sort of barbarian particularism and ad hoc solutions sanctioned by the creation of zones of discretion responsive to powerful interests alone. True corporate enclaves would thus come about, far from effectively universalistic and integrative social processes, having the market or colonized state apparatuses as their underpinnings, not to mention the expansion of (networked – but also highly hierarchical) organized crime throughout the world. We already note this in several societies across the planet, especially in the Americas and the East, implying an absolutely perverse way of bringing to fruition the network principle, which ends up captured by vested interests and powerful and exclusionary agents.[16] It may also be that, as some suggest, networks are conducive or at least may evince an 'elective affinity' with renewed forms of socialism.[17] Even if this were not the case, and at this is stage it does not appear really to be, a democratic and pluralistically respectful, integrative and dialogical development of modernity seems to hinge on how far we can link the network principle to communicative and democratic institutional forms. The present, third phase of modernity, which I have called 'mixed articulated', is open to the social struggles and the intervention of distinct social agents, of individuals and collective subjectivities. *Its precise future contours are still in the process of being delineated and will thus depend on the outcome of those struggles, as well as at least partly on our correct understanding of what is going on and may possibly emerge*, although the present situation does not look at all beautiful and a compact, although decentred, world power has set in, which answers by means of 'hybridisms' to the complexity of the ongoing phase of modernity.[18] Therefore 'power, law and money become globalized at the cost of democratic solidarity'.[19]

For all we have hitherto discussed, domination and unfreedom, inequalities and even exclusion are built into the social fabric of modernity. But we have seen too that freedom and equality constitute deep-seated features of the modern imaginary and institutions, organizing our cognitive, normative and expressive perspectives with respect to social relationships and personal fulfilment. The present chapter has tried to show that solidarity is to be framed with the same sort of approach. We cannot think of ourselves as other than free, whether in a cognitive or a normative sense. Nor can we find self-expression – individual and collective – other than in a free vein; nor simply accept that the world is not or ought not to be based on equality, not least because freedom otherwise degenerates into privilege and the particularities that lend meaning to each of us – individually and collectively – would tend to fade away. We entertain both a cognitive (especially vis-à-vis real abstractions and citizenship) and a normative standpoint regarding equality, although this is usually excessively thin in expressive terms. Solidarity is closely linked with these two categories on those three planes, frequently assuming a legal form. Cognitively solidarity has evolved in modernity from a simpler conception, which stressed the social pact and its expression in a protective state crafted to support individual rights, reaching a second stage in which a stronger and interventionist state stood out, conceived of as the guardian of society and guarantor of social ties and collective belonging. We have eventually reached a more complicated situation insofar as greater freedom and variability (reflexively elaborated) demand social institutions capable of making openness and particularity compatible with the sense of sharing a common destiny, which in turn summons the category of equality.

This is a condition of and is conditioned by a normative standpoint that deems such compatibility both necessary and healthy. Thereby people can also express themselves according to their own view, irrespective of the degree of common-sense essentialism and ideology that can be at work in this, while at the same time not choosing antagonistic identities and relations. Instead they might opt for solidary links that imply mutual recognition and collaboration, finding roots for this in the first place in equal freedom. In this regard the social construction of solidarity in more complex societal configurations typical of the third phase of modernity, in the imaginary and the institutional domains, calls for further reflexivity in the cognitive, normative and expressive dimensions, especially if we refuse to accept that it degenerates into a fragmented, despotic and exclusionary social formation. We are all, individually and collectively, implicated in such a choice, from which there is no escape, except through a relapse into 'bad faith', as Sartre would have it.

In addition we can suggest that there is a strong relationship between solidarity and transcendence. Solidarity means being open to the other, reaching out to other people, other collectivities, at least partly in their own terms. We saw in chapter 1 that modernity has placed freedom at the heart of transcendence; this means that some relationship between freedom and solidarity must be expected. This is true in all areas of social life, whether in friendship and love or in economic and social enterprises. Of course freedom may assume a rather individualistic and self-regarding outlook – this is common in modernity as well, since individualism and competition are central features of its hermeneutic fabric and institutions, not to mention the trend towards rational mastery over people and its connection to domination. Freedom may go in the other direction, though, as it often does, to variable degrees: if solidarity relations are to be built and maintained there must be some sort of openness and collaboration with others, which means that we must open up to, and engage with, other individuals and collective subjectivities. I have examined some of the principal and changing ways in which this has occurred. But there is a further complication here. We saw earlier that freedom may be self-cancelling, that reflexivity may rule itself out. The same applies in what concerns solidarity: the dialectic between freedom and transcendence may turn out to pervade solidarity, which may be built in more open-ended ways or through rigidified and dogmatic means, whether again in compulsive monogamy or in religious identities, in order to escape contingency and the responsibility attached to it. In sum, such re-embeddings may assume distinct countenances. Should compulsion or dogmatism prevail, even in this case transcendence might really come into being; and it would nevertheless operate in opposition to freedom. Freedom and equality taken in one sense as a drive for, and in another as presuppositions of, social action and movement is what may provide for transcendence in collaborative, network relationships, whereby our belonging to a common social – and natural – world may be secured. A more inclusive and communicative understanding of ourselves, which may provide patterns for our common affairs and ways for individual and collective expression may become extant against the negative tendencies of the age, which must not go unheeded.

We have reached a further stage in our investigation. It was possible initially to search for an articulation between the three categories thus far studied, bringing out their intimate ties and the possibilities open today for the future of such an articulation. We were once again confronted with the typical tensions of modernity with reference to each of those central categories when treating solidarity. The past tensions between freedom, equality and solidarity were imposed on our meditation, especially vis-à-vis the possibilities of rephrasing that tension or, on the other hand, of an agonizing contradiction between them. It also became clear that the problem of responsibility is connected to the principles of coordination of social life. Every form of solidarity implies social action and specific sorts of exercise of responsibility. This is what we have seen throughout modernity – and it is at stake once again.

Part 4

Responsibility

9 • Social Theory and Responsibility

Some Basic Issues

Responsibility has been a topic of enormous importance for the social conceptions of modernity, in regard to both definitions of individual behaviour and societal order. But it has not been a central theme of debate, remaining in the background as a crucial issue. It has certainly been more than a 'residual category', since it is not just present without being discussed, but it has not enjoyed the centrality it deserves. In order to help to change this situation, I will start my discussion by introducing the notion of responsibility in general terms, as well as investigating in particular its sociological formulations. In the following chapter we will move to a theoretical reconstruction of the historical development of responsibility in modernity, bringing out its polarization between the individual and society. Finally in the last chapter collective responsibility and responsibility in general in contemporary modernity will be at stake.

There are several ways in which responsibility must be approached; they vary historically also within the bounds of modern civilization. A minimal definition may be that: 'The condition for responsibility is causal power.' He who has acted must be held responsible for his deed, whether or not the outcome was intended, a view with, first, legal but also ethical consequences. Alternatively we could define responsibility as the 'obligation to acknowledge care (*Sorge*) for another being' that is threatened in its 'vulnerability', though here some indeterminacy creeps in, since the extent of one's duty towards the future state of such a being is not necessarily clear.[1] These are basic and proper, however minimal, definitions. Especially inasmuch as our goal here is to work out its phrasing and implications in modernity, we must now point to its relationship with the modern view of agency.

We saw with Sartre, although I was careful to distinguish what is a general ontological condition of humanity from its radicalized situation in modernity, that the situation of freedom and choice has a component which is dreadfully and wonderfully thrust upon human beings. Those who are not free – and this is the conjuring trick always tried by those who have recourse to 'bad faith' – cannot be asked to take responsibility for their choices and deeds. They are not agents, but merely patients to external social forces. Nevertheless, once we assume our freedom, this imperative moral requirement is inescapable. We must add, to recall the reasoning of chapter 2, that this is typically and foremost a predicament of modernity, regardless of a certain amount of freedom, based on even a minimal amount of power, being available to human individuals and collectivities in the most unfavourable situations. Furthermore, as Sartre remarks, by choosing a course of action for ourselves we choose it for the whole of humanity – which means that we take responsibility not only for our own personal acts but for all steps anyone else may take due to our discrete choice as well.[2] Whether or not there is an exaggeration in this view, which makes an unwarranted use of Kant's categorical imperative – which would not actually make sense in a highly individualistic conception, since it corresponds to a highly plural social world – will not be pursued here. Suffice it to note that modernity has given responsibility a particular place in the architectonics of moral reasoning and behaviour, due to its connection to freedom – as well as with equality and solidarity, a more subtle point for later. There is a proviso, to be clarified below. Although conservatism has in general given responsibility a prominent place in social thinking and institutions, its role and importance have not been restricted to this current in modernity: they cut across the whole gamut of political positions, posing a crucial question for all areas of social life.

Responsibility has been a familiar topic in juridical reasoning. In civil law it was classically defined by the 'obligation to repair the damages one has caused', in penal law, by the 'obligation of bearing punishment'. *Obligation* receives pride of place in both cases – someone is responsible and is thus under certain obligations. Further on I will examine some points related to obligation in terms of the original contract which founded the social pact, according to the liberal tenets that have to date still served as legitimation for the modern state. Let me now note that in legal reasoning *imputation* formerly had a relationship with obligation, and was in fact the notion employed, rather than responsibility. One should be *accountable* for not meeting an obligation or not abiding by that which is allowed; that is, while one should repair the situation brought about by one's missteps or suffer punishment for them, the 'hard core' of the notion of imputation was the *attribution* of the action to its 'true' author.

In moral terms, within Kantian metaphysics, this implied the 'free spontaneity' of action as causality, although the heteronomic causality of things was also operative in his view.[3] Based on internal freedom and the autonomy of the subject as well as with respect to its own principles, moral action was distinguished from action aimed at a specific end, which might assume the form of a juridical obligation, especially in order to avoid negative sanctions. In the former we are responsible before ourselves; in the latter juridical legislation entails duties that prescribe only external freedom and demand responsibility before the community. Categorical imperatives to conform freely to universal moral laws stem from the former; hypothetical imperatives, being exterior and somehow contingent, are all that can stem from the latter.[4]

Following developments have, however, tended to restrict the scope of that notion to its juridical meaning, although this was not absolute (as witnessed by Sartre's philosophical œuvre). In contrast, all the same, contemporary developments have lent responsibility a renewed and indeed thus far unknown position in social thought in a variety of areas, from philosophy and morals to juridical and political approaches, often in a somewhat loose way.[5] Why? Whereas responsibility – in either a direct or indirect manner, qua for instance *obligation* or *duty* – has performed a decisive role in modernity as a whole, it is not by chance, we may suppose, that it has recently become so visible. Underlying changes in, and demands upon, the notions of freedom and solidarity, and in particular in and upon responsibility itself, press in this direction.

Let me resume an issue that was introduced in chapters 1 and 2. Drawing upon Morse's depiction of the Iberian American path, structured by the neo-Thomism of the Second Scholastic in the sixteenth and the seventeenth centuries, as an alternative to the 'North Western design', I have outlined a distinct conception of freedom – and, implicitly, of responsibility. Sartre is patently an heir, in this as well as in other regards, to the Protestant background according to which individuals, once God left the world, were responsible for their deeds and ensuing consequences. Weber's analysis of the 'calling' (*Ruf*) that was germane to a 'vocation' (*Beruf*), which was to be applied to the ascetic transformation of this world, is one way of grasping the Protestant notion of responsibility. Another one may be directly connected to the notion of a covenant between God and men, which founded earthly communities, lying at the roots of the contractarian conceptions typical of the beginnings of the modern bourgeois era;

accordingly, 'men' are responsible for the political state of their communities as an issue that pertains to their conscience.[6] Nelson crafted a link that synthesized this idea, which was associated also to developments in the conception of knowledge: *science–conscience*. It happened in Protestantism but also in the north-western European Renaissance, in sum in early modernity.[7] Individuals were deemed responsible for what happened around them and especially for their actions and their consequences. Their conscience was now the locus of morality, which was socially somewhat emptied, insofar as state and church could no longer be seen as entities which had a specific existence; instead they were emergent realities which had morally responsible individuals as their underpinning and ultimate substratum. It is not difficult to fathom the origins of methodological individualism and all previous and later connected doctrines at least in the quite radical strands of Protestantism. The same is true in relation to the origins of Kant's notion of autonomy as the internal responsibility with respect to moral law.

In Iberian America the opposite was true. It was not that a profound renovation of political and social thought had not taken place; on the contrary, authors such as Suárez and Molina were quite inventive and *modern*. Nevertheless, morality and responsibility remained related to the individual to a great extent as *external* phenomena. As for religion, the church was kept as the spiritual body entitled to strive for faith; as for politics and the integration of the increasingly complex empires and heterogeneous populations overseen by the Iberian countries, the state was ascribed exclusive jurisdiction. Religious and political individual agents did not forcefully introject norms. This had consequences for later developments in those two modern universes, although the issue is controversial, especially concerning the conformation of subjectivity and the democratic potential of that tradition.[8] In Iberian-colonized America no political and social philosophy has explicitly worked from those definitions, but they seem to have been maintained as tacit and unspoken presuppositions. In contradistinction, in the 'North Western design' that standpoint has become a central piece of moral philosophy.

Irrespective of its connection with equality being less immediate in general (but rather close in modernity – more on that in a moment) the link between responsibility and solidarity is almost plain to see, notwithstanding other interpretations that differ from this and will be analysed in detail later. To include the other, recognize her rights and give her the appropriate esteem implies already an attitude of responsibility for the other's well-being and dignity. Taking the role of the other, proximate or 'generalized other', and thus being responsive to him or her and putting oneself in his or her shoes, is what propels us to consider our own responsibilities – our duties and their needs – towards individuals and collectivities as well as towards society as a whole. This is what Mead more or less implicitly stated.[9] How this has been carried out and evinced in modernity is not a simple story however; instead it has evolved during the last two centuries in rather distinct directions and multifarious ways. Responsibility may have itself as its own contrary: individualistically conceived of selfish responsibility may result in absolute irresponsibility vis-à-vis other people and collectivities, although it may appear as sheer recklessness, including the attitude one has towards oneself, which is one way freedom has sometimes been phrased, especially in the twentieth century. And it can pitch hierarchy against equality insofar as, combined with individualism or not, responsibility is put into the hands of powerful persons and collective subjectivities. Nonetheless – and this is normatively our best bet – the bridge between freedom qua transcendence and transcendence qua solidarity will be built, analytically mirroring what happens in reality, as we will see, through the notion of responsibility. Otherwise either the conception of freedom is highly individualistic and risks the vicinity of the loss of meaning, or solidarity eschews freedom and is captured by hierarchical, authoritarian forms of relationship, thus by domination one way or another. This is why a link between equality and responsibility, albeit neither exclusive nor absolute, must be expected in modernity too: freedom and solidarity can be joined only insofar as the former is extant, for which equality, as argued previously, is imperative. Nevertheless, the social dynamic and the contradictions of really existing modernity yield other connections between these categories, and even when the aforementioned ones come about they may appear in tandem with other elements.

If we return to Weber's work, a further initial elaboration of the problem can be accomplished. His (ideal-typical) distinction between the 'ethic of conviction' – which has eyes only for the values that must be implemented, regardless of foreseen or unexpected consequences – and the 'ethic of responsibility' – concerned with the consequences of action – is well-known, though it seems only partially explored within the general architecture of his writings.[10] Any value may be in principle subject to those two kinds of ethics; egalitarian ethics may be a case in point, as in Weber's Nietzschean example of Christ's universalist

Sermon on the Mount. The problem is that, in terms of social action, things stand on a much more hierarchical ground. After all, freedom and meaningful action regarded in their most encompassing form would pertain really only to a charismatic leader, if we took Weber at face value. For him people usually just follow such leaders or live in the limits of meaningful social action, under traditional domination in its varied expressions or in rational–legal modern meaningless domination. One can always argue that Weber is merely providing ideal-types also in terms of his typology of action. However, apart from passages such as those in 'The City', Weber is adamant about the creation of new universes of meaning by prophets and similar figures, to whom lay people attribute special qualities and of whom they become followers.[11] Those leaders alone are capable of embracing any sort of ethics in the full sense of the word. This is even more so in the case of the 'ethic of responsibility', which is explicitly cast within the bounds of leadership concerns. An 'elitist' conception of ethics and social action is here patently present. And this must be avoided.

I have elsewhere argued against Weber that creativity must be regarded as pervading social life, being always in some degree exercised by individual actors and collective subjectivities. Responsibility too must be conceived of as an issue linked to human action and collective movement as such, and the position of agents in the social hierarchy makes no difference whatsoever when this question is at stake. Nietzsche's influence on Weber was detrimental with respect to this specific aspect of ethics and a modern understanding of responsibility. This must be eschewed at the cognitive level, so that responsibility is related to action and movement irrespective of the particular historical context. Practically, the consequences of action and movement stretch unavoidably into the future, regardless of who has produced them: they are irreversible. The only two ways to respond are either forgiveness (as affirmed by Jesus) or punishment, insofar as they at least make those subject to them no longer responsible for those consequences, hence – contrary to revenge – allowing for the renewal of life.[12] At the normative level the 'elitist' outlook ought also to be resisted: the demand of equality makes responsibility something to be shared as an opportunity as well as a burden by all individuals and collectivities of modern social formations. This has indeed been present throughout modernity, featuring either the individual or the state. Collective subjectivities have been more rarely brought into this frame; the time, however, seems right for a more extensive exploration of this possibility.

Sociological Views

None of the three categories I have hitherto dwelt upon is by any means novel as a focus either for social and political or for theoretical thinking, although I hope to have thrown light on some of their aspects and developed some at least partly innovative explanatory schemes. Differently from freedom, equality and solidarity, responsibility is not a category that figures prominently either in social discourse or in theory. Of course it is a staple of everyday vocabulary, and conservative politicians have lately tried to make a public, devious case for it, resuming former liberal usage which I will examine later. But responsibility has never received comparable attention to those three former categories. These are not the only reasons for it deserving to appear alongside them in the scheme of exposition. This is so also because a certain shift in social thinking is likely to be under way. Strydom has recently suggested that the cognitive frame of responsibility is, at the beginning of the twentieth-first century, taking over from that of justice, as the latter did, during the twentieth century, vis-à-vis the paradigm of rights, prevalent in the nineteenth century.[13] While this may be an overstatement, it captures some interesting moves, besides emphasizing that responsibility does not simply substitute for the other two former historical frames. As Strydom recognizes, the sociological literature has given some attention to the topic yet this still represents short shrift compared with what should be the case. We saw above with Weber some important ideas with respect to responsibility in relation to individual orientations; let us further explore two other sociological conceptions that set responsibility in an implicit or explicit relation with more inclusive social systems, beyond individual action.

Utilizing the notion of 'duty', in regard to the distinct functions individuals performed in the division of social labour, Durkheim dealt with the idea of responsibility, although this implied a less than active position for the individual, who was 'coerced' (his more or less spontaneous choice of a role notwithstanding) within the particular morals of his profession.[14] In theoretical terms this was developed far more and in a more sophisticated manner by Parsons, to some extent bearing in mind traditional discussions of political obligation and the 'sociology of professions'. He provided a rather encompassing and general definition of 'responsibility', bringing together many concepts extracted from other dimensions of the 'social system'. Parsons was especially concerned in his functional approach – which was a theoretical construction featuring stability as a central idea, though in reality change was an ongoing process – with 'relatively stable interaction in the social system'. *Role-expectations*, functionally cast, allowed for that, since in principle they helped to overcome the 'double contingency' of interaction (which makes it unpredictable) that would otherwise prevail. Those expectations depend on 'value-standards' with a degree of 'moral significance' (that is, they are more or less deeply introjected by the personality) and 'conformity' in what was expected from the occupants of roles, and implied the fulfilment of 'obligations' by 'ego' regarding the 'larger action system'. This entailed a 'sense of responsibility' which created a *solidarity* among those orientated to 'common values', forming a *collectivity* – not exactly synonymous with the concept of social system, but one that implicated some sort of activity and awareness, regardless of the somewhat fuzzy state of such concepts at the time within Parsons's general theory. This was not connected to instrumental advantages, usually the avoidance of 'negative sanctions' in the case in point; instead it stemmed from an emotional attachment to the values of the collectivity.

Parsons chose to tie responsibility in with 'collectivity-orientation' versus 'self-orientation' in terms of the definition of his fifth 'pattern-variable' (the five supposedly possessed universal validity and could be used to interpret any social action). Moreover the 'acting in concert' of the collectivity – for which Parsons summoned his own, problematic, excessively and necessarily centred, idea of collective subjectivity – hinges directly on individuals 'taking responsibility' for 'collective goals'.[15] Parsons relates more specifically the responsibility of the occupants of specific roles to particular and variable 'competence' as well as to 'facilities' and 'rewards', the latter varying in a manner directly proportional to the former. Nevertheless he left unexplored the consequences in any depth, apart from some considerations about the role of physician, and, negatively, about the 'sick role', allowing its occupant to be 'exempted from "responsibility"', perhaps becoming a form of passive deviance with respect to the norms of the social system.[16]

Later on, in passages very relevant for discussions related to state-organized modernity, Parsons analyses responsibility in modernity bearing in mind a twofold state task vis-à-vis society. With recourse to Marshall's classical theory (cf. in chapter 3), Parsons remarked that the social 'component' of citizenship implies that the 'well-being' of citizens is 'treated as a public responsibility'. This was so to speak the benign side of his assessment, to which a more Hobbesian standpoint was adduced, related to social control and repression. Government had two 'primary functions' in an evolutionarily differentiated society: the first concerned 'responsibility for maintaining the integrity of the societal community against generalized threats', especially with reference to 'its legitimate normative order', a task which included enforcement and to some extent 'interpretation' of both that order and so-called threats, as well as the legislative creation of new norms; the second function carried the burden of taking specific measures to respond to the 'public' interest, including defence of the territory and the maintenance of 'public order'.[17] 'Effective' and 'responsible' leadership became a necessity in particular in complex societies; he supposed it could not operate without authority and a 'considerable concentration of power'.[18]

These passages from Parsons, albeit rather brief, since he did not give the topic further attention, are decisive for a preliminary understanding of responsibility in general terms but also in what concerns modernity. We have already briefly seen with Sartre and Weber that freedom and responsibility have strong connections, and that equality in modernity cannot but be implicated therein for reasons formerly discussed. Parsons has helped to bring out the relationship between responsibility and solidarity in a trenchant way, certainly drawing upon the pragmatism of authors such as Mead. His functional approach is less than adequate to allow for a proper grasp of the problem. However, an opening to the encompassing collectivity, which leads actors and other collective subjectivities away from exclusive self-reference, comes out clearly, albeit too strongly, in his discussion. Solidarity and responsibility are clearly interwoven. Other passages of his, cast at a very general theoretical level and also under the influence of pragmatism and symbolic interactionism (though these were not named due to academic power games), were much more concerned with the intersubjective construction of social life and would have been more interesting for a proper outline of the category of responsibility. Parsons's decision for functionalism as a 'second best' for sociological theorizing, in what he believed was a provisional absence of a general hypothetical–deductive scheme, prevented that move; this meant in fact an avoidance of freedom by and large as a topic of inquiry and more specifically with respect to responsibility, insofar as role-expectations functionally – that is, systemically – defined, provided values and norms which could not be openly and flexibly dealt with by their incumbents.

That is precisely what I will try to reverse in due course, in order to weave together theoretically the four categories that stand out in this study. Although I will not go into any detail here, a much more contingent view of social life and interaction, as well as a more active and flexible view of individuals and collective subjectivities, is assumed throughout this book, which sees functional statements at most as more or less useful methodological devices – prone to yield as much misunderstanding as to throw light on the workings of social life.[19] On the other hand, although Parsons was quite insightful in his account of the relationship between the welfare state and responsibility, there is no need to embrace his functionalist-conservative view of authoritarian order enforcement and interpretation by the state as a responsibility that is unavoidably (in evolutionary terms) thrust upon it. We must accept that a democratic state must strive for peace within its frontiers and with other states in order to respond properly to the duties it is trusted with by its constitutional contract. A more democratic solution for this can however be found, implying intermediate collective subjectivities, a point to be dwelt upon later.

In sum, responsibility is cognitively fundamental for our identities: the definition of who is responsible for what lies at its core. We can also make use of it expressively when we want or decide to emphasize and play out some aspect of the social roles we are supposed to perform. It is however in the normative dimension that responsibility appears as a crucial notion: what we ought or are expected to do in the world carries the main weight of its outline in the hermeneutic dimension of social systems. After having situated some of the main features of responsibility, it is time to examine its evolution in the unfolding of modernity.

10 • The Transformations of Responsibility

From Individualism to Statism

Let us explore the forms and contents responsibility has assumed in modernity, reconstructing theoretically its historical trajectory. In the beginning it was the individual and his – equal – freedom, a natural development of ideas that lay at the foundation of modern thinking as it emerged in the Renaissance and Protestantism. This founding figure of liberal thought and liberal modernity was everything in the constitution of society, hence in the overall scheme of responsibility. The state, however, had a necessary part to perform at that very beginning, lest insecurity or warfare prevail and spoil the opportunities open to 'men', literally, in nature or society, guaranteeing a minimal social solidarity. It is not possible to expand on the issue here, but it is important to note that modern thought has at its core a stark polarization between the individual and society, often represented by the state.[1] Not by chance is such a polarization concretely repeated in the two paramount and successive forms of reckoning with responsibility in modernity.

I will take two paths in order to grasp the development of responsibility in modernity: first, a brief look at the evolution of political thought, then Ewald's work will broaden the scope of analysis, which will next move towards an understanding of the contemporary reinforcement of individualism. I will examine Boltanski and Chiapello's view of the third phase of capitalism and dwell upon Giddens's support of the British 'Third Way'.

Though not a liberal, Hobbes offered the first, or at least the paradigmatic, scheme of the individualistic perspective in the political realm. The restless struggle of everyone against everyone was an intrinsic and structuring trait of the state of nature. However, in order to live well more was required: people were therefore inclined to the accumulation of power – wealth mainly – and its use against other people, either because this was an ('irrational') internal drive or due to the ('rational') necessity of being always ready to defend oneself against others, even when the individual had no special drive towards accumulation of power per se. The solution for this ongoing warfare was to give up one's sovereignty in favour of the Leviathan, to which our (prudential – that is, self-interested – and moral) duty was therefore entrusted. We should obey this sovereign power, at the peril of losing even our own lives, if we want to achieve a civilized life and preserve the pre-condition for everything else, namely security.[2]

For liberalism political obligation stemmed from the commitments men established on occasion of the original contract, introducing freedom and citizenship. Women were utterly excluded from public responsibility at this stage; the social contract was founded on the 'sexual contract', which subordinated them to men. This has only slowly changed, and not completely even today.[3] Moreover, pristine liberalism often strongly denied that all men were equally rational in political terms. For Locke this was due to the fact that in the 'state of nature' they had lost the opportunity of remaining proprietors, even integrally of their labour, which they then had to sell regularly. Hence, having joined 'civil society' already in a degraded situation and lacking both the means and the time for their enlightenment, they could not behave fully rationally, having thus no right to take part in the political affairs of the country. In principle all were able to take care of – and were therefore responsible for – themselves; some, however, proved to be incapable even of that and had to be placed under complete subjection to the state. Almost or partly deprived of rationality the members of the working class could not be admitted to the upper layers of rights of 'civil society'. They were basically subject to the state, towards which it could be said they had the duty to obey, but no political responsibility proper.[4]

In Rousseau political obligation took in turn a strict democratic shape, departing in many aspects from the liberal theory of political obligation. In no other way could political authority be legitimate: men had a duty only towards the laws which emanated from the 'general will', whereby freedom was preserved, in fact was truly established, and no one would be under somebody else's domination.[5] Yet only slowly, and after many social struggles, did a more inclusive political perspective develop overall, encompassing the whole population. For liberals, even while bereft of political responsibility, individuals could not avoid responsibility in civil terms and especially regarding their own life and destiny, except provisionally and paying a heavy price, a point which was in fact a central tenet of their world view, as will be seen below. In these liberal or democratic accounts, individualistic voluntarism and conventionalism vis-à-vis the institution of political power – an artificial construction – have had pride of place.[6] Whatever the specific content of the Iberian version of the absolutist state, in the last two centuries it has had meanwhile to adjust one way or another to the modernizing processes that take place everywhere modernity has unfolded – albeit in distinct guises and entangled with other traditions. The prevailing notion of authority has therefore been as a consequence inclined towards democracy as well.[7]

Generally speaking, '[i]n its paradigmatic form political obligation is the duty incumbent on any person or set of persons legitimately subject to a political authority to obey the legitimate commands of that authority'. Originally it was conceived of simply within the frame of the nation-state; increasingly, however, it became associated with democratic claims, which have been difficult both to fulfil and to abandon as a principle of legitimation, implying a democratic transformation of liberalism. And at least in manifest discourse democracy is indeed a banner carried by virtually anyone engaged in public life.[8] Initially, responsibility in modern political thought was to a great extent identified with the notion of *obligation* and extended piecemeal to embrace the whole population: individuals were then seen as having obligations towards the sovereign – being responsible, accountable for their actions – due to their having entered a social pact, namely the pristine contract among themselves and/or with the state (constitutional or not). The conception of 'individual moral responsibility', a modern phenomenon, was 'essential for the idea of self-assumed obligation'.[9] The rights and duties of citizenship were framed according to this, and the social contract and the enforcement of natural rights were the primary focus of solidarity during liberal modernity. From the turn of the twentieth century onwards more 'realistic' approaches – Weber providing the centre-piece – changed their angle. They took the 'elites' as properly responsible, since supposedly they alone possessed rationality.

I have argued above that Weber's notion of responsibility, due to its Nietzschean origins, was relative to political leadership only. It is not therefore difficult to grasp its links with the Roman and medieval tradition which Hegel rephrased through his notion of a universal class, the bureaucracy, which would overcome the centrifugal and individualistic forces of civil society.[10] Marx broke away from this by denouncing the state as the universal capitalist and as a class dictatorship – no political authority was seen as really legitimate, except the organized revolutionary working class during the socialist transitional phase to communism. With this idea he lent a strong dialectical twist to the idea of democracy and implicated every individual in the administration of social life and as responsible for it and for a free but fair use of common resources in the classless social formation of the future (as expressed in the sentence 'to each according to his needs').[11] In turn anarchists radicalized abstract individualism and concluded that all claims to political obligation and authority are devious.[12] Moving precisely in the opposite direction Weber swept away any real democratic claims and substituted – liberal North American translations notwithstanding – 'domination' (*Herrschaft*) for authority, domination had to be legitimate so that political order survived, yet there was no hint of democracy beyond the plebiscitary rituals enacted to select leadership and the rule of formally rationalized law.[13] Not by chance has the domination and the rule of the 'elites' come to the fore once again and become the kernel of mainstream political thought, nevertheless without recourse now to the idea of tradition (a delusion indeed of the modern age), when democracy became a problematic fact of political life for ruling collectivities. Authority involved obedience without coercion, but without persuasion too, which rests on the democratic principle of equality.[14] Rationality (or rather a supposed lack of it) substituted tradition in the job of containing mass participation and legitimating the domination of the 'elites'.

Schumpeter was adamant in his definition of the citizen as irrational and incapable of responsibility. He argued that Le Bon and Freud had shown that people have confused and vague volitions. The aggregations of such volitions cannot achieve actual coherence. The complexity of modern societies prevents people from administering the state and steering social life. At most, people can have a mind to the issues that more closely surround and interest them, though this is not even necessarily the case; finally '[t]he typical citizen drops down to a lower level of mental performance as soon as he enters the political field', becoming 'a primitive again'.[15] As he put it rather bluntly:

> This reduced sense of reality accounts not only for a reduced sense of responsibility but also for the absence of effective volition. One has one's phrases, of course, and one's wishes and daydreams and grumbles: especially, one has one's likes and dislikes. But ordinarily they do not amount to what we call a will – the psychic counterpart of purposeful responsible action. In fact, for the private citizen musing over national affairs there is no scope for such a will and no task at which it could develop. He is a member of an unworkable committee, the committee of the whole nation, and this is why

he expends less disciplined effort on mastering a political problem than he expends on a game of bridge.[16]

In virtue of social complexity and the citizen's irrationality and irresponsibility, democracy must be realistically assessed. A new definition, indeed a far cry from the far-fetched claims of traditional democratic doctrines, must be proposed, according to which 'the democratic method is that institutional arrangement for arriving at political decisions in which individuals acquire the power to decide by means of a competitive struggle for the people's vote'.[17] Responsibility, it is tacitly and unavoidably understood, is a prerogative of the 'elites' (a restrictive collective subjectivity, ultimately based on privilege). Henceforth almost all 'elitist' theories embraced this standpoint and a much more conservative and *anti-egalitarian* view of 'democracy' and responsibility was established. The functioning of state-organized modernity, including the periods of social democratic government, banked on this sort of perspective, whereby political leadership selected a package of issues and solutions which were periodically offered to the electorate, leaving little room for the expression of independent voices and social movements which were not carefully controlled by party and union machines.[18] Liberalism had come full circle and responsibility was once again seen as impossible for ordinary men and women of the modern 'democratic' societies, discarding the 'unrealistic' expectations of contractarian democratic theories. Once again we were not very distant from ideas such as 'state reason', through which Renaissance authors such as Machiavelli resumed, obliquely, the traditional notion of 'authority'.[19]

In sum, we may say that, although pristine contractarian theories do not use such a wording, he who has failed to abide by the terms of the *pact* or the *covenant* may be *imputable* for such a failure, for which he is responsible as he is for keeping his promise of abiding by those terms. As seen above, for Kant, especially vis-à-vis the conjunction between law and freedom which underpinned the categorical imperative, this had strong *moral* bearings. For others this was *prudential*, rational instrumentally, in that to survive men had no choice except to yield to the Leviathan or craft the legal state, whether or not in the last instance citizens were the ultimate source and pillar of sovereignty, or from 'need' an 'ought to' emerged.

Much of what liberalism had to say about the social pact, the original covenant, was plainly and to an enormous extent mere ideological delusion, although it offered a new solution, which harked back to classical sources, for the old problem of the political legitimation of the state. Now it appeared as the true expression of individual citizens, its creators, therefore no longer its subjects, patients to political power. They assumed the role of causal and moral agents. This blotted out the recognition of the class character of the modern state, a capitalist as well as rational–legal state, masking also the continuing importance of the collective subjectivities that were at the centre and in control of the state apparatus. Despite his 'materialistic' approach Marx perceived this in *The Eighteenth Brumaire of Louis Bonaparte*, whereas de Tocqueville had already denounced the bureaucratic and authoritarian core of the modern state, a heritage of the Old Regime, which had been nonetheless recreated everywhere modernity had penetrated (with the exception, at the time, of the United States – a thoroughly changed situation at present).[20] Therefore the theories of political obedience connected to the liberal matrix, though stressing the democratic requirements of the legitimation of the modern state, are unable to grasp it as a form of domination. 'Elitist' theories tackled the problem merely 'realistically', underscoring the fact that it conforms to a type of political domination, something that goes smoothly together with their minimal definition of democracy as a competition among political 'elites'. Following in the Marxian–Weberian footsteps sociology has however been much more concerned with the problem of domination, though frequently overlooking the problems of legitimation and political obligation that the modern state requires.[21] In addition, as seen in chapter 5, Habermas has striven to carry on along the democratic track, holding fast to the Kantian and Rousseauian heritage by placing the autonomous citizen at the core of the creation of the state through law, as emanating from and enabling individuals as free citizens. But as he himself recognizes, this is insufficient to overcome the hard core of state domination and the 'elitist' perspective he also resumes through systems theory – the political–administrative system as such remaining a 'self-regulated' body. Is this the best way out of the stalemates of the liberal political theory of political freedom and obligation? Could we not think of other 'collective subjectivities', in more democratic terms than 'elite' theories do (after all those 'elites' are moreover state-based), to move beyond the polarization between individual and society or the state? I will return to this question in chapter 11.

A different way to study the evolution of responsibility is to investigate the development of the legal and general social framework which included the overcoming of liberalism by a clearly social democratic perspective, irrespective of strong continuities. Ewald helps us through the nooks and crannies of such a convoluted evolution, in one of the very few works that has responsibility as a central topic of inquiry.

Inspired by the discontinuity of historical developments underscored by Foucault, as well as by his biopolitical studies on the state and legal regulation of social life in modernity, Ewald refines the traditional view of liberalism as a rigid and immutable doctrine. He visits the debates held in France throughout the nineteenth century, especially regarding labour accidents and also governmental and non-governmental social policies, introduced to ease the burden of workers victimized by those misfortunes. He shows that a clear-cut distinction initially made between moral 'obligations' and arrangements was juridically codified. Opting strongly for the former, nineteenth-century liberalism deemed it necessary to establish strict limits for the latter, particularly with respect to the theme of 'fraternity', since its obligations have 'no rule nor measure'. They are indefinite and unlimited; once the 'liberal limit' is crossed we enter a 'process of multiplication of juridical obligations' whose end is uncertain. Those rights depended on the 'whims of the legislator' and law would end up subordinated to politics, playing havoc with the principles of the social contract and of freedom as such, since for liberals law constitutes civil freedom by keeping underdetermined that which 'is necessary to be wanted'.[22] This entails decisive consequences for the liberal conception of responsibility:

> The liberal position about law condemns it not to recognize any right to insurance (*secour*). Positively phrased this means that *nobody may discharge on another the weight of his existence, of the blows of fate or of the evils that may befall him*, except in the case in which they had been caused by anybody who had infringed the paramount rule of the coexistence of freedoms: not to bother the others. In other words, *each one is, must be, is supposed to be responsible for his own fate, for his life, for his destiny*.[23]

Responsibility consists in the major regulatory notion of human actions, an idea that includes a precise conception of causality, trusted directly and exclusively to the individual – who is guilty for the misdeeds and accountable for the successes of his life. This allows for a regulation of individual and collective perfectibility. Poverty does not escape from this understanding of social life, emerging therefore as a responsibility of he who bears it, who *ought to* bear it: 'there are no *victims* in the liberal world'. This conception is refined by the distinction between 'causality' and 'imputation', according to which it is not enough that someone has caused a negative fact to be deemed responsible – it must be her 'fault' that she caused it. This grants the limitation of the principle of causality on the one hand, assuring on the other the punishment of those guilty for damages caused to somebody else.[24]

But liberalism does not overlook 'precariousness', 'instability' and 'uncertainty' as characteristics of social life. To conquer security is however an 'exigency of freedom', a duty rather than a right, which must be dealt with by means of 'providence', a responsibility of the agent himself. When others assume responsibility its benefits must not be dispensed as a right or in a stable manner, so as not to distort its own voluntary and extraordinary meaning, or twist those favoured by them.[25] Ewald argues that this piecemeal 'liberal diagram' became too timid. 'Pauperism', which defined the poverty of large layers of the population as a social problem, brought along a 'dangerous idea'. It made mandatory a reconsideration of the freedom to work as the exclusive solution for this sort of problem, forcing the consideration of economic, political and social causes of poverty, hence not a responsibility of the poor. To avoid such conclusions a sibylline distinction between the 'conditions' and the 'causes' of poverty was forged: if the former, which could facilitate the appearance of poverty, were due to the industrial system, the latter were maintained as a responsibility of the lack of foresight and of the perversion of the worker. Therefore poverty was reaffirmed as a 'pathology of freedom'. Since the worker could not sort out his own life in such conditions, the task of *solidarity* and social responsibility was trusted to the state, in France from 1841 onwards. A difficult consequence was that the view of equality as a presupposition of the notion of 'providence' was surpassed, at least initially, by a conception that embodied an 'imbalance of responsibilities', with the state turned into the 'bearer of a public interest'.[26]

Only later was the issue entirely settled. During the second half of the nineteenth century a 'conflict of responsibilities' raged, involving employers, workers and the state. Labour accidents and the courts lay at the core of the dispute. Social rights and a new form of solidarity, along with statistics, presented a solution to the matter, partly by thinking of (collective) *risk* in terms of *probabilities* involving groups of the population. Labour accidents and the courts lay at the core of the dispute. Insurance, centralized by the state, was the solution that stemmed from those struggles. There emerged moreover a 'new notion of responsibility' and social rights were established, as well as a new view of the social contract based on solidarity, alongside civil rights and the contracts between private agents. Overcoming the conflicts between labour and employers, the 'Providence State' was inaugurated.[27]

An important conclusion must be drawn from this evolution. The state is now responsible for the welfare of the community and, as Ewald himself has put it, not only must specific groups be targeted, but 'the citizen as such', 'without qualities', that is, as an abstract being,[28] a 'real abstraction', we may say, to refer to the theoretical issues tackled in previous chapters. This move in fact reinforces the previous patterns of that polarization which, from the very first moments of the Enlightenment, have defined the presuppositional field of modernity, namely that between the individual and society, the latter entrusted to the state. If the individual is no longer totally responsible for his destiny and the state (which originally should only oversee the contracts enacted by private agents) alters its function, becoming responsible (at least in part) for that individual, then no new entities are introduced with any centrality, in the imaginary or in legislation, despite the absolute asymmetry between those two poles. Individuals have rights, and the state, above all, has legal obligations vis-à-vis individuals. After all, as we saw in chapter 3, citizens have few duties beyond paying taxes, abiding by the law and, if necessary, dying for their motherland. I will come back to all these issues later on. From individual to collective responsibility, through its definition as 'diffuse' due to the similarly diffuse character of risk, much has changed in the unfolding of modernity.

For Ewald this led to far-reaching changes in the modern legal tradition, with a general tendency to 'give up' the reference to 'a will always susceptible of being its own master and of things'. Against his tendency to overstress the point, it must be said that by no means has the principle of imputation, individually or collectively, been dismissed, and in fact the issue has attracted renewed interest. Nonetheless, a consideration of the technical and social – always collective – processes of production in which it is inscribed has indeed crept in, representing a shift in the view of responsibility as a discrete phenomenon.[29] It is important to note too a movement which strongly pushes in another direction. As will be seen later, this stems from the recognition of the necessity of assuming collective responsibility in a number of distinct and varied ways – for several aspects of social life. It stems also from the increased scope of freedom and thus from the manifold consequences of action in advanced modernity, although this may assume a conservative guise which is not, however, mandatory.

Individualism and the Third Phase of Modernity

Modernity has therefore abided most of the time by a commitment to its two presuppositional poles – the individual and the state – also with regard to the notion of responsibility. Equality meant in principle that all should be responsible for their own destiny, including that of society as a whole, which should be at first accomplished by the acceptance of political obligation as enforced by the state, and the laws born from the social pact. This was despite the fact that many liberal thinkers tended to exclude the mass of the population from the capabilities necessary for the exercise of political responsibility since they were not deemed fit for the use of reason, insofar as they had no free time or control over their own lives. A democratization of responsibility and obligation came about in the course of the nineteenth century. However, the twentieth century celebrated once again political inequalities – through the 'realistic' recommendation of 'elites' – as necessary for the smooth functioning of democracy in complex societies. This sort of move cannot but seriously damage both equality and freedom, since one cannot prosper when no adequate space is granted to the other. Alternative ways of thinking and perhaps of living freedom were also on the rise during the second half of the twentieth century, implying a breakdown of traditional authority and the self-absorption of the individual in herself, hence an absolute lack of attention to the needs and desires of others. Once detached from the constraining role of hard worker and breadwinner, a specific sort of masculinity was revealed as especially disruptive and irresponsible, incautious even vis-à-vis the very individual agent.

Absolutely unrestrained freedom, irrespective of any consequence, underpins this sort of perspective, which is not based either on an 'ethic of conviction' or an 'ethic of responsibility'. This found expression for instance in the output of the so-called 'angry young men' during the 1950s in Britain – 'What I want is a good time. All the rest is propaganda', as declared by one of the working-class literary heroes of the time.[30] In Angela Carter's novel *Love* the same sort of behaviour can be observed, mainly in terms of the rowdy and aggressive conduct of young working-class men, as well as in terms of sexual and emotional exploitation and a lack of any commitment. The same is for instance true of many of Ernest Hemingway's novels and short stories. Research would probably show that such a view of freedom entirely detached from solidarity and responsibility – thus looking in fact dangerously close to the state of nature of liberals spread out in contemporary modernity – was linked to violence and the breakdown of morality as well as to regressive and defensive forms of narcissism.[31] This applies today in particular to the culture of criminal activity with which large parts of the young global population are involved, being unfortunately typical of a world in which 'the boundary between protest, patterns of immediate gratification, adventure, and crime becomes increasingly blurred', since opportunities look bleak for much of contemporary youth, especially in the periphery or in poor and forlorn areas of central modernity.[32]

This has as a counterpart the responsible dedication of women to the household, as wives and mothers, when they perform traditional feminine roles, a division of labour that stems from their exclusion from the social contract through a previous 'sexual contract' of subordination to men, as argued above. As Parsons put it, 'a mature woman can love, sexually, only a man who takes his full place in the world, above all its occupational aspect, and who takes responsibility for a family', while he will love she who 'is really an adult, a full wife to him and mother to his children, and an adequate "person" in her extramarital roles'.[33] One must ask, however, how much less harmful this attitude has been for society at large. Men have traditionally behaved responsibly in the economic and the public sphere, beyond the family, hence embracing more universalist patterns, although more recently, as just argued, they have revealed an irresponsible and often violent attitude, especially after the decline of the breadwinner role and the increase of social marginalization. In turn the concentration of women in the intimate domain has lent their exercise frequently a much more privatist and particularist expression, at odds with broader concepts of responsibility, irrespective of them being more emotionally charged and committed to the domestic circle.[34]

That said, some changes are noteworthy more recently, although they have not done away with those two presuppositional poles and with that conception of freedom rooted in recklessness. New sources of moral life and principles of justice, as well as connected ideas of responsibility, have been searched for and developed in recent decades, however unstable the new justifications and yardsticks may seem. How have the forces of capitalism handled the transformations of recent decades in terms of a notion of responsibility? As seen in chapter 8 networks are not by any means inimical to capitalism. But their rise has been simultaneous and linked to real changes in the nature of society's functioning, especially regarding the internal organization of the firm and management.

Boltanski and Chiapello have provided a vivid picture of such changes. Although their view is somewhat onesided, stressing novelty too much and overlooking the countless continuities that are central for the reproduction of capitalism and modernity overall, their work – which supposedly provides an ideal-type of capitalism at present – is important for characterizing what I have called the third phase of modernity. They are inspired by Wagner's account of the two previous phases of modernity and the application of a model of 'worlds' and justice developed in former publications.[35] According to them, while the first phase of capitalism was rooted in notions of saving and asceticism, and the second in those of competence, hierarchy and merit, the third phase throws up different themes, indeed partly as a response to criticisms levelled by anti-capitalist intellectuals and social and political movements.[36] The 1990s literature on management, which they chose to dive into for the transformations of capitalism, is so different and poses such distinct questions from that of the 1960s that a change in the 'spirit of capitalism' is writ large. The demand of autonomy and freedom as well as of creativity and authenticity traverses this new spirit – partly as an answer to the 'artistic critique', a sort of attack centred on the lack of those elements in the previous phase of capitalism due to hierarchies and reification. The repertoire of May 1968 was somehow transformed and absorbed by the new 'ideology' (in a broad sense) of capitalism – which suggested the overcoming of both capitalism and anti-capitalism – and fits well the new, post-Fordist and post-Taylorist processes of production and decision, frequently envisioned according to the model of networks and a view (exploitation notwithstanding) of the 'humanization' of economic and labour relationships. The multiplication of products more suited to market diversity, replacing total standardization, characterized the other face of such changes in the spirit of capitalism, answering also in part to the artistic critique. The state and social rights were not rejected as a whole but rather in their supposedly oppressive aspects, although the 'social critique' of capitalism, especially the discussion about classes, was defeated and forgotten.[37]

Managers (*cadres*) in particular have watched their way of understanding and operating in the world being radically transformed. The *project* – with its changing and contingent, challenging and unstable characteristics – assumes centre stage in the new model of administration, allowing for the fruition of the elements the artistic critique had formerly emphasized. As a 'transitory form' the project is well adjusted to an expanding network.[38] In a world of connections it is necessary to have first the desire to connect, enter relationships and weave liaisons; to know how to communicate, generate trust, openly discuss, be capable of enthusiasm, be available and active, adjustable to different situations, flexible and to possess multiple qualities and qualifications; to be a 'radar' in order to remain attentive and to collect information; to be able to play the role of a leader as a 'mediator' that links and spurs people. One must develop one's 'employability', being at ease with the flow of contemporary life, beyond bureaucracy, and keen on face-to-face relationships, 'responsibilization', trust and cooperation.[39] Workers on the shop floor have to cope with similar problems in terms of individual responsibility: they have also to adjust to the demand for autonomy, whereby the new mechanisms in the firm re-engage them and, decreasing the costs of control, stress self-control.[40]

However, despite their bias and the emphasis on the 'world of projects', Boltanski and Chiapello perceive that individualism and individualistic responsibility have not perhaps changed that much. The neomanagement literature stresses the contribution of the agent within the network to the 'common good'. But especially with reference to Ronald Burt's work (a mix of 'formal theory and advice work for ambitious managers') Boltanski and Chiapello show how individualism, and the exploitation of the advantaged positions one may build or profit from within networks, are recurrent features of the 'new spirit of capitalism'. 'Asymmetries', especially of information, and 'social capital', that is, the ensemble of personal relations an individual may master, are key in this respect, and he or she must be careful as regards investments of time and energy. Developing distant relationships, placing oneself at points of connection, building a reputation, are means by which a 'networker' may legitimately – that is, without breaching principles of justice – profit individually and in a utilitarian manner from his belonging in a network, although the principles of 'world of projects' operate precisely to control opportunistic behaviour – which is legitimate in the 'market world' but not in a world of networks. Moreover, one's destiny is one's responsibility.[41]

The problem is, nevertheless, that contemporary social life is concretely characterized by a mixture of principles of organization. Therefore the network projects may be overridden by calculations of unilateral advantage typical of market relationships (apart from common good indirect consequences as a result of that). The literature on management seems unwarrantedly and ideologically (in the traditional sense of clouding reality due to the prevalence of sectional interests) to mix the actual difference and intertwinement in companies of principles of market, hierarchy and network. Although aiming at a sort of phenomenologically based and sophisticated critical theory, Boltanski and Chiapello appear to outline the network principle – in this regard in consonance with the neomanagement literature – as the *exclusive* principle operating in the third phase of capitalism (interpreting even Castel's work, formerly analysed, which is patently committed to a return to the models of the second phase of modernity, as though it spoke of a network society[42]). The whole argument of chapter 8 endeavours to bring out the increased importance of networks in the third phase of modernity; nonetheless, it stresses both that this is not absolute – networks have *not* become, analytically defined as 'voluntary collaboration', the dominant principle today – and how much it has been present, with less weight, in previous phases of modernity. It is true that in a world of increasing complexity, wherein disembedded individuals and collectivities are pressed into much more contingent and fleeting social relationships, the maintenance and extension of contacts may be of extreme importance for success in whatever sphere of social life. But this does not mean, contrary to what Boltanski and Chiapello tend to imply, that networks and this sort of behaviour are an absolute novelty associated with the new phase and the new spirit of capitalism; nor should that be taken as what should be defined as, in a theoretically strong sense, network relations: rather those connections may consist merely in an instrument of market (that is, based on exchange) or hierarchical (that is, articulated by command) ties which operate in a more fluid and complex social world.

Lip service paid to broad principles and discourses – whether relative to market or network principles of justice – may merely conceal a recklessness marked by the absorption in one's interests, even confining them perhaps to the short term. This is a problem with which traditionally the literature on management has been obliged to cope: free riders have been a very common phenomenon. Moreover this new form of individualism is both conditioned and contributes to the insecurity that reigns today in societies in which strong deregulation, privatization, firm restructuring, economic policies, etc. have followed the neoliberal recipe. This is what some have spotted in the transformation of 'character' in contemporary North American liberal, tough, individualistic and utilitarian society. Since there are no established paths and people must care for themselves alone in the midst of extreme professional and personal instability, only a very flexible and empty sort of personality, to which nothing must be allowed to 'stick' and which is ready to make the most of opportunities, can survive. No strong ties to other people (except perhaps – and in a tense manner – within the love couple) but merely a utilitarian and strategically orientated interaction with them is to be expected from agents subjected to such harsh conditions of life in contemporary capitalism. In such a whirlpool responsibility consists almost in a bravado – one can hardly control even one's own life and destiny.[43] Even the neomanagement literature is traversed by a tension between the demand for authenticity in personal relations, which would be fundamental for the good functioning of the 'world of projects' and the solidity of networks, and the instrumental and often individualistic use to which personal relations – including friendship – may be submitted precisely in order to make networks effective and extended. A commodification of relationships seems to be widespread, due in particular to the disappearance of a sharp division between the public sphere of interest and that private one wherein disinterested interactions take place.[44]

The position in the internal hierarchy may constitute, albeit not necessarily, a pre-condition for such 'self-orientation' versus 'collectivity orientation' (to take up Parsons's expressions, discussed in the previous chapter), even though intermediate 'cadres' may certainly play this sort of self-interested, utilitarian game. As we can learn also from Boltanski and Chiapello, to some extent in contrast with what may happen with agents placed in the lower layers of the firm or of a specific project, and especially with workers and subordinates in general, responsibility becomes an imperative which is utilized by hierarchically dominant echelons in organizations so as to accomplish finer forms of control and increase productivity. The 'common good' in such a situation becomes a stark constraint. By accepting in part the anti-capitalist 'artistic critique' which denounced its hostility towards autonomy, authenticity and creativity, capitalism has instrumentalized it for its own purposes. Instead of being basically submitted to management, workers now directly control other workers: conflicts have their centre of gravity dislocated to the working group. Furthermore, the price paid for 'the growth of autonomy and responsibility' has been a 'decrease of protections' of the previous phase of modernity, due to prosperous economic conditions as well as to a favourable balance of power.[45]

Directly influenced by Thatcherism and neoliberalism's decades of dominance, as well as by the Clintonian version of the United States Democratic Party compromise with the New Right, Giddens expresses this in his writings. A crucial principle of Third Way politics, he argues, aims at a 'new social contract'. This should be based on a 'theorem': 'no rights without responsibilities'. The access to social goods should imply responsible use and the delivery of something to the 'wider community' in return. This would be a feature of citizenship, applied to politicians and citizens, the rich and the poor, as well as to business corporations.[46] This must hold centre stage in a contemporary reform of the welfare state, beyond of course communism but also the 'statist zeal' of old social democracy, corresponding to 'positive welfare' and the empowerment of individuals. Thereby autonomy and 'individual and collective responsibility' (never clearly defined) would be linked.[47] This is what should be at stake when crime is tackled, for instance, the same obtaining for family life. This is in spite of Giddens having been softer on this just a while before, when he restated his view of the family as undergoing profound changes that actually responsibly engage men and women, and possibly children too.[48] Certainly bearing in mind ideas such as those of Jonas and a widespread concern, which will be touched upon below, Giddens introduces the topic of 'corporate responsibility', especially regarding ecological issues and their conduct in poor countries, which must be promoted both through active encouragement and the rigorous policing of corporate behaviour.[49] But responsibility is not merely duty for him, since it implies 'the spelling out of reasons, not blind allegiance', consisting in a 'clue' for agency as well as being connected to reflexivity and the solidarity that springs from democratic dialogue.[50]

Although his arguments often sound specious, I do not want to suggest that the problems underlying Giddens's account are not real enough. A number of authors have indeed been drawing attention to them for years, especially regarding the fact that, by intervening so deeply in society, welfare states have taken over many responsibilities, hence leading to a 'decline in a sense of individual moral responsibility'.[51] This problem obviously sits oddly in relation to the evolution of collective responsibility such as discussed above and it will, along with individual responsibility, be resumed in the last chapter of this book. This tension is nevertheless constitutive of our time and cannot be discarded out of hand.

I have, in sum, analysed the development of responsibility pointing to some of its connections with freedom, equality and solidarity. The constitutive polarization of modernity between the individual and society – often represented by the state – has stood out. The only exception to this seems to have been 'elites', introduced in political thought as a normative and actual alternative to 'mass' democracy, giving rise to a restrictive, unequally based 'collective subjectivity' that celebrates hierarchy. Openings to collective subjectivities of different kinds will feature in chapter 11. If the future does not look bright in principle, it is not altogether bleak in relation to new possibilities.

11 • Responsibility Today: Horizons of Development

Collective Responsibility

In the concluding decades of the twentieth century and at the turn of the twenty-first, the theme of responsibility has been posited in a new dimension, more directly collective, beyond the polarization between individual and society. This has been happening at both the theoretical and the more empirical level, conjuring up new dimensions of collective subjectivity vis-à-vis ecological problems, international governance, social policy and so forth, while authors such as Jonas and Apel have crafted new concepts to tackle the issue. The former tends towards a politically authoritarian view, or at least cannot project the mobilization of society and intersubjectivity in the public sphere as the vehicle for the development of what he calls 'collective responsibility'. But the latter lends the topic a decisive democratic and intersubjective dimension. I will first analyse their contribution. Then I will try to suggest a connection between responsibility and the notion of recognition, a key topic in debates of contemporary social theory, in order to rethink individualism, as well as some further tensions of modernity. The last section of the chapter will introduce some more specific issues of contemporary modernity.

Jonas was especially concerned with the relationship between humanity and nature. He was fiercely critical of the 'unbound' Prometheus of modernity, which capitalism and Marxism alike express – that is, he attacked the other side of the 'autonomy' project of the modern age, the forceful and relentless desire of 'rational mastery' in particular of nature. He refused utopia (especially in the form of Marxism and its phrasing by Ernest Bloch), which would irremediably be entangled with that project. But he retained the potential of hope as a basic quality of action. He did so in the name of an ethic of responsibility that might secure the world for the forthcoming generations of the human species, as well as rescuing and saving nature from the destruction yielded by the ever-expanding and unforgiving powers of human technology; in so doing, a new conception of the ties between humanity and the future was outlined. Politically, nonetheless, his ground-breaking stress on collective responsibility is, if not openly authoritarian, careless in regard to democracy and the interactive processes which must underlie a renewal and change of humanity's thinking about and relationship with its natural soil and environment. Statesmen – who he was prone to equate with parents – appear as the main public agents for guaranteeing a future-orientated responsibility.[1] In turn Apel systematically addresses these shortcomings: he is eager to establish a bond between collective responsibility and democratic, communicative principles of social interaction, to which he attributes a utopian dimension.

Apel proposed a new relationship with freedom, by eschewing individualism: '[a]s sheer arbitrary will of decision freedom is indeed not only incapable of an ethic of responsibility'; it is equally 'politically impotent' – and even more so than the purely interior freedom of the Kantian ethic of conviction (*Gesinnungsethik*).[2] Individualist conceptions of morals and action are deficient and have become too exhausted to cope with the problems the human species now has to face. By the same token he rejected positivism, which would pretend to be scientifically objective and supposedly neutral in terms of values, and is a companion to the subjective and individualistic conception of freedom. To this pair he opposed the 'potential solidary responsibility', without however taking it onto the plane of an undifferentiated collectivity, rather rooting it in intersubjective, communicative processes. A new situation demands new forms of framing the issue: we do not need an 'ethic of conviction' resting on 'ultimate irrational decisions', either as an ethic of responsibility related to the situation of political decision, as suggested by Weber, or as related to the borderline existential situation, which Sartre's Existentialism elaborated. Neither corresponds to the 'demand of the moment'. In the present crisis of the 'techno-scientific civilization in a planetary scale' there is a demand for 'something as an ethic of humanity's common solidary responsibility in the sense of a communicative mediation of interests (*Interesenvermittlung*) and deliberative situation (*Situationsberatung*)'.[3]

But how would it be possible to base its 'intersubjective validity' rationally, beyond values ultimately unjustifiable, which stem from a Nietzschean–Weberian battle of multiple gods? Apel searched for a 'third way', beyond the 'freedom without ethical substance and solidary responsibility' typical of 'Western capitalism' and the 'compulsory solidarity' characteristic of 'totalitarian socialism', although he stated that offering 'political recipes' was not his goal, thus sticking to the general domain of philosophical inquiry. His horizon consisted of the institutional democratic reform towards a 'partial realization of the ideal communicative community', a project which, for many years, he has shared with Habermas.[4] While this ideal future comes to the fore in his reflection, its backdrop is explicitly the crisis diagnosis proposed by Jonas. Apel, however, does not believe in the possibility of a refusal of progress and utopia he professes, unless we simply accept a neo-Darwinist solution for the growth of the population – a Hayekian solution incompatible with a *universalist ethics*, such as Kant's, and the 'regulative ideal' of a realization of justice in a planetary scale, moreover orientated to responsibility as to the *future* (contrary to the atemporality of the Kantian categorical imperative). Finally, Apel underscored that the principle of intersubjectivity and the demand for the construction of that ethics should *not* draw upon an abstract universalization similar to Kant's. On the contrary it should be projected with reference to 'actual communities of communication', whose participants cope with problems of the real world as agents capable of 'understanding' (*Verständigung*), bearing in mind also the piecemeal realization of the model and affirmation of human dignity.[5]

This can be instructively contrasted with the individualistic – and inconsistent – position of Rawls's theory. He outlined theoretically the issue in a systematic manner through ideas such as those of a 'rational plan of life' and 'deliberative rationality', reaching the corollary that 'the principle of responsibility to self resembles a principle of right: the claims of the self at different moments must be so adjusted that the self at each time can affirm the plan that has been and is being followed'. People must not be able to 'complain' about themselves at another stage. However, Rawls introduced the responsibility of each individual before the coming generations in the 'original position' (examined in chapter 4), a proposition which only through ad hoc reasoning and an abstract rendering of time – which suspends the actual unfolding of generations and is thus inimical to the contemporary view of space–time previously upheld here – can be treated by a utilitarian or even a social contractarian conception.[6] Apel's historical standpoint and his concern with actual problems and processes promise therefore to be much more fruitful than the Rawlsian view, especially with respect to the introduction of collective subjectivities into the conceptualization. Responsibility must be reckoned with, regarding actual relationships and space–time trajectories of individuals, multifarious and specific collective subjectivities and generations in particular. Only by taking this more concrete angle can we assess the possibilities and necessities for the further reorganization of responsibility in advanced modernity.

Nevertheless, it is not immediately evident what Apel had in mind when he mentioned the institutionalization of communicative and responsible communities as an alternative to individualism, and idealism too. In Habermas's case and his version of 'discourse ethics', this is highly problematic. His intersubjective approach still proves to be very individualistic, since it is only to the interaction between individuals that Habermas makes reference. Furthermore, although Habermas argues that it cannot be conceived of as abstract, in the sense of overlooking specific social interests, it evinces little institutional substance.[7] Apart from his general support for citizenship in the constitutional state and the idea that today there would be interstitial public spheres (ideas studied in some detail in chapter 5), Habermas stops short of a substantial proposition, in contrast to some interesting and instructive ideas adumbrated by Apel.

In the first place it is evident that Apel implies the whole of humanity in his proposals. He wants an ethic of *co*-responsibility, that is, intersubjectively built, rather than a collective ethics that might warrant the authoritarian intervention of a national state not democratically constituted, or of an international organization displaying a similarly authoritarian countenance (which lurks in Jonas's groundbreaking work).[8] The problem of freedom and democracy was central for Apel's reasoning. It is of paramount importance to stress, in contradistinction, that he has a sharp notion of the limits which an individualistic, although intersubjective, conception of action imposes upon our thinking, whether in general philosophical terms or at the level of institutional arrangements. Far-reaching consequences result from this, even though it is not expressed in an articulated way. Nor has Apel related it to the typical modern presuppositional polarization between the individual and society or the state, and especially to its overcoming. That said, how has he understood the 'organization of collective responsibility?'

> When questions are asked about the empirically graspable quotidian subjects (individual subjects and collective subjects) of responsibility, two ideal types sharply crafted can be distinguished: they are juridical persons and juridical *quasi*-persons which must be attributed responsibility as subjects responsible for actions (*Handlungen*) and omissions (*Unterlassungen*) in the sense of positive law.[9]

This does not mean that everything might be juridified, since a community of communication is surely broader than that. But the possibilities of institutionalization of 'collective action' can be thereby indicated – an issue present since Augustine of Hippo within the Catholic Church. These possibilities branch off on many planes, from taking part in the enactment of laws to the running of a kindergarten. However, it is not a case of acknowledging the validity either of initiatives deprived of direct interest in the participants or of those rooted merely in 'good will'. On the contrary, the inclusion of individual and collective actors geared towards 'rational strategic action' and 'self-conservation' must be at the core of a new way of thinking. The possibility of taking part in the 'organization of responsibility' must be institutionally attributed to individuals, families, groups, interest associations, the state, etc., if this is in fact to 'have a chance'. It is not the acceptance of 'sheer egoism' that is at stake, but the recognition of the following of one's own interest in a system of rules.[10] It is just as obvious that, by carrying out this conceptual operation, Apel places the theme of collective subjectivity at the heart of contemporary responsibility. Instead of merely individuals who can freely organize and communicate, collectivities, that is, social systems with their specific, collective causality, assume centre stage in the discussion. He even requires that they are institutionalized and entrusted with specific tasks and responsibilities, although he does not spell out how this could be in reality carried out.

It is important to realize at this stage that an implicit divergence with Habermas reveals itself, since Apel does not look for a division of domains between life-world and communicative action on the one hand, and instrumental and strategic action and self-steered systems on the other. This is pressed home in his discussion of an ethic for the economy, although no direct confrontation with Habermas's position is articulated, and no specific institutional arrangements are suggested. Apel insists on the differentiation of society but argues that, as a regulative ideal that must be gradually brought into being, communicative action needs to be somehow practically mediated with strategic rationality in the economic domain also. Hence this takes up a role beyond a mere 'ideal principle' and allows for the actual coming about of discourse ethics as an ethic of responsibility – a 'historically related task'.[11] In another, connected piece of work, both issues return: we cannot concretely think of an ethic of responsibility in tandem with a stark division of rationalities (consensual–communicative–ethical versus strategic or communicative versus systemic) even if we attribute to them an ideal-typical character (as he did vis-à-vis Habermas's approach, in what I believe is a charitable interpretation); nor can an ethic of responsibility be conceived of in terms of a competence which is not both context-sensitive and universalist, that is, which is simultaneously evolutionarily advanced and historically based, as well as searching for its realization in the actual and possible interactive settings of contemporary societies.[12]

In sum, while the empirical or theoretical developments previously analysed have shown the importance of responsibility for social thought, Apel's musings on the topic bring out an especially instructive form of conceptualizing the issue theoretically at the collective level, leaving behind the polarization between individual and state which is typical of modern thought in general, and has shown itself clearly in relation to responsibility. With this in mind and in order to conclude this book, let me now address the problems of individualism and then some areas in which some collective problems will receive pride of place.

Impasses and Entanglements

But are modern forms of individualism and collective responsibility compatible? Collective responsibility seems to demand the overcoming of radical, atomistic forms of individualism, although by no means implying a refusal of individualization. In order for collective responsibility to become central in social life, new ways of reckoning with relationships and new forms of social praxis vis-à-vis other agents are required. This means that in particular freedom, a presupposition and a goal of modern individualism, must be rephrased, so that collective responsibility can find a more encompassing reach and deeper significance. That is what I will analyse now. The other, institutional questions that link up with the position of collective responsibility today, as a possible alternative to the typical polarizations of modernity, will be taken up later.

I have argued in this book that freedom is a central category, in the imaginary and institutionally, in the universe of modernity. The more encompassing and deeper it becomes (though the economic and the political domains have been especially shielded against its development), the more encompassing responsibility, or its requirement, is. The more identity continuously changes, the more we must 'respond' to such changes as well.[13] Of course one may back off from being responsible for one's own behaviour and its consequences, insofar as this may make little sense in situations in which, either due to the background of past memories or the lack of prospects regarding the future, responsibility is not posed as a demand and a challenge. If we intend, suppose or desire to become socially collectively responsible, it is necessary to go beyond this, as well as beyond the restricted model of responsibility. But this does not seem either simple or evident, as shown by an analysis of depression as a 'pathology of freedom'.

Moving in an ambience that evokes Sartre, Ehrenberg aims to understand the contemporary individual. According to him, depression has become a mass phenomenon in the aftermath of the Second World War. It 'instructs us about our present experience of the person, since it is the pathology of a society in which the norm is no longer founded in guilt and discipline, but in responsibility and initiative'. The notions of project, motivation and communication cut across all domains of social activity, from business management to the politics of reinsertion. This often represents an excess of requirements for the subject, who feels 'insufficient' to cope with especially the inevitable insecurity of identity this entails. Thus '[t]he anguish of being oneself turns into a tiredness (*fatigue*) of being oneself'.[14] And, instead of the traditional psychological diseases and disturbances (mainly the Freudian neuroses), which had in guilt and conflict their propelling power, a new, freer, less stable form of individuality – for more *disembedded* – produces depression as an expression of a lack of internal tension and strength, since individuals cannot discern within themselves the power to change their lives and the world. Instead of the Freudian interpreted exigency of civilization as a renunciation of drives and satisfaction, we suffer in depression now because of the illusion that everything is possible and depends on our choice and action.[15]

Should freedom, nonetheless, be indicted in this regard? Or had we not better shift the focus of the highly individualistic presuppositions that lie at the core of such a notion of freedom? Could not a more collectively orientated perspective of freedom be more adequate, taking people as free indeed, but according to which self-realization and meaning can be attained only if we reach out to others, if we aim at collective endeavours? Could not freedom – and thus responsibility – be disentangled from the principle of performance, to take up Marcuse's phrase, which, as seen formerly with recourse especially to Boltanski and Chiapello's work, so starkly encompasses it? It is also worth eschewing right away – cognitively, normatively and expressively – the idea that a solution for this might be a return to tougher social norms, a hardening of the authoritarianism of the 'superego', that is, a diminution of freedom. On the one hand, what is at stake is how to reckon with the requirements for individuals and collective subjectivities to take on responsibility for the *other*; on the other hand, we need to think how this would fit in the normative bounds of modernity and in terms of its institutions, in the coordinates of freedom and equality, or in those of domination and inequality.

We can start with the idea that being seen as a full member of social life is a condition for taking responsibility for the outcome of one's action, a point which is implied also, notwithstanding its excessive harmonic tone, in Mead's account of the 'generalized other' (that is, all the other members of society in their specific roles) as built and rebuilt through social interaction, as introduced in chapter 9. In this regard we may speak of a *balance of responsibility*, which is demanded as a mutual form of recognition in that the other's needs are taken care of and looked after, or minimally attended to; this is especially true if the state is not directly introduced, which, as seen in chapter 10, tends to establish a top–down imbalance vis-à-vis individuals in terms of responsibility. However, insofar as responsibility is not confined to an individualist conception, it is not only freedom that lies at the heart of modern conceptions and feelings of responsibility. Solidarity is there as well, and we can thus think of circuits of libidinal investment that would bring people together[16] and overcome the sort of pathology depression so clearly expresses. Responsibility may be regarded as an imperative that extends into the future, as demanded by Jonas; but there is no reason to forget its exercise among contemporaries – Apel's main, democratized intuition. Surely responsibility is sometimes a one-sided phenomenon, a situation epitomized by the ties between parents and children.[17] Lest someone be prone to universalize such an imbalance of responsibility, it must be said that this is far from always being the case: especially if we take the whole of social interactions. It then becomes patent that to fulfil responsibly, at least to some extent, the expectations of others requires that one be responsibly dealt with by those others; otherwise it is unlikely that responsibility will be forthcoming. In the short run this may happen, yet as time goes by the probability of a responsible attitude being abandoned and the social fabric collapsing increases and recklessness is likely to take over – not to mention the very impossibility of responsibility thriving if children do not find it in their environment, above all (though not only) in relation to themselves.

Hierarchical ideologies can be and are operative in several domains of social life, often entwined with individualist conceptions. There are nevertheless limits for those ideologies in the imaginary of modernity and I have identified some tensions in this respect throughout this book. In terms of changes in the direction of collective responsibility, along with a post-individualist view, the centrality of equality is hence crucial for an understanding of the balance of responsibility and its viability. To some extent this is what Honneth seems to adumbrate when he proposes love, rights and the esteem due to specific forms of life as the three aspects of intersubjective recognition in the differentiated life world of modernity.[18] However, he does not investigate the relations between *difference* and *equality*. In chapter 6 I suggested that the former refers to pluralism versus homogeneity, while the latter implies a sort of universality that is opposed to inequality, rather than to difference. We may agree in some measure with Fraser[19] and state that 'equality of status' – guaranteed by equal rights and entailing equal freedom – should be placed at the heart of *justice* and *redistribution* (even if we doubt, as I do, that this can be solved merely on the plane of morals instead of ethics; what might imply a division between recognition of the first and second order, the former making possible the definition of a common humanity and universal rights – a point I cannot follow up here). In turn difference would demand an answer on the plane of *recognition* (of the second order, to refer to the point just made) within the limits of equality and freedom, that is, insofar as it does not intend to establish forms of hierarchy, stratification or domination. Although the prospects of socialism look dim today and Marx's solution seems in many ways untenable or highly problematical, the classical Hegelian dialectic of master and slave still has strong purchase. We should not be oblivious to it: within the modern imaginary, to have one's humanity – in its generality as well as specificity – recognized we need to be able to recognize others as equal in the first place, otherwise our own recognition inevitably remains itself partial.[20]

A new form of thinking responsibility, implied in its collective translation, in daily life and at the level of large historical developments, can probably only be reached if overarching hermeneutic and institutional changes come about, with some bearing on the overcoming of radical individualism and the promotion of equality and freedom. In what follows I want to examine some contemporary configurations and possibilities that may – or may not – lead in this direction.

Towards New Forms of Responsibility?

Does this mean that advanced modernity has actually achieved or will in principle achieve that status of mutual recognition as a universally or even prevalent phenomenon? Unfortunately not. A functionalist approach is not assumed here, to restate a point already made. Keeping as a backdrop a more interactive and contingent understanding of social life, let us finally examine some institutional domains of contemporary modernity and see how the question of responsibility appears, in connection with the other categories hitherto studied. I will in some measure return to the axes of the social space upon which I dwelt in chapter 7, since collective responsibility is at stake in them, along with other issues relating directly to the evolving of that category today.

I examined also in chapter 7 the problems besetting the recognition of difference between collectivities in contemporary, highly complex and plural societies. The same problem arises in connection with the ideological refusal of the role and relevance of social classes and related inequalities today. On the other hand, in many domains, for instance and particularly in the family, the dynamic of economic development and the unfettered requirements it places on people's lives have made the care of children and the responsibility for them an increasingly difficult task to cope with, regardless of conservative or Third Way (often empty) claims of bringing such topics back to the top of the agenda.[21] This has little to do with conservative or even communitarian conservative fears, expressed by authors such as Bell – who speaks of the decline of the Protestant ethic, and the rise of 'hedonism', which implicitly means a dissipation of responsibility – and Lasch – who mourns the decline of the traditional family and the loss of both parental authority and responsibility.[22] Instead, a new ethic of responsibility is required, which must face up to the realities of changed life patterns and morals and in particular to the decentring of the family. More individualized – but to some extent necessarily less individualist – and plural societies demand a responsibility based less on internal repression and pre-established role-models and more on dialogical constructions, whether of a more practical or rationalized reflexivity. Superego repression is unlikely to be adequate in a society with a high level of variability, in which contingency and changing patterns and interactions cross people's paths almost everyday in their mutual dealings, which are hence open to negotiations, compromises and new consensus building. What we should actually be aware and wary of is the fact that the more the world becomes uncertain and hazardous, the more parents are pushed to take responsibility, protecting their children and trying hard to improve their lot, sometimes leading to stressful situations or an excessive pampering due to exaggerated emotional investment.[23]

We have still to learn how to live with this extended, networked type of family. This is by no means painless. But unless we give in and remain prisoners of old ideologies of the nuclear family, we are compelled to find our way through the changing reality of its new decentred form, whether in sexual, emotional or responsible terms. By means of such reasoning we have in any case already trod the path of collective responsibility in advanced modernity. In accordance with the arguments of chapter 8, although individual and state responsibility are not at all irrelevant (on the contrary), networked responsibility appears as a particularly relevant form of responsibility today, in virtue of course of the very structure of social solidarity, which has included with greater centrality the network principle of coordination, alongside market interchange and hierarchy. In the case of the family it is closely connected to the surpassing – however incomplete this still remains – of patriarchal relations of subordination originating in the marriage contract (and not in the feudal system) and divides the public from the private–intimate sphere,[24] the hierarchy of that ordering is either more slowly or more quickly crumbling, being replaced by more egalitarian, network-type ties, and thus, to return to categories developed in that same chapter, 'voluntary collaboration' substitutes for 'command'. This is true during marriage as much as in its aftermath, whereby those changes in the idea of responsibility (and of obligation) are produced, although a total transformation of the relations between men and women is far from having been accomplished.

Has this trend towards greater weight being placed on responsibility affected one of the pillars of modern social life, namely economic firms, and especially corporate business? We saw that within enterprises the networked 'world of projects', to take up Boltanski and Chiapello's description of the 'new spirit of capitalism', has given responsibility pride of place, touching management first, but including workers as well. This means that there is a clear path opening towards collective responsibility. However, within the bounds of the 'mixed articulation' characteristic of the third phase of modernity it may be easily captured in the concrete interactive systems of especially, but not only, capitalist relations, a problem correctly perceived by those two authors. Whether it will develop into more democratic and egalitarian, not manipulative nor hierarchical, relationships is still to be seen, although at present general social conditions do not seem conducive.

Outside firms and corporations, that is, in their relations with society at large, this topic has also become of increasing importance. Ecology has been a paramount issue in this regard, alongside other problems. It may even be argued that the depoliticization of the link between business, government and science has been undone: politics is now back to economics, and many social actors have the possibility of influencing or at least disputing or bringing to light business decisions and their consequences. The answer from economic organizations of this kind has been a 'new piety': 'ecological morality, ethics and responsibility are proclaimed for public relations effect on entire newspaper pages and the glossy pages of magazines'.[25] Is such a cynical view warranted? Whether this is merely a matter of superficial expressive behaviour, a 'make-believe', or includes actual normative and cognitive concerns will remain an open question here. Suffice it to adduce two considerations. First, if we take seriously the growing importance of the notion of responsibility we had better consider that it is likely that its impact will not bypass economic life and business firms, small and large alike. On the other hand, the dynamic and ethos of capitalism make it unlikely that the impositions and habits of competition will be abandoned beyond paying mere lip service to issues involving responsibility, should this be detrimental to the strategy such organizations envision.

At any rate few in the corporate world would follow today Milton Friedman and simply state that 'the social responsibility of business is to increase its profits'.[26] Social responsibility more broadly conceived of seems to consist in a theme that has consolidated itself in corporate discourse. *Impact* on the 'surrounding community', in a positive or negative manner – and not only the responsibility of executives to stockholders – is a topic that mobilizes corporate imagination. 'Stakeholders' thus include customers and consumers (especially in an age when consumerism is such an important feature of identity), employees, suppliers and external contractors, as well as the public in general and the environment. Moral issues are present, but even apologists of business and 'free' corporate enterprise acknowledge that profits can undoubtedly be made from a company's image as socially responsible.[27]

Regardless of the main propelling factor it is interesting to note that such literature actually distinguishes the responsibility of the individual from that of the corporation, insofar as its impact is a product of processes channelled through the 'corporate internal decision' structure – that is, it appears as a *highly centred* collective subjectivity, whereby its collective causality as a 'formal organization' authorizes even judicial imputation.[28] In this third phase of modernity it would in any case be necessary to go beyond this in order to consider shared responsibility, internally and to the environment, since the new entrepreneurial networks imply new networks of causality, which cannot be grasped merely by individualism or by the model of formal and centred collectivities. A new principle of imputation also at the juridical level, ought to be developed.[29]

I pointed out in chapter 7 that a number of initiatives may be envisaged in social policy taking intermediate collective subjectivities into account. In philanthropy – the liberal and neoliberal preferred solution for social problems and poverty – this usually engages business and citizens initiatives from the top–down. However, a patronizing and inegalitarian attitude is comprised in philanthropy, making social policy a private and not rights-based activity, not to mention its inefficiency against poverty and for empowering people as free citizens. A different tack must be taken, vindicating social policy as rights-orientated and requiring citizen responsibility as well as a more active way of thinking about solidarity. One crucial problem, to begin with, concerns how free time is ideologically framed in capitalist (and patriarchal) society, since people regard themselves as freer precisely when they are supposedly allowed to do nothing. 'Leisure' time has assumed this task in a society with stark inequalities, in which people have difficulty in understanding their actions as achieving any meaningful impact. But instead of being swallowed by consumer culture a more active attitude, which recognizes our responsibility towards other people as well as towards nature, can and must be taken – especially when full-time jobs are increasingly scarce[30] (a redistribution of work time, 'free' time and socially dedicated time consisting in a problem to be put on the social policy agenda).

Certainly such moral demands must be posed to individuals and collectivities. Nevertheless, we can and need to go much further than that and outline a distinct *institutional design* which moves beyond the traditional distinction between public and private, according to which we usually (though not necessarily) find the collectivity captured by the state and filling the public domain, while individuals are the centre-piece of the private. A *social sphere* wherein multiple collective subjectivities feature as responsible for social solidarity – without abandoning the frame of universal rights or giving up on the role of the state – may be imagined in which the administration of important areas of social police becomes a collective responsibility that is not confined to the state. A balance of responsibility is thereby intimated. A reconstitution of social ties beyond privatized individualism is feasible, and depends on our creative institutional imagination.[31] As even sculptors of the state-based welfare society recognize, 'mutual aid' organizations have qualities which are absent from the public services, although contrary to voluntary associations these are accountable to the public in general; links between these forms of social service should therefore be supported.[32]

In terms of public security the same path emerges as viable and positive, an alternative to the criminalization of marginalized social collectivities which are not recognized in their full expression as citizens, as members of society: male blacks in the United States, immigrants, the very poor and drug addicts in Europe, or the black and poor in Brazil by and large, with similar phenomena obtaining in the American Spanish-speaking countries. The role of justice in this respect may be paramount, preventing the break-up of social relations and the wearing out of the social fabric. In order to escape from the hierarchical, even authoritarian, imposition of the rule of law and criminalization by a state which is the keeper of social order and mores, being responsible for social control, only a juridical pre-emptive strategy can probably succeed. It would be aimed at forestalling the degeneration of a rather pluralistic and complex social fabric into conflicts which must otherwise be tackled by repressive means.[33] Neither reckless individualism, so rampant today among the youth and misrecognized collectivities, nor state law and order enforcement are conducive to a democratic, freedom and egalitarian-orientated maintenance of the social fabric. Instead networks of responsibility and solidary action and movement are a need of our increasingly complex and non-a-priori manageable societies, which demand attention for the concrete, particular contexts in which so to speak 'anomic' problems come up.

Also here a social sphere is at stake, which is neither confined to the private life of individual citizens nor rests content with public state action, but draws upon our communicative capabilities and willingness to behave in a way orientated to voluntary collaboration. Law has many facets and cannot be reduced to a 'single simple type': some of them are 'mandatory' (as Hobbes supposed), others provide individuals with 'facilities', while others prescribe 'formalities' and conditions to be followed so that contracts and wills in general are valid – in order that what people want becomes legally effective. In its penal variant, law is indeed mandatory and based on 'command', on state-defined obligations which impose duties of behaviour upon individual citizens – force actually backing up the enforcement of such legally binding orientations.[34] But if the issues raised above are brought to bear, instead of operating repressively and through command a posteriori, the constitution of plural social networks linking state and social organizations appears as a need and perhaps even a condition of social peace in increasingly complex societies. They seem a requirement, not only as a means to prevent penal offences, but to connect people in a more positive and integrative vein by making them co-responsible for the fabric of social life. That is not tantamount to saying that this is enough to break through the warfare atmosphere of contemporary societies, although even penal law must conversely give up its a-priori character in order to become context-sensitive. It does, however, offer a possibly interesting and innovative way forward.

In fact what is explicit in the technical vocabulary of jurisprudence is valid for the other areas discussed in this section. 'Command' is indicative of hierarchical structurings. In contemporary complex societies it is rather voluntary collaboration, which can facilitate the smooth evolving of social relationships, that must advance and take on a more prominent position. This has been occurring in recent decades but a more inclusive and even peaceful development of social life is likely to be fostered through greater recourse to this sort of mechanism of coordination, rather than a concentration on command or market-based voluntary exchange. Connected to these elements we find the idea of *trust*, which has been in one way or another present in a great number of approaches that conceptualize phenomena with cooperative relationships at their centre. Trust is not only present in cooperative relationships (expectations of technical expertise or the continuity of social order and patterns also imply trust, for example); in addition it cuts across all social domains, including family and love ties as much as economic and productive structures. In all these domains trust is becoming increasingly important, within social life itself and as an object of inquiry for the social sciences. Why? If we define trust the reason for this is not difficult to explain. Trust may be conceptualized as 'believing in; in fact, to trust is to believe despite uncertainty'.

And what we believe in is that people will responsibly fulfil their obligations towards us – which, in the context of cooperative relationships, means mutual trust, duties and responsibilities.[35]

We have seen that we live in more plural societies, in which individuals are more disembedded, uncertainty therefore becoming rife. Although this does imply that previous societies did not depend very much on trust – usually they did so a lot – the fact is that in societies in which fluidity has become the norm, trustworthy ties become more necessary, allowing for the continuity of social life and the response to expectations out of which individual and collective identities are to a great extent crafted. Social solidarity and meaning thus hinge more on trust than they possibly did at least in previous stages of modern society. insofar as trust requires mutual responsibility in cooperative processes it appears moreover that it is precisely in network links and its underlying principle of coordination, voluntary collaboration, that trust has a particularly important role to play, although markets and even hierarchies by no means exclude its operation as a key feature.

One caveat must however be added as regards the organization of intermediate collectivities as the way to foster collective responsibility. I have strongly stressed the voluntary character of this organization. But there is no reason to devise the displacement of the state, which can be seen instead as one element in a more extended solidary network and as responsible for keeping a universalist outlook. This leads to a second point. We live in a society of rights, whose bottom line is the statute of citizenship. How could responsibility link up with a sense, and the institutions, of duty and new sorts of social and political obligation? Changes are likely to be required here too if egalitarian collective responsibility is to thrive.

The field of international relations also strongly evinces this trend towards the centrality of responsibility, although nothing similar to the nation-state seems actually to be at stake. It is true that theoreticians of this discipline have normally (and in a never conceptually debated way) worked with collective subjectivities – the nation-states. However, this has been carried out by attributing to them characteristics similar to those of individual actors. If there is some plausibility in this, since states are social systems with a *high level of centring*,[36] such a formulation is excessively ad hoc and blunt in theoretical terms. Whatever the case may be, the 'international society' perspective, represented especially by Hedley Bull's studies, has thought of the international system as the normatively, albeit strategically orientated, based interaction of those actors. For some this was typical of the system of relations of the Cold War, regardless of the originators of the theory not being aware of the fact, and even while the theory granted a vision beyond that period of balance of power and impasses. This was an improvement in relation to the 'realist' (as well as the now restated 'neo-realist') perspective, which nevertheless captures important aspects of the reality of international relations in the modern world; authors in this tradition see states as first of all concerned with their security, their survival in a hostile and anarchical world, which reproduced Hobbes's state of nature outside the boundaries of internally pacified societies.[37] Responsibility, therefore, it can be argued, was exercised by state actors exclusively towards themselves in the international order of states, similarly to what was true of individuals within national societies, with the additional complication that outside state borders no rule of law was available, beyond wishful thinking. More recently, against realism, and neo-realism, but also as a departure from the 'international society' theory, the perspective of the 'world society', as argued by Shaw, has come to the fore, insofar as state boundaries become less sacred and a global 'civil society' emerges. Furthermore, this new configuration is accompanied by a concept of 'global responsibility', concerning especially ecological questions and human rights all over the world, although strong resistances by national states are likely to postpone its effective realization.[38]

Shaw's discussion is centred on the Kurd crisis in Iraq and the dissolution of Yugoslavia; he hardly touches upon the behaviour of the 'Great Powers', namely countries such as the United States. It is interesting to observe that a civil society, albeit nationally based during the cold war period, was extremely active (regardless of being permanently defeated) in the denunciation of the activities of the winners of that confrontation and in the fight against the most noxious aspects of their behaviour – interventions in the 'Third World' and the weapons race, themes underplayed in Shaw's argument. Obviously, if those problems possess enormous importance – since dictators and aggressive regional powers must be repressed and controlled by a policy of global responsibility – one cannot close one's eyes to the behaviour of the United States and Europe. Responsibility and the search for egalitarian relationships at the international level must be brought together. This is the only way 'discourse ethics' may be imagined, something not particularly vivid on the horizon today.[39] Evidently we have a very long road to travel; nonetheless, to resume Apel's proposition, it is one that must be started on right now so that that regulative model is accomplished practically some day. Thus once the question of responsibility is put in global terms, 'sub-national' collective subjectivities – non-governmental organizations and social movements, plus ethnic groups – assume centre stage, although undoubtedly the nation-states and possibly the big international organizations (such as the United Nations, among others) still rule in the global arena. But here we must begin to contemplate the need to *consider the institutionalization of channels that combine participation and responsibility*.

Let us pause for a moment and return to the discussion of social solidarity broadly defined. We saw in chapter 8 that different institutional mechanisms are operative in the weaving of social solidarity, assuming centrality at different phases of the imaginary of modernity. If we now focus on participation we meet this issue again. The duties of the citizen were seen in chapter 3 as merely implying equality in obligatorily abiding by the law (or obeying the state *tout court*, in less democratic perspectives), carrying out warfare if the state so demanded and paying taxes. Whatever further duties one was expected to shoulder would be of a moral kind, being thus relative, not mandatory. Certainly, a very important strand of political thought has tried to attribute an *active* character to citizenship – as pointed out in chapter 4. This remains nevertheless largely confined to the realm of morals: there are few, secondary provisions to make it workable in practical, institutional terms. That is not to say that in many respects citizens have not become more active; indeed they have, and this has to do with increased possibilities open for action in societies that have more or less deeply entrenched democracy as a basic principle.[40] But overall it is not enough that moral responsibility – however sophisticatedly elaborated in discursive terms and articulated by mass communication means, for instance – is postulated.[41]

Contemporary debates about the role of civil society as a third sphere alongside the market and the state point already in this direction, implying the self-organization of society and the influence of citizens in the more independent domains of politics and economics, especially through social movements.[42] The same may be said of those systematic reflections (in my view rather imprecise and wrongly apolitical) that emphasize the importance of social capital, of civic life and the links between government, society and, in some respects, business networks, which suppose some institutions of mutual coordination.[43] On the whole Western societies might be undergoing changes in political behaviour and prevailing conceptions of democracy. Instead of looking at democracy from an authoritarian angle – as the delegation of power to state authorities and 'elites' – people may perhaps be developing a view of democracy as self-mobilization in diverse areas, many of which mould a field of sub-politics. This is more indirectly related to the state, but is linked in some ways to it, to economic systems and technological politics. *Authority* moves away from politicians and bureaucrats without further ado (or sometimes with much ado), and political obligation towards the state becomes looser and disjointed from responsibility, which is more clearly assumed by citizens and social movements.[44]

Perhaps some good effects may be expected from a sort of ethic of good feelings and good will with regard to citizen participation within the present institutional mould of citizenship. This implies changes of the social moral framework, according to which people embrace duties regarding the general functioning of social life and are solidary co-responsible for their fellow citizens and public life in general, as well as for the situation of nature today and in the future.[45] It is quite possible, however, that this will remain merely as a good intention, insofar as there are no mechanisms whereby participation can take on more than symbolic and public opinion pressure roles. It is mandatory that innovative mechanisms, which intersect the fate of individuals and collectivities in their functioning, are envisioned and institutionalized so that participation may have greater impact on society at large, and in particular on the political system. This is what Delanty clearly recognizes at the international, global level, in which individuals are far too removed from power centres, possible legislative and decision-making nuclei. His passing mention to 'social actors' at the national level both raises the issue and leaves it undeveloped:

> Transnational political governance, that is cosmopolitan democracy, mediates between, on the one side, legal cosmopolitanism and, on the other, national and subnational governance. It is becoming an important domain for social movement actors. I would like to suggest that the appropriate kind of democratic citizenship for the transnational level is collective or group citizenship. Social actors are operative on all levels of governance, in particular on the national level where they are particularly effective. But with respect to some of the key challenges to democratic citizenship, such a question of an economically sustainable society, the global regulation of justice, migration, human rights and security, it is only on the transnational level that such problems can be solved.[46]

My discussion of 'elitism' showed that the complexity of contemporary social life is usually taken as an excuse to disqualify popular participation in political debates and decision-making processes of democratic states. This is not a tenable assumption insofar as it is based on a conception of rationality that denies its possession by the 'masses'. However, we must accept that complexity brings about problems for participation and that the individual citizen is excessively distant from the state to be really able to interfere directly with its workings. What could be the role of organized collective subjectivities in this regard? In fact only by bringing collectivities onto the centre stage can the promises of freedom and equality of early modernity be properly answered at the stage at which we find ourselves now.

During the twentieth century – apart from party and union-based leftist movements, which did not however break away from traditional views of representation – only corporatism seems to have reflected on how politics should be thought about, institutionally, beyond the individual level. Its historical association with fascism snatched away the legitimacy necessary for its arguments to be regarded as plausible, while neocorporatism seemed a rather restricted manner, in democratic terms, of running the economy and society during the period of state-organized modernity, when state, business and workers representatives met at the top and alone decided the principal policy problems and solutions in each country in the short, medium and long term.[47] This arrangement is by and large no longer viable. New ways of organizing political power and interest mediation have emerged, as I have pointed out in previous chapters, implying a decentring of the state and its intermeshing with social entities sometimes ambiguously established. The pluralization of society has led to a much more diffuse representation of interests and even to a colonization of the state, in particular by business groups which circumvent the democratic institutions of the advanced modern state.[48] Is there anything to be done about this, or should we rest content with the hollowing out of democracy by this sort of political dynamic and institutional design? Although the argument to be made now is likely to be contentious, I believe that only such a move will be able to respond to problems which have come out of the increased complexity of advanced modernity and the demands of responsibility which have been thrust upon us by its development.

Drawing inspiration partly from Apel's reasoning on co-responsibility and the role collective subjectivities forcibly play in his institutional proposals, we may think also of representation along collective lines, which, in highly complex societies, do not substitute for, but may be complementary to, individual citizens, and in many cases constitute the sole entities that may take part in a public sphere and in civil society. Even at the local level representation and participation in the processes of administrative power which brings together – in principle, considerably centred – organizations, either for specific purposes or with more general intent, may evince features and dynamics that are more democratic than thinking of individuals as the basis of democracy. At the regional, national and global level this makes even more sense for a democratizing agenda. Its effects might unfold in several directions: generating debate, taking part in administrative processes, furnishing support for technical decisions, among other possibilities, as well as moving once again downward to their bases. We would have a process that, by creating a distinct *social* sphere, breaks through the split between state and society, public and private, universalism and particularism. The democratization of the state would go, hopefully, hand in hand with a strengthening of those societal organizations, whose importance would grow due to the greater relevance attributed to their role in social life, which would not be confined to the struggle against, or even for, something. They would become less intermittent, as assuredly new issues would arise and new movements and organizations develop.

There is perhaps a risk of rigidifying such organizations, or of their cooptation, since they become partners of the state; there is also the danger of having particularisms prevailing to the detriment of solutions at times necessarily universalist.[49] But we will not get rid of such problems by clinging to old models of representation and administration. If the rolling back of the state has been somehow or other associated with its colonization by private interests of different sorts, democratizing state–society networks and lending not only a more plural character to that colonization – with the state transformed into a site of both collaboration and struggle – but turning them also into processes to be carried out in the public eye, is possibly the best strategy to fight the intimidating threats of the third phase of modernity. As citizens and as intellectuals our responsibility may be demanded precisely at this juncture, so that freedom, equality and solidarity remain values that orientate the twenty-first century and the new paths modernity has been taking, and which will broaden in the coming years.

Although we must not by any means become oblivious to the class mobilization and the powerful working-class movements of the nineteenth and the twentieth centuries (without which the development of modernity cannot even begin to be grasped, an obvious fact that only too many are now inclined to forget) or downplay the importance of the instituting struggles for rights during the same period, the analysis of recent trends in the development of citizenship has shown a more context-bound, less abstract conception of individuals and collectivities, which have in some aspects become less passive as well. The further tendencies I have just brought up and the suggestion of an evolving 'social' sphere may push that forward, towards a broader overcoming of the connection between citizenship and 'real abstractions'. Along with this a different perspective of the space–time dimension is introduced, one which is also less abstract, bridging the past and the future through a concentration on active solidary relations of free and equal agents in concrete space–time configurations of the present. There are powerful currents that may prevent the species from treading a path that preserves the promises and conquests of modernity; especially in the economic domain where the prevalence of inequality and domination seems much less auspicious, a shortcoming bound to affect citizenship negatively. This notwithstanding, the hopes on which we can more promisingly rely were tentatively summarized and discussed in this and foregoing chapters, within a 'realist utopian' perspective – that is, with a view to actual developments, but taking this as the starting point for an exploration through the mind's eye.

The other side of the development of the notion of responsibility in terms of the relations between human beings, individuals and social collectivities, is the flipside of the project of rational mastery of the world that was tied in with the project of autonomy and freedom. We must be attentive to an organized irresponsibility which ensues from technological development and its often deleterious consequences, especially when it goes unchecked, as well as to the mere use and abuse of nature that draws upon such sort of technical recourse, since in such a situation 'corresponding to the highly differentiated division of labour, there is a general complicity', which 'is matched by a general lack of responsibility'. Being always in some measure cause and effect of what happens, no-one is eventually responsible for problematical or even disastrous outcomes, at least until social movements get organized to challenge such a gap.[50] The unintended, though already widely known, effects of the attempt at rational mastery of nature abound and are not always responsibly handled. As we have seen theoretically with Jonas and Apel, this is a pressing issue. It has become exposed, sometimes greatly so, to public opinion in many countries, and responsibility in practice has to some extent, albeit still far too timidly, been taken up by a myriad of social agents from the local up to the global level, risks deriving from technological developments are increasingly on the agenda of modernity.[51]

Also, and perhaps especially in this domain, responsibility will inevitably become a prominent question in the future. This is not to suggest that the situation looks particularly bright. All in all, however, if it is seriously and deeply embraced, responsibility towards nature may be conducive to changes in the relations within society, if such a distinction can still be made so sharply. Once the rational mastery of nature no longer keeps its traditionally modern features, modernity as a whole – or, in this case, postmodernity – cannot escape far-reaching changes. When and how this will take place is an open question, one that present and future generations will have to answer at some point in the evolution of the species.

We can conclude therefore that the tensions we found in relation to the other categories of modernity are present also in what refers to responsibility. Freedom is directly linked to responsibility but it may, due to the radical individualistic way in which it is phrased today, lead in an opposite direction, to overall recklessness and even the negation of freedom. Moreover equality and solidarity demand recognition, which is forthcoming only insofar as hierarchies are eschewed, if the normative directives of modernity are to prevail. Responsibility would thus depend on the affirmation of equality, and solidarity would hinge on a balance of responsibility between free and equal individuals. Hierarchies and inequalities cut across modern social life, though, and this produces problems not only for freedom, equality and solidarity, but for responsibility, which is caught up in a polarization between atomic individualism and hierarchy and inequalities. Can we surpass this? Can we find new ways to deal with nature, beyond 'rational control', a mainstay of our individual and collective view of freedom? History is open and modernity continues its trajectory. Let us hope these tensions will be resolved in an emancipatory direction.

Notes

1 Freedom and Domination

1. See Peter Wagner, *A Sociology of Modernity* (London: Routledge, 1994); Boaventura de Sousa Santos, *Toward a New Common Sense* (London: Routledge, 1995), pp. 22ff.
2. Allan Megill, *Prophets of Extremity* (Los Angeles and Berkeley: University of California Press, 1985), p. xiii.
3. Ibid., pp. 33–4.
4. I will concentrate here on European thinkers and not pursue an analysis of North American pragmatism, which, albeit with somewhat distinct roots, shares similar problems.
5. Georg Simmel, *Philosophie des Geldes* (Frankfurt am Main: Suhrkamp, [1900] 1996), ch. 1.
6. Eugene Fleischmann, 'De Weber à Nietzsche', *Archives européenes de sociologie*, 5 (1964).
7. Max Weber, 'Wissenschaft als Beruf' (1919), in *Schriften zur Wissenschaftlehre* (Stuttgart: Philipp Reclam, 1991), pp. 258ff.
8. Fleischmann, 'De Weber'.
9. M. Weber, 'Zwischen zwei Gesetzen' (1916) and 'Deutschland unter den europäischen Weltmächten' (1916), in *Gesammelte Politische Schriften* (Tübingen: J. C. B. Mohr [Paul Siebeck], 1988), respectively pp. 145, 176–7.
10. These arguments are present in M. Weber, 'Objektive Möglichkeit und adäquate Verursachung in der historischen Kausalbetrachtung' (1906), in *Schriften zur Wissenschaftlehre*; plus 'Vorbemerkungen' (1905) and 'Die protestantische Ethik und der Geist des Kapitalismus' (1904–5), p. 204, both in *Gesammelte Aufsätze zur Religionssoziologie*, vol. 1 (Tübingen: J. C. B. Mohr [Paul Siebeck], [1920] 1988).
11. See José Maurício Domingues, '*The City*: rationalization and freedom in Max Weber', *Philosophy and Social Criticism*, 26 (2000).
12. Megill, *Prophets*, p. 118.
13. Lucien Goldmann, *Heidegger et Lukács* (Paris: Denöel, 1973).
14. Despite the position of authors more sympathetic to Heidegger (cf. Megill, *Prophets*, p. 360, n. 21), in his first main book there is at least one explicit indication of the debate between he and Lukács, when he speaks of authenticity and reification (*Verdinglichung des Bewusstseins*). Martin Heidegger, *Sein und Zeit* (Tübingen: Max Niemeyer, [1927] 1993), § 10, p. 46. His opposition between *Dasein* and *Zuhandene* ('ready-to-hand')

goes the same way. The 'decision' for 'authenticity' and the refusal of the immersion of Being-there in daily, inauthentic life sounds clearly like an alternative to Lukács's notion of reification.

15. Heidegger, *Sein und Zeit*, §§ 5–6, pp. 15ff.
16. Ibid., § 29, p. 135; and § 31, pp. 142ff.
17. Ibid., § 27, pp. 126–30; § 38, pp. 175ff; § 40, pp. 184ff.
18. Ibid., § 44b, pp. 221–2.
19. Ibid., §§ 54–60, pp. 267–301.
20. Ibid., § 72, p. 376; § 75, p. 391.
21. Heidegger, 'Bekenntnis zu Adolf Hitler und dem Nationalsozialistischen Staat' (1933), in Guido Schneeberger (ed.), *Nachlese zu Heidegger* (Berne: Buchdrukerei AG, 1962), pp. 148–50, where there is no talk of freedom at all. Cf. Jürgen Habermas, *Der philosophische Diskur der Moderne* (Frankfurt am Main: Suhrkamp, [1985] 1988), esp. pp. 171, 177, 186.
22. Heidegger, *Sein und Zeit*, § 74, pp. 384, 386.
23. Heidegger *Über den Humanismus* (Brief an Jean Beaufret) (Frankfurt am Main: Vittorio Klustermann, [1944] n.d.).
24. Jean-Paul Sartre, *L'Existentialisme est un humanisme* (Paris: Nagel, [1946] 1970).
25. Idem, *L'Être et le néant* (Paris: Gallimard, [1943] 1992), pp. 56ff, 82ff, 123ff, 128, 487ff, 690–1.
26. Ibid., pp. 497ff, 517ff, 536–7, 623ff. We do not necessarily have 'knowledge' of the original project (p. 630).
27. Ibid., pp. 59–60, 74ff.
28. Idem, *Critique de la raison dialectique*, vol. 1 (Paris: Gallimard, [1960] 1985), pp. 76–7.
29. Ibid., vol. 1, pp. 318–19, 362–4, 376, 407, 410, 423–4, 425ff, 449ff, 543, 631, 883.
30. Ibid., pp. 491–2. Whatever the limitations of his (Cartesian) notion of *centring* (freedom of praxis, 'translucidity', that is, consciousness, organization and so on versus the practico-inert), Sartre is among the few thinkers to craft a theory of 'collective subjectivity', its less than accomplished exposition notwithstanding. I cannot expand on the concept of collective subjectivity here, although I will return to it at several stages. It is however worth noting that my definition of the 'philosophy of the subject' differs from Benhabib's, who rightly refuses its underlying presuppositions: the 'unitary mode of activity' as 'objectification', 'the model of transitive (collective) subject' and history as its history, as well as the identity between subject and object. They actually lingered on in the Frankfurt School's critical theory, including that of Habermas. Seyla Benhabib, *Critique, Norm and Utopia* (New York: Columbia University Press, 1986), pp. 54, 330, 393, n. 37. For a full account of collective subjectivity, see J. M. Domingues, *Sociological Theory and Collective Subjectivity* (London and New York: Macmillan and St Martin's Press, 1995).

31 Sartre, *Critique de la raison dialectique*, vol. 1, p. 816, and *passim*; plus vol. 2 (Paris: Gallimard, 1985), *passim*.
32 Ibid., vol. 1, pp. 157–9, 182–4, 748–9, 893–4; vol. 2, p. 13.
33 See J. M. Domingues, 'Creativity and master trends in contemporary sociological theory', *European Journal of Social Theory*, 3 (2000).
34 Anthony Giddens, *The Consequences of Modernity* (Stanford: Stanford University Press and Cambridge: Polity, 1990); *Modernity and Self-Identity* (Cambridge: Polity, 1991); *The Transformation of Intimacy* (Cambridge: Polity, 1992).
35 Ulrich Beck, *Risk Society* (London: Sage, [1986] 1992).
36 Alberto Melucci, *The Playing Self* (Cambridge: Cambridge University Press, 1996), pp. 45, 147–8. See also his *Nomads of the Present: Social Movements and Social Needs in Contemporary Society* (Philadelphia: Temple University Press, 1989) and *Challenging Codes* (Cambridge: Cambridge University Press, 1996).
37 J. M. Domingues, *Social Creativity, Collective Subjectivity and Contemporary Modernity* (London and New York: Macmillan and St Martin's Press, 2000), chs 5, 7.
38 Beck, *Risk Society*, pp. 116, 195.
39 Frédéric Vandenberghe, *Une Histoire critique de la sociologie allemande* (Paris: La Découverte and MAUSS, 1997–8).
40 Benhabib, *Critique*, pp. 328–9.
41 Vandenberghe, *Histoire critique, passim*.
42 Charles Taylor, *Hegel* (Cambridge: Cambridge University Press, 1975), chs 1–3, 20.
43 Karl Marx, *Das Kapital*, vol. 1, *Mega* II-5 (Berlin: Dietz, [1867] 1987), pp. 66–7, 102ff.
44 G. Simmel, 'Der Begriff und die Tragödie der Kultur' (1911), in *Philosophische Kultur* (Berlin: Klaus Wagenbach, 1986).
45 Idem, *Philosophie des Geldes*, esp. pp. 13, 380ff, 392ff, 400, 609ff. K. Marx and Friedrich Engels, *Manifest des kommunistischen Partei* (1848), in Marx and Engels, *Werke*, vol. 4 (Berlin: Dietz, 1939).
46 For a broad view of rationalization, see Weber, 'Vorbemerkungen'; his stress on instrumental rationalization is in 'Die protestantische Ethik und der Geist des Kapitalismus' and in 'Wissenschaft als Beruf', as well as, partly, in his *Wirtschaft und Gesellschaft* (Tübingen: J. C. B. Mohr [Paul Siebeck], [1921–2] 1976). This last book provides a more formal-legal, universalizing conception of rationality.
47 Gyorg Lukács, *Geschichte und Klassenbewusstsein*, in *Werke*, vol. 2 (Berlin: Luchterhand, [1923] 1977), p. 385.
48 Ibid., p. 257.
49 Ibid., pp. 271ff.
50 Ibid., pp. 286ff.

51 Ibid., pp. 262–7.
52 Max Horkheimer, 'Traditionelle und kritische Theorie' (1937), in *Traditionelle und kritische Theorie* (Frankfurt am Main: Fischer, 1980), p. 30.
53 Theodor W. Adorno and M. Horkheimer, *Dialektik der Aufklärung* (Frankfurt am Main: Fischer, [1944] 1984), pp. 31, 37.
54 Ibid., pp. 7, 15.
55 Ibid., pp. 151ff.
56 Ibid., pp. 113–15. See Herbert Marcuse, 'Über den Affirmativen Charakter der Kultur' (1937), in *Herbert Marcuse: Kultur und Gesellschaft* (Frankfurt am Main: Suhrkamp, 1965).
57 M. Horkheimer, *Eclipse of Reason* (New York: Oxford University Press, [1946] 1974), ch. 1.
58 Ibid., pp. 23, 37.
59 T. W. Adorno, *Minima Moralia* (Frankfurt am Main: Suhrkamp, [1944–5] 1997), esp. pp. 9–10; § 97, p. 197; § 132, p. 275.
60 Idem, *Negative Dialektik* (Frankfurt am Main: Suhrkamp, [1966] 1980), pp. 17ff, 42.
61 M. Horkheimer, 'Kritische Theorie Gestern und Heute' (1970), in *Gesellschaft im Übergang* (Frankfurt am Main: Fischer, 1981).
62 Adorno, *Negative Dialektik*, p. 218.
63 Ibid., pp. 59–60. Adorno dedicated a piece exclusively to Heidegger and 'authenticity' (originally planned as part of *Negative Dialektik*): *Jargon der Eigentlichkeit: Zur Deutschen Ideologie* (Frankfurt am Main: Suhrkamp, 1964).
64 Adorno, *Negative Dialektik*, p. 259. He maintains that Lukács had an idealist position, since he was concerned basically with consciousness. Ibid., pp. 190–1.
65 Ibid., pp. 213–14, 261–2.
66 Ibid., p. 215.
67 H. Marcuse, *Onedimensional Man* (Boston: Beacon, [1964] 1968), pp. xii–xvi, 168. Sartre's later writings probably reminded him of his own early efforts of bringing together his teacher's (Heidegger) sort of 'Existentialism' and Marxism. See his 'Beiträge zu einer Phänomenologie des historischen Materialismus' (1928), in *Schriften*, vol. 1. *Frühe Aufsätze* (Frankfurt am Main: Suhrkamp, 1978).
68 Idem, *Onedimensional Man*, pp. 4–5.
69 Ibid., pp. 4, 6–8, 915, 19ff, 29ff, 49–50, 223, 84.
70 Ibid., pp. 72–8, 222–3, and idem, *Eros and Civilization* (Boston: Beacon, [1955] 1966).
71 Idem, *An Essay on Liberation* (London: Penguin, 1969), esp. pp. vii–viii; and *Counterrevolution and Revolt* (Boston: Beacon, 1972).
72 Domingues, *Sociological Theory*, ch. 3; *Social Creativity*, chs 4, 7.

73 Idem, *Strukturwandel der Öffentlichkeit* (Frankfurt am Main: Suhrkamp, 1962).
74 Idem, *Erkenntnis und Interest* (Frankfurt am Main: Suhrkamp, [1971] 1991). For Horkheimer's efforts, see his 'Traditionelle und kritische Theorie'.
75 Habermas, *Theorie des kommunikativen Handelns* (Frankfurt am Main: Suhrkamp, [1981] 1988), vol. 2, ch. 6 and 'Schlussbetrachtungen'.
76 Ibid., pp. 182ff.
77 Idem, 'Die Moderne: Ein unvollendetes Projekt', in *Kleine politische Schriften*, vols 1–4 (Frankfurt am Main: Suhrkamp, 1981).
78 Idem, *Faktizität und Geltung* (Frankfurt am Main: Suhrkamp, 1992).
79 Idem, *The Future of Human Nature* (Cambridge: Polity, 2003).
80 Jean Baudrillard, *La Société de consommation* (Paris: Gallimard, 1970); *A l'Ombre des majorités silencieuses* (Paris: Cahiers d'Utopie, 1978).
81 Fredric Jameson, *Postmodernism, or, The Cultural Logic of Late Capitalism* (Durham, NC: Duke University Press, 1991); *Late Marxism: Adorno, or, the Persistence of Dialectic* (London: Verso, 1990).
82 Weber, 'Wissenschaft als Beruf'; Habermas, *Theorie des kommunikativen Handelns*, vol. 1, pp. 332ff, 462ff.
83 K. Marx, 'Vorwort' (1859), in *Zur Kritik der politischen Ökonomie*, in Marx and Engels, *Werke*, vol. 13 (Berlin: Dietz, 1962).

2 Projects, Dialectic and History

1 José Maurício Domingues, *Social Creativity, Collective Subjectivity and Contemporary Modernity* (London and New York: Macmillan and St Martin's Press, 2000), ch. 2; and 'Reflexividade, individualismo e modernidade' (2002), in *Ensaios de sociologia* (Belo Horizonte: Editora UFMG, 2004).
2 Gyorg Márkus, 'On freedom: positive and negative', *Constellations*, 6 (1999), 280–2, 285.
3 Claus Offe, 'The utopia of the zero option' (1987), in *Modernity and the State. East, West* (Cambridge: Polity, 1996), pp. 17–18. It must be said that, contrary to many views, including Offe's own, only in a very restricted (along with Marx) and today dubious sense can one speak of the 'revolutionary' character of markets as opposed to conservatism in moral terms – as indeed his example evinces.
4 Ibid., pp. 5–10.
5 Hans J. Eysenck, 'Social attitude and social class', *British Journal of Sociology*, 1 (1950); Antônio Flávio Pierruci, *Ciladas da diferença* (São Paulo: Editora 34, 1999), pp. 14–19.
6 Teresa Matus Sepúlveda, *A revisitação dos Deuses: Ensaio sobre cultura e modernização nas sociedades periféricas* (Ph.D. thesis, IUPERJ, 2000), esp. pp. 207ff.

7 Márkus, 'On freedom', p. 274.
8 Amartya Sen, *Development as Freedom* (New York: Anchor Books, 1999). See J. M. Domingues, 'Amartya Sen: o desenvolvimento e a liberdade', in *Do ocidente à modernidade: Intelectuais e mudança social* (Rio de Janeiro: Civilização Brasileira, 2003).
9 Anthony Giddens, *The Consequences of Modernity* (Cambridge: Polity, 1990), esp. pp. 18–19, 22–5, 27–8.
10 Ibid., pp. 63–5, 108–9. See also David Harvey, *The Condition of Postmodernity* (Cambridge, MA: Blackwell, 1990), chs 12–18. I will articulate a specific concept of space–time in part 2.
11 Peter Wagner, *A Sociology of Modernity* (London: Routledge, 1994).
12 Piet Strydom, *Discourse and Knowledge: The Making of Enlightenment Sociology* (Liverpool: Liverpool University Press, 2000), pp. 9–10. See also John B. Thompson, *The Media and Modernity* (Cambridge: Polity, 1995).
13 Sigmund Freud, *Hemmung, Sympton und Angst* (1926), in *Studienausgabe* (Frankfurt am Main: S. Fisher, 1971), vol. 6, pp. 302ff.
14 Idem, *Die Zukunft einer Illusion* (1927), in *Studienausgabe* (Frankfurt am Main: S. Fisher, 1974), vol. 9, esp. ch. 4.
15 Idem, *Das Unbehagen in der Kultur* (1930), in *Studienausgabe*, vol. 9 (Frankfurt am Main: S. Fisher, 1974), pp. 248–9, 270.
16 Adam Phillips, *Monogamy* (London: Faber & Faber, 1996) and Niklas Luhmann, *Liebe als Passion* (Frankfurt am Main: Suhrkamp, 1982); J. M. Domingues, *Sociologia e modernidade: Para entender a sociedade contemporânea* (Rio de Janeiro: Civilização Brasileira, 3rd edn 2005), esp. ch. 4.
17 Michael Oakeshott, 'On being conservative', in *Rationalism in Politics* (London: Methuen & Co., 1962).
18 Axel Honneth, 'Die soziale Dynamik von Missachtung' (1994), in *Das Andere der Gerechtigkeit* (Frankfurt am Main: Suhrkamp, 2000).
19 See, though inattentive to that manic response, Alberto Melucci, *The Playing Self* (Cambridge: Cambridge University Press, 1994), pp. 20–1.
20 Charles Taylor, *Sources of the Self* (Cambridge: Cambridge University Press, 1989), p. 12; and 'The politics of recognition', in Amy Guttman (ed.), *Multiculturalism* (Princeton: Princeton University Press, 1992), pp. 31ff.
21 See Michael Mann, *The Sources of Social Power*, vol. 1 (Cambridge: Cambridge University Press, 1986), pp. 301ff, 397–8, 412; Richard Morse, *El espejo de Próspero* (Mexico: Siglo XXI, 1982), ch. 1, as well as my 'Richard Morse and the "Iberian-American" path', *Revista interamericana de bibliografia*, 45 (1995). Weber's piece on the medieval city depicts important stages in the development of freedom in the West, especially insofar as the internal dynamic of such social systems is concerned, though within the inclusive society freedom was still conquered and kept as a privilege, and ended up being dissolved by the absolutist state. See M. Weber, 'Die nichtlegitime Herrschaft (Typologie der Stadt)' (1921), in

Wirtschaft und Gesellschaft, (Tübingen: J. C. B. Mohr [Paul Siebeck], [1921–2] 1976), and my '*The City*: rationalization and freedom in Max Weber', *Philosophy and Social Criticism*, 34 (2000).
22. But see Jean-Paul Sartre, *Critique de la raison dialectique*, vols. 1–2 (Paris: Gallimard, [1960] 1985 and 1985, respectively).
23. See in any case for the great traditional world religions, M. Weber, *Die Wirtschafsethik der Weltreligionen* ('Zwischen Betrachtungen') (1915–19), in *Gesammelte Aufsätze zur Religionssoziologie*, vol. 1 (Tübingen: J. C. B. Mohr [Paul Siebeck], [1920] 1988). Weber, however, was as usual so concerned with rationalization that he lost sight of the very demand for freedom that can be found in Protestant theology, especially perhaps, but certainly not exclusively, in its late developments.
24. Weber, 'Die protestantische Ethik und der Geist des Kapitalismus' (in *Gesammelte Aufsätze zur Religionssoziologie*, vol. 1), 'Zwischen Betrachtungen' and *Wirtschaft und Gesellschaft*, pp. 314–19; and Talcott Parsons, 'A tentative outline of American values' (1959–60), in Roland Robertson and Bryan S. Turner (eds), *Talcott Parsons, Theorist of Modernity* (London: Sage, 1991).
25. H. Marcuse, 'Über den Affirmativen Charakter der Kultur' (1937), in *Herbert Marcuse: Kultur und Gesellschaft* (Frankfurt am Main: Suhrkamp, 1965).
26. Domingues, *Sociologia e modernidade*, ch. 4.
27. Márkus, 'On freedom', p. 288, n. 5. I will expand on the relationship between power and freedom vis-à-vis equality in part 2. Let me now cursorily state that they are not the same thing: capabilities give us power which is a condition of freedom.
28. Domingues, *Social Creativity*, ch. 2.
29. Theodor W. Adorno and Max Horkheimer, *Dialektik der Aufklärung* (Frankfurt am Main: Fischer, [1944] 1984), pp. 7ff, 12.
30. Cf. Wagner, *Sociology of Modernity*, p. 14 (who draws upon Castoriadis).
31. Adorno and Horkheimer, *Dialektik*, pp. 42ff.
32. Michel Foucault, *Surveiller et punir* (Paris: Gallimard, 1975); *Histoire de la sexualité*, vol. 1, *La Volonté de savoir* (Paris: Gallimard, 1976).
33. Ulrich Beck, *Risk Society* (London: Sage, [1986] 1992), chs 2, 7–8.
34. Giddens, *Consequences*, pp. 15–16, 22, 26ff, 38–42, 79ff, 112ff.
35. Boaventura de Sousa Santos, 'Reinventar a democracia: entre o pré-contratualismo e o pós-contratualismo', in Agnes Heller et al., *A crise dos paradigmas nas ciências sociais e os desafios para o século XXI* (Rio de Janeiro: Contraponto and Corecon-RJ, 1999), p. 68.
36. Cornelius Castoriadis, 'L'Epoque du conformisme generalisé', in *Le Monde morcelé* (Paris: Seuil, 1990). See also Johann P. Anarson, 'The imaginary constitution of modernity', *Revue europeéne des sciences sociales*, 20 (1989).

[37] See Domingues, *Social Creativity*, p. 163.
[38] Idem, *Sociological Theory and Collective Subjectivity* (London and New York: Macmillan and St Martin's Press, 1995), and *Social Creativity*, esp. ch. 4.
[39] Of course my perspective is at variance with the simultaneously structuralist and almost subjectivist conception of history Lévi-Strauss polemically introduces against Sartre. See Claude Lévi-Strauss, *La Pensée sauvage* (Paris: Plon, 1962), ch. 9.
[40] Domingues, *Social Creativity*, p. 163.
[41] See idem, 'A teoria sociológica alemã contemporânea: evolução, criatividade e modernidade', in Leopoldo Waizbort (ed.), *A ousadia crítica* (Londrina: Editora da Universidade Estadual de Londrina, 1996).
[42] Therefore I only partly agree with Seyla Benhabib, *Critique, Norm and Utopia* (New York: Columbia University Press, 1986), pp. 276–7.
[43] Adorno and Horkheimer, *Dialektik*; M. Horkheimer, *Eclipse of Reason* (New York: Oxford University Press, [1946] 1974), ch. 1.
[44] J. Habermas, *Zur Rekonstruktion des historischen Materialismus* (Frankfurt am Main: Suhrkamp, 1976) and *Theorie des kommunikativen Handelns* (Frankfurt am Main: Suhrkamp, [1981] 1988). See Domingues, *Social Creativity*, ch. 4, for a full account of this debate and a proposal that centres on contingency and reconstructive models.
[45] Weber, *Die Wirtschaftsethik der Weltreligionen*, especially pp. 521–2.
[46] See Morse, *El espejo de Próspero*; and Jessé Souza, 'A ética protestante e a ideologia do atraso brasileiro', in J. Souza (ed.), *O malandro e o protestante* (Brasília: Editora UnB, 1999).
[47] For a definition of 'imaginary', see Domingues, *Social Creativity*, ch. 2.

3 Citizenship and Equality

[1] Boaventura de Sousa Santos, 'Reinventar a democracia: entre o pré-contratualismo e o pós-contratualismo', in Agnes Heller et al., *A crise dos paradigmas em ciências sociais e os desafios para o século XXI* (Rio de Janeiro: Contraponto and Corecon-RJ, 1999), p. 33.
[2] Alexis de Tocqueville, *De la Démocratie en Amérique* (Paris: Gallimard, [1835–40] 1951); *L'Ancien Régime et la Révolution* (Paris: Gallimard, [1856] 1953). I draw also upon Marcelo Jasmin, *Alexis de Tocqueville: A historiografia como ciência política* (Rio de Janeiro: Access, 1997).
[3] De Tocqueville, *De la Démocratie*, mainly vol. 1 ii, ch. 4, and vol. 2 ii, chs 4–8.
[4] Idem, *L'Ancien Régime*, pp. 73–4.
[5] Ibid., pp. 74, 105, 222–3. The situation is probably replicated by women today.
[6] Idem, *De la Démocratie*, vol. 1, p. 5.

7. Ibid., vol. 2, pp. 74, 147–8, 324–5.
8. Jean L. Cohen, 'Changing paradigms of citizenship and the exclusiveness of the demos', *International Sociology*, 14 (1999), 248.
9. Norberto Bobbio, *L'età dei diritto* (Turin: Einaudi, [1990] 1997), pp. ix–xv and 61. It is worth noting that Bobbio outlines four generations of rights: civil, political and social, plus those which accrue to ecology, reproduction and so forth – whose elements and characteristics are still in their making. It may be added that not all legal states are constitutional states (for example, Great Britain). For the struggle for social rights, see Adam Przeworski, *Capitalism and Social Democracy* (Cambridge: Cambridge University Press, 1985).
10. Max Weber, *Wirtschaft und Gesellschaft* (Tübingen: J. C. B. Mohr [Paul Siebeck], [1921–2] 1976), pp. 122ff.
11. Piet Strydom, *Discourse and Knowledge: The Making of Enlightenment Sociology* (Liverpool: Liverpool University Press, 2001), chs 6–7.
12. Michel Foucault, *Surveiller et punir* (Paris: Gallimard, 1975), pp. 259, 292–8.
13. Bobbio, *L'età dei diritto*, pp. 46, 62–4, 67–70.
14. Feminists have stressed this feature of modernity. See Carole Pateman, *The Sexual Contract* (Stanford: Stanford University Press, 1988); and Nancy Fraser, 'What's critical about critical theory? The case of Habermas and gender' (1985), in *Unruly Practices* (Minneapolis: Minneapolis University Press, 1989) plus 'Rethinking the public sphere: a contribution to the critique of actually existing democracy' (1991), in *Justice Interruptus: Critical Reflections on the 'Postsocialist' Condition* (New York: Routledge, 1997).
15. Bobbio, *L'età dei diritto*, p. 72. As a liberal Bobbio naturally states (pp. 40–2) that the freest societies are those in which there is less justice – those values are for him 'antinomic'. I have argued precisely the opposite of that, although not unconditionally, in chapter 2, and will resume the argument below.
16. Ibid., pp. xvi–xvii.
17. Gerard Delanty, *Citizenship in a Global Age* (Buckingham: Open University Press, 2000), pp. 11ff.
18. Thomas Humphrey Marshall, 'Citizenship and social class' (1950), in *Class, Citizenship, and Social Development* (Garden City, NY: Doubleday & Co., 1964), pp. 71–2.
19. Ibid., pp. 72ff, 76–7.
20. See José Maurício Domingues, *Social Creativity, Collective Subjectivity and Contemporary Modernity* (London and New York: Macmillan and St Martin's Press, 2000), ch. 4.
21. Marshall, 'Citizenship', pp. 70ff, 79ff.
22. Ibid., pp. 87–8. See also Roberto Mangabeira Unger, *The Critical Legal Studies Movement* (Cambridge, MA: Harvard University Press, [1983] 1986), p. 36.
23. Marshall, 'Citizenship', pp. 93–4.

[24] Anthony Giddens, *The Nation-State and Violence* (Cambridge: Polity, 1985), pp. 200ff; see also his 'Class division, class conflict and citizenship rights', in *Profiles and Critiques in Social Theory* (London: Macmillan, 1982). He draws upon Marshall.

[25] Marshall, 'Citizenship', p. 75.

[26] For criticisms see Michael Mann, 'Ruling class strategies and citizenship' (1987), in Bryan S. Turner and Peter Hamilton (eds), *Citizenship: Critical Concepts*, vol. 1 (London: Routledge, 1994) and B. S. Turner (ed.), *Citizenship and Social Theory* (London: Sage, 1993). Other key references are the evolutionist theses of Talcott Parsons, *The System of Modern Society* (Englewood Cliffs, NJ: Prentice Hall, 1971); and the globally and historically orientated approach of Reinhard Bendix, *Nation-Building and Citizenship* (Berkeley and Los Angeles: University of California Press, [1964] 1977).

[27] Marshall, 'Citizenship', pp. 93–4, 101ff.

[28] For a general analytical view, see Bryan Barry, *Political Argument* (London: Routledge & Kegan Paul, 1965), pp. 152–4; for World Bank (and the International Monetary Fund) policies, Joan M. Nelson, 'Poverty, equity, and the politics of adjustment', in Stephan Haggard and Robert R. Kaufman (eds), *The Politics of Economic Adjustment* (Princeton: Princeton University Press, 1992), esp. pp. 234–5, 244; for discriminated collectivities, N. Fraser, 'After the family wage: a postindustrial thought experiment' (1994), in *Justice Interruptus*.

[29] Marshall, 'Citizenship', pp. 105ff.

[30] See for instance G. H. D. Cole, *The British Co-operative Movement in a Socialist Society* (London: Georg Allen & Unwin, 1951).

[31] Isabel A. Ribeiro de Oliveira, 'Princípios de justiça e legitimação do Estado contemporâneo', *Sociedade e Estado*, 12 (1997), 115.

[32] Goran Esping-Andersen, *Politics against Markets: The Social-Democratic Road to Power* (Princeton: Princeton University Press, 1985), pp. 245ff; *The Three Worlds of Welfare Capitalism* (Princeton: Princeton University Press, 1990), part i.

[33] See Wanderley Guilherme dos Santos, *Cidadania e justiça* (Rio de Janeiro: Campus, 1979); Hobart Spalding Jr, *Organized Labor in Latin America* (New York: Harper & Row, 1987); and Domingues, *Social Creativity*, ch. 7.

[34] Alan Ware and Robert E. Goodin, 'Introduction'; Richard Parry, 'Needs, services and political success under the British conservatives'; Joakin Palme, 'Models of old-age pensions', all in A. Ware and R. E. Goodin (eds), *Needs and Welfare* (London: Sage, 1990), pp. 5, 100, 110, respectively.

[35] These issues were studied by, among others, A. Giddens, *A Contemporary Critique of Historical Materialism* (London: Macmillan., 1981), pp. 11, 125–8, 165, 212–14; Jürgen Habermas, 'Technik und Wissenschaft als Ideologie', in *Technik und Wissenschaft als Ideologie* (Frankfurt am Main: Suhrkamp, 1968); and Robert Castel, *Les Metamorphoses de la question sociale* (Paris: Fayard, 1995).

36 As celebrated in Karl Marx and Friedrich Engels, *Manifest des kommunistischen Partei* (1848), in Marx and Engels, *Werke*, vol. 4 (Berlin: Dietz, 1939).
37 See Amartya Sen, *Inequality Reexamined* (Cambridge, MA: Harvard University Press, 1992); and Sabina Alkine, *Valuing Freedoms* (Oxford: Oxford University Press, 2002).
38 Bobbio, *L'età dei diritto*, p. 69.
39 Ibid., p. 71.

4 Inequalities and Real Abstractions

1 Gilberto Velho, 'Prestígio e ascensão social: dos limites do individualismo na sociedade brasileira', in *Individualismo e cultura* (Rio de Janeiro: Zahar, 1981), p. 53.
2 See Reinhard Kreckel, *Politische Soziologie der sozialen Ungleicheit* (New York and Frankfurt am Main: Campus, [1992] 1997), pp. 16, 29.
3 See Anthony Giddens, *The Class Structure of Advanced Societies* (London: Hutchinson & Co., 1973).
4 Gerard Delanty, *Social Theory in a Changing World* (Cambridge: Polity, 1999), p. 184.
5 Pierre Bourdieu, *La Distinction* (Paris: Minuit, 1979), pp. 135–6.
6 José Maurício Domingues, *Sociological Theory and Collective Subjectivity* (London and New York: Macmillan and St Martin's Press, 1995), pp. 132ff; 'Sociological theory and the space–time dimension of social systems', *Time and Society*, 4 (1995). And see the beautiful panel by Ernest Cassirer, *The Philosophy of the Enlightenment* (Princeton: Princeton University Press, [1931] 1951), ch. 6.
7 Talcott Parsons, 'An approach to psychological theory in terms of the theory of action', in S. Koch (ed.), *Psychology: The Study of a Science*, vol. 3 (New York: McGraw-Hill, 1959).
8 Jeffrey C. Alexander, 'Contradictions: the uncivilizing pressures of space, time, and function', *Soundings*, 16 (2000). This is so despite his structuralist conception of culture, according to which a *binary code* is necessarily subsistent in social life – what seems in this case to entail inevitably some sort of exclusion – and his functionalist bias – which accepts inequalities in the other main spheres of social life in the name of differentiation.
9 John Rawls, *A Theory of Justice* (Oxford: Oxford University Press, [1972] 1990), § 3, p. 12; § 20, pp. 120–1. I refrain from analysing his other works here. See in any case his *Political Liberalism* (New York: Columbia University Press, 1993), where he emphasizes his intention to present a *political* version of liberalism and justice in that previous book, and shifts towards a more discursive approach to justice, leaving at least some of the heavy

abstractions of his former work behind, especially when discussing the 'steps' of an overlapping consensus (Lecture IV, §§ 6–7, pp. 158ff, 164ff).

[10] Idem, *Theory of Justice*, § 22, pp. 126–30; § 23, p. 140. The discussion about 'responsibility' will be resumed in ch. 11.

[11] Robert P. Wolff, *Understanding Rawls* (Princeton: Princeton University Press, 1977), pp. 204, 210.

[12] Rawls, *Theory of Justice*, § 40, p. 253.

[13] Ibid., § 4, p. 19; § 24, pp. 136–42; § 25, pp. 142–50.

[14] Ibid., § 2, pp. 7, 9; as well as § 10, p. 54.

[15] Ibid., § 8, pp. 42–3.

[16] Ibid., § 11, p. 60.

[17] Not even ibid., § 82, pp. 541–8 – supposedly the decisive passage.

[18] Ibid., § 11, pp. 61–2; § 13, pp. 75ff; and further on in § 16, pp. 96–7. Note, however, that he rejects both meritocracy and the 'principle of redress' to deal with the issue in § 17, pp. 100–1.

[19] Robert A. Dahl, *A Preface to Economic Democracy* (Berkeley and Los Angeles: University of California Press, 1985).

[20] John Dunn, 'Property, justice and common good after socialism', in John Hall and I. C. Jarvie (eds), *Transitions to Modernity* (Cambridge: Cambridge University Press, 1992).

[21] Rawls, *Theory of Justice*, p. 258; § 43, pp. 274–84.

[22] Ibid., § 32, p. 209.

[23] A. Giddens, *Central Problems in Social Theory* (London: Macmillan, 1979), pp. 68–9, 88ff.

[24] T. Parsons, 'On the concept of political power' (1963), in *Sociological Theory and Modern Society* (New York: Free Press, 1967); Michael Mann, *The Sources of Social Power*, vol. 1 (Cambridge: Cambridge University Press, 1986), pp. 6ff, 27ff. The distinction between the concepts of 'action' and 'movement' is important for the theory of collective subjectivity. See J. M. Domingues, *Social Creativity, Collective Subjectivity and Contemporary Modernity* (London and New York: Macmillan and St Martin's Press), ch. 1.

[25] Max Weber, *Wirtschaft und Gesellschaft* (Tübingen: J. C. B. Mohr [Paul Siebeck], [1921–2] 1976), pp. 28–9.

[26] Probably the best overall treatment of this is still Barrington Moore Jr, *The Basis of Dictatorship and Democracy* (Boston: Beacon, 1966).

[27] See J. M. Domingues, 'Globalização, reflexividade e justiça' (2002), in *Ensaios de sociologia* (Belo Horizonte: Editora UFMG, 2004).

[28] K. Marx, *Das Kapital*, vol. 1, *Mega* II-5 (Berlin: Dietz, [1867] 1987), *passim*.

[29] Idem, *Zur Juden Frage* (1844), in Marx and Engels, *Werke*, vol. 1 (Berlin: Dietz, 1956).

[30] Theodor W. Adorno, *Minima Moralia* (Frankfurt am Main: Suhrkamp, [1944–5] 1997), pp. 23, 130.

[31] Luc Boltanski and Laurent Thévenot, *De la Justification* (Paris: Gallimard, 1991), p. 99.

32. Jürgen Habermas, *Theorie des kommunikativen Handelns*, vol. 2 (Frankfurt am Main: Suhrkamp, [1981] 1988), pp. 489ff, 499.
33. Ibid., vol. 2, pp. 522–31, 539, 548–9; and vol. 1, p. 346ff.
34. Michel Foucault, *Surveiller et punir* (Paris: Gallimard, 1975) and 'Two lectures', in C. Gordon (ed.), *Power/Knowledge* (Brighton: Harvester, 1980). For the administrative development of the state, see A. Giddens, *The Nation-State and Violence* (Cambridge: Polity, 1985).
35. For a wide-ranging historical account of law, especially in the modern state, see Roberto Mangabeira Unger, *Law in Modern Society* (New York: Free Press, 1977).
36. David Held, *Models of Democracy* (Cambridge: Polity, 1987), pp. 72ff, 288–9.
37. Bryan S. Turner, 'Outline of a theory of citizenship' (1990), in B. S. Turner and Peter Hamilton (eds), *Citizenship. Critical Concepts*, vol. 1 (London: Routledge, 1994).
38. Reinhard Bendix, *Nation-Building and Citizenship* (Berkeley and Los Angeles: University of California Press, [1964] 1977), p. 24.
39. Rawls, *Theory of Justice*, §§ 18–19, pp. 113–17.
40. Hegel's criticism of Kant's theory of abstract morality, for which he substitutes a concrete *Sittlichkeit*, as well as his ambivalent relation to the modern state, is the foremost classical expression of this attitude before critical theory.
41. A few authors seek such a global synthesis. See Boaventura de Sousa Santos, 'Toward a multicultural conception of human rights', *Zeitschrift für Rechtssoziologie*, 18/1 (1997).

5 Justice, Real Abstractions and the Return to Context

1. Niklas Luhmann, *Die Gesellschaft der Gesellschaft* (Frankfurt am Main: Suhrkamp, 1997).
2. Idem, *Das Recht der Gesellschaft* (Frankfurt am Main: Suhrkamp, [1993] 1997), pp. 30, 33. An older, more historically orientated and closed-systems approach is his *Rechtssoziologie* (Opladen: Westdeutscher Verlag, [1980] 1987).
3. Idem, *Das Recht*, pp. 124ff, 138–9.
4. Ibid., pp. 59ff, 77ff, 156–7, 165ff, 216ff. Brief remarks on equality are found in pp. 110–17 and 223ff. At any rate the obsolescence of the natural or rational rights terminology for a description of the legal system is evident for him, in contradistinction to Habermas (p. 528).
5. Ibid., pp. 100–2. The target of the polemic is explicitly Habermas.
6. Ibid., p. 97 and ch. 8, for the 'self-observation' of the system.
7. Max Weber, *Wirtschaft und Gesellschaft* (Tübingen: J. C. B. Mohr [Paul Siebeck], [1921–2] 1976), pp. 387ff. An approach that depicts the different

types of rationalization as an alternative to both Weber and systems theory is found in Klaus Eder, 'Prozedurale Rationalität: Moderne Rechtentwicklung jenseits von formaler Rationalisierung', *Zeitschrift für Rechtssoziologie*, 7 (1986).

[8] Gunther Teubner, 'The two faces of Janus: rethinking legal pluralism', *Cardoso Law Review*, 13 (1992). His pristine, more orthodox Luhmannian approach can be seen in 'How the law thinks', *Law and Society Review*, 23 (1989).

[9] Marcelo Neves, 'From the autopoiesis to the allopoiesis of law', *Journal of Law and Society*, 28 (2001).

[10] Alfons Bora, 'Grenzen der Partizipation? Risikoentscheidungen und Öffentlichkeitsbeteiligung im Recht', *Zeitschrift für Rechtssoziologie*, 15 (1994).

[11] Jürgen Habermas, *Der philosophische Diskur der Moderne* (Frankfurt am Main: Suhrkamp, 1985), pp. 426ff; *Faktizität und Geltung* (Frankfurt am Main: Suhrkamp, 1992), p. 16.

[12] Idem, *Faktizität und Geltung*, pp. 12–13.

[13] Ibid., pp. 41–5.

[14] Gerard Delanty, *Social Theory in a Changing World* (Cambridge: Polity, 1999), p. 87.

[15] Habermas, *Faktizität und Geltung*, p. 44. See also his 'Zur Legitimation durch Menschrechte', in *Die postnationale Konstellation* (Frankfurt am Main: Suhrkamp, 1998).

[16] Idem, *Faktizität und Geltung*, pp. 17–18, plus 22, 33.

[17] Ibid., pp. 45ff, 119ff, 136ff; and 51, 56–7, 59–60, 117, 397–8.

[18] Ibid., p. 108.

[19] Ibid., p. 117.

[20] Idem, 'Kampf um Annerkenung in demokratische Rechtstaat' (1993), in *Die Einbeziehung des Anderen* (Frankfurt am Main: Suhrkamp, 1996), pp. 242–3. In any case he is critical of the concentration purely on rights, to the detriment of duties for the 'artificially created status of bearers of subjective rights'. Idem, 'Zur Legitimation', esp. pp. 171–2.

[21] Idem, *Faktizität und Geltung*, pp. 155–6, 167–8.

[22] Ibid., p. 168.

[23] Ibid., pp. 170, 182; and his 'Arendts Begriff der Macht' (1976), in *Philosophisch-politische Profile* (Frankfurt am Main: Suhrkamp, 1981).

[24] Idem, *Faktizität und Geltung*, pp. 360ff, 367ff, 373–4, and ch. 8, esp. pp. 435ff. See also his 'Drei normative Modelle der Demokratie' (1992), in *Die Einbeziehung des Anderen*.

[25] Idem, *Strukturwandel der Öffentlichkeit* (Frankfurt am Main: Suhrkamp, 1962).

[26] A well-taken critical point is that Habermas would have learnt more from the realists and critical legal studies currents than from liberal and

republican theorists, especially regarding the problematic thesis of the self-reference and closure of economic and political systems. William E. Forbath, 'Short-circuit: a critique of Habermas's understanding of law, politics and economic life', in Michel Rosenfeld and Andrew Arato (eds), *Habermas on Law and Democracy: Critical Exchanges* (Los Angeles and Berkeley: University of California Press, 1998). In his reply to the contribution in the same volume, Habermas chooses to bypass this criticism.

27 See J. Habermas, 'Treffen Hegels Einwände gegen Kant auch auf die Diskursethik zu?' (1985), in *Erläuterungen zu Diskursethik* (Frankfurt am Main: Suhrkamp, 1991); and 'Kampf um Annerkenung'.

28 See Boaventura de Sousa Santos, 'A sociologia dos tribunais e a democratização da justiça', in *Pela mão de Alice: O social e o político na pós-modernidade* (São Paulo: Cortez, 1995).

29 He first set out these ideas in K. Eder, *Geschichte als Lerneprozess?* (Frankfurt am Main: Suhrkamp, 1985).

30 Idem, 'Prozedurales Recht und Prozeduralisierung des Rechts', in Dieter Grimm (ed.), *Wachsende Staatsaufgaben: Sinkende Steuerungsfähigkeit des Rechts* (Baden-Baden: Nomos, 1990); and *Geschichte als Lerneprozess?*

31 Idem, 'Prozedurales Recht', pp. 165ff.

32 Idem, 'Prozedurale Rationalität'. See also his 'Die Autorität des Rechts: Eine soziale Kritik prozeduraler Rationalität', *Zeitschrift für Rechtssoziologie*, 8 (1987).

33 See, respectively, B. de Sousa Santos, *Toward a New Common Sense* (London: Routledge, 1995), p. 87; and Roberto M. Unger, *What Should Legal Analysis Become?* (London: Verso, 1996), pp. 1, 106, 113.

34 Sousa Santos, *New Common Sense*, pp. 2, 22ff.

35 Ibid., pp. 112–15.

36 Ibid., ch. 4.

37 Ibid., pp. 240, 248.

38 Germán Palacio, 'Pluralismo jurídico, neoamericanismo y postfordismo: notas para decifrar la naturaleza de los cambios jurídicos de fines de siglo', *Crítica jurídica: Revista latinoamericana de política, filosofía e derecho*, 17 (2000). See also José Eduardo Faria, *O direito na sociedade globalizada* (São Paulo: Malheiros, 1999).

39 See Mauro Cappelletti and Bryan Garth, *Access to Justice: The Worldwide Movement to Make Rights Effective* (Milan: Dott A. Giuffrè, 1978).

40 Antoine Garapon, *Le Gardien des promesses* (Paris: Odile Jacob, 1996), pp. 20–4, 44–5.

41 Ibid., pp. 47–9, 58, 61, 69. Garapon insists in particular on the role played by a rationalist and absolute notion of truth, which, especially under the influence of the media, would be immediately available to society, represented by the judicial system (pp. 66, 73ff). Furthermore this assumes an aspect of increasing 'penal preference' – pointing to revenge and a depoliticized, sacrificial attitude (pp. 95ff).

42 Ibid., 116–17, 120–3, 126, 135–6, 182, 195.
43 Ibid., p. 140.
44 Ibid., pp. 155ff.
45 Ibid., ch. 11.
46 Unger, *What Should Legal Analysis Become?*, pp. 36–7, 51ff, 72. He thinks however that, pushed further, rationalizing legal analysis can be put to the service of criticism and the far-reaching reconstruction of society. Ibid., pp. 129ff.
47 Ibid., pp. 81–2, as well as 46–7, 57, 93. But if Unger is an outspoken supporter of radical, though piecemeal, reformism, it is evident that he holds a very traditionally modern view of the state and law, which is regarded by him as state-centred and strictly universalist; moreover its enactment and execution, however influenced by citizen participation, are to be placed in the hands of professionals.
48 G. Teubner, 'The transformation of law in the welfare state' and 'After legal instrumentalism? Models of a post-regulatory law', as well as especially François Ewald, 'A concept of social law', all in G. Teubner (ed.), *Dilemmas of Law in the Welfare State* (Berlin and New York: Walter de Gruyter, 1986).
49 G. Teubner, 'La Juridicisation: concepts, caractères, limites et alternatives' (1984), in *Droit et reflexivité: L'Auto-référence en droit et dans l'organisation* (Paris: LGDJ and Bruyant, 1996), pp. 89–98.
50 Jean L. Cohen, 'Personal autonomy and the law: sexual harassment and the dilemma of regulating "intimacy" ', *Constellations*, 6 (1999).
51 Unger, *What Should Legal Analysis Become?*, p. 103.
52 See M. Cappelletti, *The Judicial Process in Comparative Perspective* (Oxford: Clarendon, 1989), esp. chs 1, 3.
53 For instance Saskia Sassen, *Losing Control? Sovereignty in an Age of Globalization* (New York: Columbia University Press, 1996).
54 Sousa Santos, *New Common Sense, passim*, although he supports a form of legal pluralism that is more radical and problematic than the one I think is healthier and more likely to prevail.
55 Cappelletti, *Judicial Process*, pp. 297ff.
56 Pierre Rosanvallon, *La Crise de l'État-Providence* (Paris: Seuil, 1981), p. 5.

6 Solidarity and Complexity

1 However, I cannot see a direct connection between the scope of justice and equality (which would be 'complex' and dependent upon a plurality of goods and values) and modernity and differentiation – especially if we bear the pre-Neolithic record in mind – contrary to the standpoint of Michael Walzer, *Spheres of Justice: A Defense of Pluralism and Equality* (New

York: Basic Books, 1983), p. 315. In any case his view of different spheres of justice is somehow adequate to the modern world, although we should be much more incisive than his liberalism allows for, in terms of the basic institutions of social life and inequality today.

2 As suggested by Émile Durkheim, *De la Division du travail social* (Paris: Presses Universitaires de France, [1893] 1973), pp. xlii–xliii, 28–34.

3 For a brief account of this idea in contemporary physics, see W. H. Newton-Smith, 'Space, time and space–time: a philosopher's view', in Raymond Flood and Michael Lockwood (eds), *The Nature of Time* (Oxford: Blackwell, 1986).

4 Instead of directing the reader to Freud's numerous texts, I refer to my own synthesis of his main ideas with other strands of thought in social theory: José Maurício Domingues, *Social Creativity, Collective Subjectivity and Contemporary Modernity* (London and New York: Macmillan and St Martin's Press, 2000), ch. 2.

5 See, in the nineteenth century, Herbert Spencer, *Structure, Function and Evolution*, ed. Stanislav Andreski (London: Michael Joseph, 1971), p. 78.

6 Durkheim, *De la Division*, pp. 205–6ff, 212ff, 236ff, 244, 253, 267ff.

7 Ibid., pp. 272ff.

8 Ibid., pp. 343ff, 397.

9 Ibid., p. 290; 'Preface de la seconde édition: Quelques remarques sur les groupements professionels' (1912), in *De la Division*, pp. xxviii, xxxii.

10 Idem, *Leçons de sociologie* (Istanbul: Presses Universitaires de France, [1898–1900] 1950), pp. 60–2.

11 Talcott Parsons, *The System of Modern Societies* (Englewood Cliffs, NJ: Prentice-Hall, 1971), pp. 12–13, 26–8. His general view of social evolution is found in *Societies: Evolutionary and Comparative Perspectives* (Englewood Cliffs, NJ: Prentice-Hall, 1967).

12 Georg Simmel, *Über soziale Differenzierung* (1890), in *Gesammtausgabe*, vol. 2 (Frankfurt am Main: Suhrkamp, 1989), pp. 239–44. For Parsons's use of such ideas – featuring the analytical concept of the 'individual' as a bundle of statuses and roles – see his *The Social System* (London: Routledge, [1951] 1979), pp. 25–6.

13 Parsons, *System of Modern Societies*, pp. 11ff. Similarly to Durkheim, albeit in another strand of his body of work, Parsons was adamant that the state enjoyed centrality as the organizer of social life and of social mobilization, once again, we may adduce, regardless of the high level of social differentiation of modernity. Parsons, 'On the concept of political power' (1963), in *Sociological Theory and Modern Society* (New York: Free Press, 1967).

14 Idem, *System of Modern Societies*, pp. 26–7.

15 Ibid., p. 99. As usual Parsons is here highly apologetic and acritical regarding his own country.

16 Idem, 'Full citizenship for the Negro American?' (1965), in *Sociological Theory*, p. 454. He also mentions the point in his general account of modernity, without apparently being aware of any conceptual problems, however. Cf. idem, *System of Modern Societies*, p. 89.
17 Idem, 'Full citizenship', pp. 424–5.
18 Contemporary neofunctionalists, although remaining faithful to the idea of differentiation as a 'master-trend', have tried to overcome this sort of problem by entwining it with historical narrative, of a contingent character. See Jeffrey C. Alexander and Paul Colomy (eds), *Differentiation Theory and Social Change* (New York: Columbia University Press, 1990).
19 Anthony Giddens, *The Consequences of Modernity* (Cambridge: Polity, 1990), p. 21.
20 See J. M. Domingues, *Sociologia e modernidade: Para entender a sociedade contemporânea* (Rio de Janeiro: Civilização Brasileira, 3rd edn 2005), p. 58.
21 Cf. Nestor Garcia Canclini, *Culturas híbridas: Estratégias para entrar y salir de la modernidad* (Mexico City: Grijalbo, 1990); and J. M. Domingues, 'Globalização, sociologia e cultura', *Contexto internacional*, 15 (1993).
22 Jürgen Habermas, *Theorie des kommunikativen Handelns* (Frankfurt am Main: Suhrkamp, [1981] 1988), vol. 1, pp. 230, 303ff; vol. 2, pp. 229ff. Adaptation does not turn up in his theory as such, but the basis of society (sometimes the economy, in a Marxist way) throws up problems to be coped with in other spheres and prompting differentiation, although it is by no means apparent which are the explicative variables of evolution. Ibid., vol. 2, pp. 72ff, 251, 464.
23 Wolfram Eberhart, 'Problems of historical sociology', in Reinhard Bendix (ed.), *State and Society* (Boston: Little, Brown & Co., 1968).
24 See Peter Wagner, *A Sociology of Modernity* (London: Routledge, 1994).
25 I carried out a detailed analysis of this issue, especially with reference to contemporary literature, in Domingues, *Social Creativity*, ch. 4.
26 Alasdair MacIntyre, *After Virtue* (Notre Dame: University of Notre Dame Press, [1981] 1984), pp. 3, 8ff.
27 J. Habermas, 'Diskursethik: Notizen zu einem Begründungsprogramm', in *Moralbewusstsein und kommunikativen Handelns* (Frankfurt am Main: Suhrkamp, 1982); and 'Was macht ein Lebensform rational' (1984), 'Treffen Hegels Einwände gegen Kant auch auf die Diskursethik zu?' (1985) and 'Erläuterungen zu Diskursethik' (1991), all in *Erläuterungen zu Diskursethik* (Frankfurt am Main: Suhrkamp, 1991).
28 For instance idem, *Theorie des kommunikativen Handelns*, vol. 1, pp. 15–151; and, for more flexible and recent positions, *Faktizität und Geltung* (Frankfurt am Main: Suhrkamp, 1992), pp. 151ff.
29 T. Parsons, *The Structure of Social Action* (New York: Free Press, [1937] 1966), pp. 90ff.
30 J. M. Domingues, 'Social integration, system integration and collective

subjectivity', *Sociology*, 34 (2000). Habermas's argument is found in his *Theorie des kommunikativen Handelns*, pp. 229ff.
31. Cf. J. C. Alexander, 'Differentiation theory: problems and prospects', in Alexander and Colomy, *Differentiation Theory*, pp. 2, 5, 11–12. Despite his use of differentiation in place of complexity he states that that 'master-trend' is followed by integration at higher levels only contingently.
32. See Carole Pateman, *The Sexual Contract* (Stanford: Stanford University Press, 1988), pp. 77–82.

7 The Fundamental Forms of Contemporary Solidarity

1. Talcott Parsons, 'The American family: its relations to personality and to the social structure', in T. Parsons and Robert F. Bales, *Family, Socialization and Interaction Process* (New York: Free Press, 1955), pp. 16–17.
2. Chiara Saraceno, 'Isolamento della famiglia nucleare contemporanea: ideologia o realtà', in *Anatomia della famiglia* (Bari: De Donato, 1976).
3. Carole Pateman, *The Sexual Contract* (Stanford: Stanford University Press, 1988), pp. 3–4, 7, 148ff, 158, 231.
4. See, for a comparison between France and Brazil, Clarice H. Peixoto, 'Avós e netos na França e no Brasil: a individualização das transmissões afetivas e materiais', in C. H. Peixoto, François de Singly and Vincenzo Cicchelli (eds), *Família e individualização* (Rio de Janeiro: Editora FGV, 2000).
5. See Karl Mannheim, 'Das Problem der Generationen' (1928), in *Wissenssoziologie* (Berlin and Neuwied: Hermann Luchterhand, 1964); Shmuel Eisenstadt, *From Generation to Generation* (New York: Free Press, 1956), esp. ch. 1; Alberto Melucci, *Challenging Codes* (Cambridge: Cambridge University Press, 1996), ch. 6.
6. For an interesting, however somewhat strange system-orientated, account of such evolution, see Niklas Luhmann, *Liebe als Passion* (Frankfurt am Main: Suhrkamp, 1982).
7. Charles Lindholm, 'Love and structure', in Mike Featherstone (ed.), *Love and Eroticism* (London: Sage, 1999), p. 243.
8. Ibid., pp. 247–8.
9. Anthony Giddens, *The Transformation of Intimacy* (Cambridge: Polity, 1992), pp. 37–8. Lindholm ('Love', pp. 249–57) spots three types of 'social configuration' in which romantic love would emerge: (1) systems with extreme ecological and social pressures, entailing struggle and competition, as well as hierarchies: romantic love runs counter to and is lived as a risk in such configurations; (2) fluid societies in which the couple is important as mutual help and as a bond in situations of competition and harshness – either in hunting-and-gathering societies or in modernity; (3) group-orientated

societies, with strictly controlled marriage, wherein pre-marital romance appears as a compensation.

10. Ulrich Beck and Elisabeth Beck-Gernsheim, *The Normal Chaos of Love* (Cambridge: Polity, [1990] 1995), pp. 12, 147–8, plus pp. 175ff.
11. A. Giddens, *Modernity and Self-Identity* (Cambridge: Polity, 1991), pp. 88–98.
12. Idem, *Transformation of Intimacy*, p. 61.
13. Bertrand Russell, *Marriage and Morals* (London: Unwin, [1929] 1986), p. 12. For accounts of the role of fidelity, see, for Finland, Elina Haavio-Mannila, J. P. Roos and Osmo Kontula, 'Repression, revolution and ambivalence: the sexual life of three generations', *Acta Sociologica*, 39 (1996); for Holland, Cas Wouters, 'Balancing sex and love since the 1960s sexual revolution', in Featherstone (ed.), *Love and Eroticism*; and, for Brazil, José Maurício Domingues, *Sociologia e modernidade: Para entender a sociedade contemporânea* (Rio de Janeiro: Civilização Brasileira, 3rd edn 2005), p. 47. An instructive general commentary is found in Mariam Lau, 'Humanitora. Eine Kolumne. Die Revolution enttäuscht ihre Kinder', *Merkur*, 54/4 (2000).
14. Little has changed since this was noted by Jeffrey Weeks, *Sex, Politics, and Society* (London: Longman, [1981] 1989), pp. 274, 289 (n. 6). See also Claus Offe and Rolf G. Heinze, 'Beyond the labour market: reflections on a new definition of "domestic" welfare production', in C. Offe, in *Modernity and the State: East, West* (Cambridge: Polity, 1996), p. 125.
15. Beck and Beck-Gernsheim, *Normal Chaos*, p. 7.
16. Giddens, *Modernity and Self-Identity*, p. 13; Beck and Beck-Gernsheim, *Normal Chaos*, pp. 149–50.
17. For a discussion of conceptual matters regarding emotions and family structure, see Mark Poster, *Critical Theory of the Family* (Connecticut: Seabury, 1978), esp. ch. 7.
18. C. Offe, 'The utopia of the zero option' (1987), in *Modernity and the State*, pp. 17–18.
19. See Giddens's more recent, almost conservative, 'back to basics', 'Third Way' revaluing of the traditional family structure he had previously understood to be on the wane, in *The Third Way and its Critics* (Cambridge: Polity, 1999), pp. 45–8.
20. Cf. Mark Granovetter, 'The strength of weak ties', *American Journal of Sociology*, 78 (1973).
21. Alasdair MacIntyre, *After Virtue* (Notre Dame: University of Notre Dame Press, [1981] 1984), pp. 155–6.
22. See respectively Georg Simmel, 'Psychologie der Diskretion' (1906), in *Schriften zur Soziologie* (Frankfurt am Main: Suhrkamp, 1995), and Giddens, *Modernity and Self-Identity*, pp. 88–98.
23. See Simon Critchey, 'The other's decision on me', *European Journal of Social Theory*, 1 (1998).
24. Craig Calhoun, *Critical Social Theory* (Cambridge, MA: Blackwell, 1995), pp. 215–16, and 232–3 for class and nation specifically.

25 Ibid., p. 220.
26 Benedict Anderson, *Imagined Communities* (London: Verso, [1983] 1991), p. 7. For a different list of characteristics, see Anthony Smith, *National Identity* (Harmondsworth: Penguin, 1971), p. 11; and pp. 59ff for the 'three revolutions' – administrative, economic and cultural – underlying the rise of the 'first nations'. Smith nonetheless held an arguably 'ethnic' view of the nation, which has become attenuated lately.
27 Anderson, *Imagined Communities*, pp. 6, 199–201.
28 Cf. A. Giddens, *The Nation-State and Violence* (Cambridge: Polity, 1985), pp. 116ff, 148ff; Anderson, *Imagined Communities*; Smith, *National Identity*, pp. 16, 69, 91ff, 116ff. Giddens saw nationalism, in an arguable step, mainly as a psychological phenomenon.
29 Giddens, *Consequences of Modernity*, p. 64.
30 Roland Robertson, *Globalization: Social Theory and Global Culture* (London: Sage, 1992); and R. Robertson, Mike Featherstone and Scott Lash (eds), *Global Modernities* (London: Sage, 1995).
31 The literature on the topic is immense. In addition to the works by Giddens and Robertson already quoted, see M. Featherstone (ed.), *Global Culture* (London: Sage, 1990); Anthony King (ed.), *Culture, Globalization and the World System* (Binghamton, NY and London: State University of New York and Macmillan, 1991); Renato Ortiz, *Mundialização e cultura* (São Paulo: Brasiliense, 1994). I have partly reviewed this literature in J. M. Domingues, 'Globalização, sociologia e cultura', *Contexto internacional*, 15 (1993).
32 Charles Taylor, 'The politics of recognition', in Amy Guttman (ed.), *Multiculturalism* (Princeton: Princeton University Press, 1992); Will Kymlicka, *Multicultural Citizenship* (Oxford: Clarendon Press, 1995). See also Boaventura de Sousa Santos, *Toward a New Common Sense* (New York: Routledge, 1995), pp. 313ff, for a globalizing perspective.
33 Jürgen Habermas, 'Kampf um Anerkennung im demokratischen Rechtstaat' (1993), in *Die Einbeziehung des Anderen* (Frankfurt am Main: Suhrkamp, 1997).
34 See J. M. Domingues, 'Desencaixes, abstrações e identidades' (1999), in *Do ocidente à modernidade: Intelectuais e mudança social* (Rio de Janeiro: Civilização Brasileira, 2003).
35 See Hans Joas, *Die Entstehung der Werte* (Frankfurt am Main: Suhrkamp, 1997).
36 Nancy Fraser, 'Multiculturalism, antiessentialism, and radical democracy' (1996), in *Justice Interruptus: Critical Reflection on the 'Post-Socialist' Condition* (New York: Routledge, 1997), p. 186. See also, in the same volume, her 'From redistribution to recognition? Dilemmas of justice in a "postsocialist" age' (1995), esp. p. 16; and Antônio Flávio Pierruci, *Ciladas da diferença* (São Paulo: Editora 34, 1999).
37 Fraser, 'From redistribution to recognition?', p. 13.
38 Domingues, *Sociologia e modernidade*, ch. 4.

[39] Erik Olin Wright, *Class Counts* (Cambridge: Cambridge University Press, 1997), pp. 45–58. For the application of Wright's scheme to Brazil, see José Alcides F. Santos, *Estrutura de posição de classe no Brasil: Mapeamento, mudanças e efeitos na renda* (Belo Horizonte and Rio de Janeiro: Editora UFMG and IUPERJ, 2002), esp. ch. 2.

[40] Karl Marx and Friedrich Engels, *Manifest des kommunistischen Partei* (1848), in Marx and Engels, *Werke*, vol. 4 (Berlin: Dietz, 1939); and K. Marx, *Misère de la Philosophie* (1847), in *Œuvres*, vol. 1 (Paris: Gallimard, 1963), p. 135. See also J. M. Domingues, *Sociological Theory and Collective Subjectivity* (London and New York: Macmillan and St Martin's Press, 1995), ch. 4.

[41] See David Harvey, *The Condition of Postmodernity* (Cambridge, MA: Blackwell, 1990), pp. 152ff, 192ff.

[42] Zigmunt Bauman, 'The left as the counter culture of modernity', *Telos*, 70 (1986–7), 83.

[43] C. Offe, 'Work: the key sociological category?' (1982), in *Disorganized Capitalism* (Cambridge: Polity, 1985), esp. pp. 135–42. His point of view has some resemblance to that of André Gorz, *Adieux au prolétariat* (Tours: Galillé, [1980] 1981), although this author derives much more radical consequences from the idea that work has become unimportant for the construction of individual and collective identities. Both tend to believe that workers evince a much more *instrumental* attitude now, moving away from what could be deemed its *expressivist* dimension, closely linked to identity building.

[44] Scott Lash and John Urry, *The End of Organized Capitalism* (Cambridge: Polity, 1987), pp. 5–6, 8, 283, 310–12. For a somewhat distinct standpoint, see their *Economies of Sign and Space* (London: Sage, 1994). For class inequalities and an 'underclass' developing out of the new 'mode of information', see S. Lash, 'Reflexivity and its doubles: structure, aesthetics, community', in U. Beck, A. Giddens and S. Lash, *Reflexive Modernization* (Cambridge: Polity, 1994), pp. 119–35.

[45] Melucci, *Challenging Codes*; and Michel Maffesoli, *Le Temps des tribus* (Paris: Méridiens Klinksieck, 1988).

[46] Stephen Crook, Jan Pakulski and Malcom Waters, *Postmodernization: Change in Advanced Societies* (London: Sage, 1992), pp. 137ff.

[47] Melucci, *Challenging Codes*, pp. 113ff. Personal quests, quotidian affective and communicative needs of participants are meshed together in the movement's build-up (p. 115). That the same can be said of course of traditional working-class movements – regardless of the importance of big union and party machines – curiously eludes Melucci's understanding, probably because of his eagerness to underline the novelty of new social movements.

[48] Amy Bartholomew and Margit Mayer, '*Nomads of the Present*: Melucci's contribution to "new social movement" theory', *Theory, Culture and*

Society, 9 (1992). This criticism was aimed at his previous work, but it holds for his later publications as well.
49 Luc Boltanski and Eve Chiapello, *Le Nouvel Esprit du capitalisme* (Paris: Gallimard, 1999), pp. 429–35.
50 U. Beck, *Risk Society* (London: Sage, [1986] 1992), pp. 19ff.
51 Ibid., pp. 87ff.
52 Including data gathered from diverse countries, see Adalberto M. Cardoso, 'A filiação sindical no Brasil', *Dados*, 44 (2001). For a distinct view, see Leôncio M. Rodrigues, *Destino do sindicalismo* (São Paulo: EDUSP, 1999).
53 Marx and Engels, *Manifest*; Wright, *Class Counts*; Leslie Sklair, *Sociology of the Global System* (London: Harvester Wheatsheaf, 1991), ch. 3.
54 Klaus Eder, *Kulturelle Identität zwischen Tradition und Utopie* (Frankfurt am Main: Campus, 2000), pp. 96ff.
55 Jean L. Cohen, 'Changing paradigms of citizenship and the exclusiveness of the demos', *International Sociology*, 14 (1999), p. 248.
56 See Abraham de Swaan, *In Care of the State* (Cambridge: Polity, 1998).
57 Goran Esping-Andersen, *Politics against Markets* (Princeton: Princeton University Press, 1985), pp. 33–5, 171, 289ff.
58 Idem, *The Three Worlds of Welfare Capitalism* (Princeton: Princeton University Press, 1990), p. 25. He went further especially in relation to problems ensuing from globalization in his 'After the golden age? Welfare state dilemmas in a global economy', in G. Esping-Andersen (ed.), *Welfare States in Transition* (London: Sage, 1996).
59 Christopher Pierson, *Beyond the Welfare State?* (Cambridge: Polity, 1991).
60 Cohen, 'Changing paradigms', pp. 249–52, 256.
61 Ibid., pp. 257ff.
62 Ibid., p. 262.
63 Robert Castel, *Les Metamorphoses de la question sociale* (Paris: Fayard, 1995), pp. 13ff, 410–12.
64 Ibid., chs. 2–4 and pp. 217ff.
65 Ibid., pp. 268ff.
66 Ibid., pp. 418ff, 459.
67 Pierre Rosanvallon, *La Crise de l'État-Providence* (Paris: Seuil, 1981), pp. 7–10, 13ff, 20ff, 40–8.
68 Ibid., pp. 114–16.
69 Ibid., pp. 111ff, 121–4, 137–8. For his self-managed socialism, see *L'Age de la autogestion* (Paris: Seuil, 1976).
70 Idem, *La Nouvelle Question sociale* (Paris: Seuil, 1995), pp. 7–8, 11–30.
71 Ibid., pp. 57–62. See ch. 4 for an analysis of Rawls's argument, which has nothing to do with such a pedestrian thesis.
72 Rosanvallon, *Nouvelle Question*, pp. 92ff, 192ff, 202–11, 219–21. Once again emphasizing social heterogeneity, he has altered his position towards a less radical stance (even quoting Castel approvingly) in P. Rosanvallon and Jean-Paul Fitoussi, *Le Nouvel Age des inégalités* (Paris: Seuil, 1996).

8 Complexity and Mixed Articulation

1. Claus Offe, 'State action and structures of will formation: elements of a social-scientific theory of the state' (1990), in *Modernity and the State: East, West* (Cambridge: Polity, 1996).
2. Idem, *Contradictions of the Welfare State* (London: Hutchison, 1984); Scott Lash and John Urry, *The End of Organized Capitalism* (Cambridge: Polity, 1987); Peter Wagner, *A Sociology of Modernity* (London: Routledge, 1994); José Maurício Domingues, *Social Creativity, Collective Subjectivity and Contemporary Modernity* (London and New York: Macmillan and St Martin's Press, 2000), ch. 7; Luc Boltanski and Eve Chiapello, *Le Nouvel Esprit du capitalisme* (Paris: Gallimard, 1999).
3. See Domingues, *Social Creativity*, ch. 6. In her *The Sexual Contract* (Stanford: Stanford University Press, 1988, ch. 8) Carol Pateman is for instance adamant on and detailed in her argument about the nature of capitalist labour contracts: if they are based on the idea of free exchange of property, they in fact imply the subordination of workers to capitalists – their unfreedom – which only then allows for exploitation. She forces the argument a bit in her dismissal of contract as mere illusion in this case (as well as in that of marriage) but if modified it may be used to show that labour contracts include *both* free exchange and hierarchy, the latter being as modern and typical of modernity as the former.
4. I have discussed this partly in Domingues, *Social Creativity*, ch. 6. For comprehensive empirically orientated and theoretically informed perspective, see S. Lash and J. Urry, *Economies of Sign and Space* (London: Sage, 1994), part 2; and Manuel Castells, *The Rise of the Network Society* (Cambridge: Blackwell, 1996). For further analytical as well as empirical material, see Jeniffer Francis et al., *Markets, Hierarchies and Networks* (London: Sage, 1991) and Richard Swedberg (ed.), *Explorations in Economic Sociology* (New York: Russel Sage Foundation, 1993), especially Perrow's piece on small firms networks.
5. Waldimir Pirró e Longo and Antônio R. Pimentel de Oliveira, 'Pesquisa cooperativa e centros de excelência', *Parcerias estratégicas*, 9 (2000). See for a discussion of development strategies from this standpoint, J. M. Domingues, 'Modernidade, subjetividade e desenvolvimento' (1999), in *Do ocidente à modernidade: Intelectuais e mudança social* (Rio de Janeiro, Civilização Brasileira, 2003).
6. Boltanski and Chiapello, *Le Nouvel Esprit*, pp. 208ff.
7. Cf. Robert Perruci and Harry R. Potter, 'The collective actor in organizational analysis', in R. Perruci and H. R. Potter (eds), *Networks of Power: Organizational Actors at the National, Corporate, and Community Levels* (New York: Aldine de Gruyer, 1989), p. 10.
8. Castells, *Rise of Network Society*, respectively pp. 474, 61–2.
9. A previous and shorter outline of this thesis is found in J. M. Domingues,

'Modernity, complexity and mixed articulation', *Social Science Information*, 41 (2002).
10. Idem, *Social Creativity*, ch. 7.
11. Boaventura de Sousa Santos, 'Reinventar a democracia: entre o pré-contratualismo e o pós-contratualismo', in Agnes Heller et al., *A crise dos paradigmas em ciências sociais e os desafios para o século XXI* (Rio de Janeiro: Contraponto and Corecon-RJ, 1999), p. 67.
12. Douglas A. Chalmers, Scoot Martin and Kerianne Piester, 'Associative networks: new structures of representation for the popular sectors?', in D. A. Chalmers et al. (eds), *The New Politics of Inequality in Latin America* (New York: Oxford University Press, 1997).
13. Ilse Scherer-Warren, *Cidadania sem fronteiras* (São Paulo: Hucitec, 1999); Kathryn Sikkink, 'La dimensión transnacional de los movimientos sociales', in Martín Abregú and Silvina Ramos (eds), *La sociedad civil frente a las nuevas formas de institucionalidad democrática* (Buenos Aires: CEDES/CELS/Cuadernos del Foro, 2000).
14. Friedrich Hayek, 'The use of knowledge in society', in *Individualism and Economic Order* (London: Routledge & Kegan Paul, 1949); Niklas Luhmann, 'Die Zukunft der Demokratie' (1986) and 'Enttäuschungen und Hoffnungen', in *Soziologische Aufklärung* (Opladen: Westdeutscher Verlag, 1987).
15. Leon Trotsky, *History of the Russian Revolution*, vol. 1 (London: Sphere Books, 1967 [1932–3]), ch. 1.
16. Many examples are found in M. Castells, *Rise of Network Society*, and *End of Millenium* (Cambridge: Blackwell, 1998). Private security and surveillance systems in the USA, as well as organized crime in Colombia or Russia, are outstanding aspects of such perverse developments, but the case of Singapore and the creation of zones controlled exclusively by multinational corporations epitomizes the dramatically negative potential of the current situation. See Aihwa Ong, 'Graduated sovereignty in South-East Asia', *Theory, Culture and Society*, 4 (2000).
17. For instance Hilary Wainright, *Arguments for a New Left* (Cambridge: Cambridge University Press, 1994).
18. Despite its revolutionarism, to be strongly criticized, and the downplaying of the role of the USA, see Michael Hardt and Antonio Negri, *Empire* (Cambridge, MA: Harvard University Press, 2000).
19. Hauke Brunkhorst, *Solidarität: Von bürgerfreudschaft zur globalen Rechtsgenossenschaft* (Frankfurt am Main: Suhrkamp, 2002), p. 18.

9 Social Theory and Responsibility

1. Hans Jonas, *Das Prinzip Verantwortung* (Frankfurt am Main: Suhrkamp, [1979] 1984), pp. 172, 391.

2. Jean-Paul Sartre, *L'Existentialisme est un humanisme* (Paris: Nagel, 1947).
3. Paul Ricoeur, 'Le Concept de responsabilité: essai d'analyse sémantique', in *Le Juste* (Paris: Esprit, 1995), pp. 41–9.
4. Noberto Bobbio, *Diritto e stato nel pensiero di Emanuele Kant* (Turin: G. Giappichelli, 1969), ch. 2.
5. Ricoeur, 'Le Concept', pp. 43, 51.
6. Max Weber, 'Die protestantische Ethik und der Geist des Kapitalismus' (1904–5), in *Gesammelte Aufsätze zur Religionssoziologie*, vol. 1 (Tübingen: J. C. B. Mohr [Paul Siebeck], [1920] 1988), pp. 63ff; David Zaret, *The Heavenly Contract* (Chicago: Chicago University Press, 1985), pp. 7, 135ff.
7. Benjamin Nelson, 'Conscience and the making of early modern cultures: the Protestant ethic beyond Max Weber', *Social Research*, 36 (1969).
8. Richard Morse, *El espejo de Próspero* (Mexico: Siglo XXI, 1982), ch. 1. See also José Maurício Domingues, 'Richard Morse and the "Iberian-American path"', *Revista interamericana de bibliografia*, 45 (1995); and Isabel A. Ribeiro de Oliveira, 'Direito subjetivo: base escolástica dos direitos humanos', *Revista brasileira de ciências sociais*, 41 (1999), as well as her 'Direito subjetivo e sociabilidade natural: uma revisão do legado ibérico', paper given at the First Latin American Congress of Political Science, Salamanca, 2002.
9. Georg H. Mead, *Mind, Self and Society* (Chicago: University of Chicago Press, [1934], 1962), pp. 152–64.
10. M. Weber, 'Politik als Beruf' (1919), in *Gesammelte politische Schriften* (Tübingen: J. C. B. Mohr [Paul Siebeck], 1971), pp. 552ff. A neo-Kantian ethical approach, in tandem with an erudite reading of Weber's view of ethic and values, which stresses his opposition to the direct, eudemonic enjoyment of life, is found in Wolfgang Schluchter, *Religions und Lebensführung* (Frankfurt am Main: Suhrkamp, 1991), ch. 3.
11. M. Weber, *Wirtschaft und Gesellschaft* (Tübingen: J. C. B. Mohr [Paul Siebeck], [1921–2] 1976), pp. 1–30; and 'Die nichtlegitime Herrschaft (Typologie der Städt)', in the same volume. See also J. M. Domingues, '*The City*: rationality and freedom in Max Weber', *Philosophy and Social Criticism*, 26 (2000).
12. Hannah Arendt, *The Human Condition* (Chicago: University of Chicago Press, 1958), ch. 1.
13. Piet Strydom, 'The challenge of responsibility for sociology', *Current Sociology*, 47 (1999), 69ff; *Discourse and Knowledge: The Making of Enlightenment Sociology* (Liverpool: Liverpool University Press, 2000), pp. 61–4, 72–5.
14. See the first lectures of Émile Durkheim, *Leçons de sociologie* (Istanbul: Presses Universitaires de France, [1898–1900] 1950).
15. Talcott Parsons, *The Social System* (London: Routledge & Kegan Paul, [1951] 1979), pp. 41, 97ff.
16. Ibid., pp. 159, 437–47. Deviance can moreover appear as either 'compulsive

avoidance of responsibility' or as, instead, exaggerated, 'compulsive responsibility'. Ibid., pp. 322–5.
17 Idem, *The System of Modern Societies* (Englewood Cliffs, NJ: Prentice Hall, 1971), pp. 16, 21.
18 Ibid., pp. 100–4.
19 I studied and criticized Parsons's work, including his view of collective subjectivity, in J. M. Domingues, *Sociological Theory and Collective Subjectivity* (London and New York: Macmillan and St Martin's Press, 1995), ch. 5; and *A sociologia de Talcott Parsons* (Niterói: EdUFF, 2001).

10 The Transformations of Responsibility

1 I tried to overcome this shortcoming with the concept of 'collective subjectivity' in José Maurício Domingues, *Sociological Theory and Collective Subjectivity* (London and New York: Macmillan and St Martin's Press, 1995).
2 Crawford B. Macpherson, *The Political Theory of Possessive Individualism* (Oxford: Oxford University Press, 1962), ch. 3; John Dunn, 'Political obligation', in David Held (ed.), *Political Theory Today* (Cambridge: Polity, 1991), pp. 28ff.
3 See Carole Pateman, *The Sexual Contract* (Cambridge: Polity, 1988).
4 Macpherson, *Political Theory*, ch. 5. In any case, especially for the ruling and ascending bourgeois collectivities, the opposition of *interests* to *passions* seems to have been germane to the development of the liberal idea of freedom and responsibility, insofar as it allowed for constancy and foresight. See Albert O. Hirschman, *The Passions and the Interests* (Princeton: Princeton University Press, 1977). Something related to this will be clear also in Ewald's account below. Let me stress at this point, however, that I do not intend to reconstruct here the complex and multiple views of authority, obedience and responsibility that were present in the Enlightenment – and in usually conservative reactions to it – but merely to lay the groundwork for subsequent developments in this book.
5 Ernest Cassirer, *The Problem of Jean-Jacques Rousseau* (Bloomington and London: Indiana University Press, [1932] 1963), pp. 56–64; C. Pateman, *The Problem of Political Obligation* (Chichester: John Wiley & Sons, 1979), pp. 7, 145ff.
6 Pateman, *Problem of Political Obligation*, ch. 1.
7 J. M. Domingues, 'Imaginário social e esfera pública no Rio de Janeiro dos anos 30' (1997), in *Do ocidente à modernidade: Intelectuais e mudança social* (Rio de Janeiro: Civilização Brasileira, 2003).
8 Dunn, 'Political obligation', pp. 23–4.

[9] Pateman, *Problem of Political Obligation*, p. 2. As Hans Jonas in *Das Prinzip Verantwortung* (Frankfurt am Main: Suhrkamp, [1979] 1984, p. 234) put it, '[t]he concept of responsibility implies that of ought to (*Sollen*)'; the same can be said of ideas such as 'obligation' and 'duty', although the former implies an act of conscious will and, in terms of political obligation, a self-chosen commitment. See Pateman, *Problem of Political Obligation*, pp. 106–7. Curiously enough, only in passing were responsibility and duty connected in Michael Walzer, *Obligations: Essays on Disobedience, War and Citizenship* (Cambridge, MA: Harvard University Press, 1975), ch. 1.

[10] Reinhard Bendix, *Max Weber: An Intellectual Portrait* (Berkeley and Los Angeles: University of California Press, [1960] 1977), p. 486. However, he mistakenly, with a strong bias and strangely enough for a German, translated *Herrschaft* as 'authority' (p. 292, note). This helps in an unintended way to evince Weber's connection with previous political theory, but conceals the sea-change contained in his use of the notion of 'domination'.

[11] Karl Marx, *Kritik des Gothaer Programms* (1875), in Marx and Engels, *Werke*, vol. 19 (Berlin: Dietz, 1962).

[12] Pateman, *Problem of Political Obligation*, pp. 134ff.

[13] Max Weber, *Wirtschaft und Gesellschaft* (Tübingen: J. C. B. Mohr [Paul Siebeck], [1921–22] 1976), part 1, ch. 3.

[14] Hannah Arendt, *Between Past and Future* (New York: Viking, [1954] 1968), pp. 92–3, 118–24.

[15] Joseph A. Schumpeter, *Capitalism, Socialism and Democracy* (New York: Routledge, [1943] 1994), pp. 252–62.

[16] Ibid., p. 261.

[17] Ibid., p. 269, and the whole of ch. 22.

[18] See Jürgen Habermas, 'Drei normative Modelle der Demokratie', in *Die Einbeziehung des Anderen* (Frankfurt am Main: Suhrkamp, [1996] 1997), for political theory; and Peter Wagner, *A Sociology of Modernity* (London: Routledge, 1994), ch. 6, for political practice.

[19] Arendt, *Between Past and Future*, pp. 136–8.

[20] K. Marx, *Der 18te Brumaire des Louis Bonaparte* (1852), in Marx and Engels, *Werke*, vol. 8 (Berlin: Dietz, 1960); Alexis de Tocqueville, *L'Ancien Régime et la Révolution* (Paris: Gallimard, [1856] 1953).

[21] For an overview of the sociological literature and a good solution, see Michael Mann, *The Sources of Social Power*, vol. 2 (Cambridge: Cambridge University Press, 1993), ch. 3.

[22] François Ewald, *L'État Providence* (Paris: Grasset & Fasquelle, 1986), pp. 53ff, 59–62.

[23] Ibid., p. 64.

[24] Ibid., pp. 64–7, 69–70.

[25] Ibid., pp. 66, 77ff.

[26] Ibid., pp. 91–4.

27 Ibid., esp. pp. 195, 212ff, 225–33, 249–50, 285, 316. I think that he goes too far – tensions and discontinuities notwithstanding – when stating that social rights and the rules of judgement attached to them (that is, the substitution of juridical imputation by the notion of professional risk) imply a 'political rationality foreign to liberal rationality' (p. 35). Or at least this is what the arguments provided in chs 3 and 4 of this book lead me to believe, a view which passages of Ewald's own book in fact reinforce, insofar as social rights rephrase 'real abstractions', in terms of time perspective, of who crafts them and of their encompassing reach, but by no means do away with those reified entities.
28 Ibid., p. 335.
29 Ibid., p. 444.
30 Allan Sillitoe, quoted in Lynne Segal, *Slow Motion: Changing Masculinities, Changing Men* (London: Virago, 1990), p. 13.
31 Jurandir Freire Costa, 'Narcisismo em tempos sombrios', in Heloísa R. Fernandes (ed.), *Tempo de desejo* (São Paulo: Brasiliense, 1989).
32 Manuel Castells, *End of Millennium* (Oxford: Blackwell, 1998), p. 205.
33 Talcott Parsons, 'The American family: its relations to personality and to the social structure', in T. Parsons and Robert F. Bales, *Family, Socialization and Interaction Process* (New York: Free Press, 1955), p. 22.
34 See L. Segal, *Is the Future Female? Troubled Thoughts on Contemporary Feminism* (London: Virago, 1987), pp. 145–9.
35 Luc Boltanski and Laurent Thévenot, *De la Justification* (Paris: Gallimard, 1991); L. Boltanski, *L'Amour et la justice comme compétences* (Paris: Métailié, 1990).
36 L. Boltanski and Eve Chiapello, *Le Nouvel Esprit du capitalisme* (Paris: Gallimard, 1999), pp. 37ff.
37 Ibid., pp. 148–53, 178, 255, 289–90, 417–18.
38 Ibid., p. 167.
39 Ibid., pp. 166ff.
40 Ibid., p. 418.
41 Ibid., pp. 198, 414, 437ff, 467ff.
42 Ibid., p. 428.
43 Richard Sennett, *The Corrosion of Character* (New York: W. W. Norton & Co., 1998), esp. ch. 1.
44 Boltanski and Chiapello, *Le Nouvel Esprit*, pp. 552ff, 574.
45 Ibid., pp. 516–20.
46 Anthony Giddens, *The Third Way and its Critics* (Cambridge: Polity, 2000), pp. 52, 106.
47 Idem, *Beyond Left and Right* (Cambridge: Polity, 1994), p. 18; *Third Way and Critics*, pp. 2, 4–5, 56.
48 Idem, *Beyond Left and Right*, p. 162; *The Third Way* (Cambridge: Polity, 1999), pp. 89–98, 162; *Third Way and Critics*, pp. 45, 47, 49.

49 Idem, *The Third Way*, pp. 62–3; *Third Way and Critics*, pp. 146–7.
50 Idem, *Beyond Left and Right*, pp. 20–1, 127.
51 Alan Wolf, *Whose Keeper? Social Science and Moral Obligation* (Berkeley and Los Angeles: University of California Press, 1989), pp. 180–1.

11 Responsibility Today: Horizons of Development

1 Hans Jonas, *Das Prinzip Verantwortung* (Frankfurt am Main: Suhrkamp, [1979] 1984), *passim*.
2 Karl Otto Apel, 'Die Konflikt unserer Zeit und das Erfordernis einer ethisch-politischen Grundorientierung' (1975), in *Diskur und Verantwortung* (Frankfurt am Main: Suhrkamp, [1988] 1997), p. 30.
3 Ibid., pp. 23–4.
4 Ibid., pp. 34, 40.
5 Idem, 'Verantwortung Heute: Nur noch Prinzip der Bewahrung und Sebstschränkung oder immer noch der Befreiung und Verwirklichung von Humanität?' (1986), in *Diskur*, pp. 182–98, 201.
6 John Rawls, *A Theory of Justice* (Oxford: Oxford University Press, [1972] 1990), respectively § 64, p. 423; § 24, p. 140; § 44, pp. 284ff.
7 See the essays collected in Jürgen Habermas, *Erläuterungen zu Diskursethik* (Frankfurt am Main: Suhrkamp, 1991).
8 Piet Strydom, 'The challenge of responsibility for sociology', *Current Sociology*, 47 (1999), 67–8.
9 Apel, 'Verantwortung Heute', pp. 206–7.
10 Ibid., pp. 206–9.
11 Idem, 'Diskursethik als Verantwortungsethik und das Problem der ökonomischen Rationalität' (1987), in *Diskur*, esp. pp. 291ff, 296–8.
12 Idem, 'Die transzendentalpragmatische Begründung der Kommunikationsethik und das Problem der höchsten Stufe einer Entwicklungslogik des moralischen Bewusstsein' (1986), in *Diskur*, pp. 362, 368.
13 Alberto Melucci, *The Playing Self* (Cambridge: Cambridge University Press, 1996), pp. 48, 148.
14 Alain Ehrenberg, *La Fatigue d'être soi* (Paris: Odile Jacob, 1998), pp. 14–15, 52, 120, 148, 242–3.
15 Ibid., pp. 29, 45ff, 236. I will refrain here from scrutinizing critically his theses. Suffice it to say that his reading of Freud is rather biased; moreover a thesis which affirms that the subject today is beyond – or does not reach – intra-psychic conflicts and the confrontation with limits is hardly tenable.
16 Joel Birman, *Mal-estar na atualidade* (Rio de Janeiro: Civilização Brasileira, 1999).
17 Jonas, *Prinzip* pp. 177–8.
18 Axel Honneth, *Kampf um Anerkennung* (Frankfurt am Main: Suhrkamp,

1994), which however pays no attention to the economic question in psychoanalysis. See also J. Habermas, 'Gerechtigkeit und Solidarität: Zur Diskussion über "Stufe"' (1986), in *Erläuterungen zur Diskursethik* (Frankfurt am Main: Suhrkamp, 1991), pp. 70–1. Whether it makes sense to link Meadian concepts to a strong Kohlbergian evolutionary– teleological approach, in which responsibility (together with autonomy) features in the post-conventional stage, is nonetheless something that begs the question. In fact it seems to me excessively Western-biased, despite arguments introduced in J. Habermas, 'Moralbewusstsein und kommunikatives Handeln', in *Moralbewusstesein und kommunikatives Handeln* (Frankfurt am Main: Suhrkamp, [1983] 1988), p. 174.

[19] Nancy Fraser, 'From redistribution to recognition? Dilemmas of justice in a post-socialist age' (1995), in *Justice Interruptus: Critical Reflections on the 'Post-Socialist' Condition* (New York: Routledge, 1997); and 'Recognition without ethics', *Theory, Culture and Society*, 18 (2001).

[20] See Michel Misse, 'O Senhor e o Escravo como tipos-limite de dominação e estratificação', *Dados*, 39 (1996).

[21] See, for British conservatism, Martin Durham, *Sex and Morality: The Thatcher Years* (London: Macmillan, 1991).

[22] Daniel Bell, *The Cultural Contradictions of Capitalism* (New York: Basic Books, [1976] 1978), pp. 54ff; Christopher Lasch, *Heaven in a Heartless World: The Family Besieged* (New York: Basic Books, 1977). Moreover, if responsibility may be onesidedly exercised, this is not always the case. In any event this already exposes a crucial problem, suggesting that we should reject Jonas's (*Prinzip*, pp. 189ff) assertion that the liaison between parents and children is the model for all relations of responsibility, including the behaviour of statesmen.

[23] Ulrich Beck and Elisabeth Beck-Gernsheim, *The Normal Chaos of Love* (Cambridge: Polity, [1990] 1995), pp. 109, 118.

[24] Carole Pateman, *The Sexual Contract* (Cambridge: Polity, 1988), ch. 5, esp. p. 118.

[25] U. Beck, *The Reinvention of Politics* (Cambridge: Polity, [1996] 1997), p. 120 (and ff). *Trust* by the public is a key variable in this respect.

[26] Milton Friedman, 'The social responsibility of business is to increase its profits', *New York Times* (13 September 1970), quoted in Robert C. Solomon, *The New World of Business: Ethics and Free Enterprise in the Global 1990s* (Lanham: Rowman & Littlefield, 1993), p. 213.

[27] Solomon, *New World*, pp. 203ff, 208–9.

[28] Ibid., pp. 218–23. A short and informal but insightful discussion of the notion of responsibility is found on pp. 70–2.

[29] Gunther Teubner, 'La Coupole invisible: de l'attribution causale à l'attribution collective de la responsabilité écologique' (1992), in *Droit et reflexivité: L'Auto-référence en droit et dans l'organisation* (Paris: L.G.D.J and Bruyant, 1996).

30 Chris Rojek, *Leisure and Culture* (London: Macmillan, 2000), pp. 207–12.
31 José Maurício Domingues, *Social Creativity, Collective Subjectivity and Contemporary Modernity* (London and New York: Macmillan and St Martin's Press, 2000), ch. 7.
32 Thomas Humphrey Marshall, 'Voluntary action' (1949), in *Class, Citizenship, and Social Development* (Garden City, NY: Doubleday & Co., Inc., 1964), pp. 317–18.
33 Antoine Garapon, *Le Gardien des promesses* (Paris: Odile Jacob, 1996), ch. 4. For data on incarceration and the groups targeted in different contexts, see Loïc Wacquant, *As prisões da miséria* (Rio de Janeiro: Zahar, 2001). There is no repair to be made regarding his fierce indictment of neoliberalism. However, restoring the social fabric certainly demands more than just returning strength to the welfare state, or indeed creating it where it has never actually existed.
34 I draw upon the distinctions outlined by Herbert L. A. Hart, *The Concept of Law* (Oxford: Clarendon Press, [1961] 1970), esp. pp. 9, 24, 27–8, 32.
35 Barbara A. Misztal, *Trust in Modern Societies* (Cambridge: Polity, 1996), esp. pp. 2, 14, 18–19, 23–4.
36 J. M. Domingues, *Sociological Theory and Collective Subjectivity* (London and New York: Macmillan and St Martin's Press, 1995), p. 155.
37 As a synthetic exemplar of the enormous literature on the topic, see Scott Burchill, 'Realism and neo-realism', in S. Burchill, Andrew Linkater et al., *Theories of International Relations* (London: Macmillan, 1996).
38 Martin Shaw, 'Global society and global responsibility: the theoretical, historical and political limits of "international society"', in Rick Fawn and Jeremy Larkins (eds), *International Society after the Cold War* (London: Macmillan, 1996), esp. pp. 56–7. For the global civil society, especially non-governmental organizations, see Liszt Vieira, *Os argonautas da cidadania: A sociedade civil na globalização* (Rio de Janeiro: Record, 2001).
39 J. Habermas, *Glauben und Wissen* (Frankfurt am Main: Suhrkamp, 2001), esp. p. 11; J. M. Domingues, 'Globalização, reflexividade e justiça' (2002), in *Ensaios de sociologia* (Belo Horizonte: Editora UFMG, 2004).
40 Gerard Delanty, *Citizenship in a Global Age* (Buckingham: Open University Press, 2000), p. 130.
41 John Thompson, *The Media and Modernity* (Cambridge: Polity, 1995), pp. 258–65.
42 Jean Cohen and Andrew Arato, *Civil Society and Political Theory* (Cambridge, MA: MIT Press, 1992).
43 Robert Putnam, *Making Democracy Work: Civic Traditions in Modern Italy* (Princeton: Princeton University Press, 1993); *Bowling Alone* (New York: Simon & Schuster, 2000).
44 U. Beck, *Risk Society* (London: Sage, [1986] 1992), ch. 8; see also his *Reinvention of Politics*.

45 A concern conservatives have usually displayed with greater emphasis, as regards the notion of responsibility, than has been the case with other political currents. See Delanty, *Citizenship*, p. 10.
46 Ibid., p. 135.
47 Philippe C. Schmitter, 'Still the century of corporatism?', *Review of Political Studies*, 36 (1974); 'Modes of interest intermediation and models of societal change in Western Europe', *Comparative Political Studies*, 10 (1979).
48 Claus Offe, 'State action and structures of will formation: elements of a social-scientific theory of the state', in *Modernity and the State: East, West* (Cambridge: Polity, 1996); Wolfgang Streeck and P. C. Schmitter, 'From national corporatism to transnational pluralism: organized interests in the single European market', *Politics and Society*, 19 (1991).
49 Cf. the debate in Joshua Cohen and Joel Rogers (eds), *Associations and Democracy* (London: Verso, 1995).
50 Beck, *Risk Society*, pp. 49, 60, 214.
51 Piet Strydom, *Risk, Environment, and Society* (Buckingham: Open University Press, 2001), ch. 8.

Index

absolutism 87
abstract man 70, 84
abstraction 74–5, 76–82, 119
    see also real abstractions
accommodation 51, 81
    see also adaptation
accountability 174
action and agency 22, 29, 31, 154, 161, 192, 234 n.24
    and responsibility 173–4, 192, 198, 201, 203, 204
    see also praxis
active citizenship 57, 88–9, 217–18
active subject 116
activism 42
adaptation 124, 125, 240 n.22
administrative power 98, 99, 220
Adorno, Theodor W. 19–23, 28, 45, 47, 50, 84, 161
aesthetic perspective 16, 18, 21
    identity 4
affect see emotions
affirmative culture 42
agency see action and agency
Alexander, Jeffrey C. 75
alienation 7, 9, 16, 18, 23, 86
anarchism 59, 100, 186
ancient Greece 51, 126
    friendship 138–9
'angry young men' 192–3
anomie 105, 109, 119, 128
anti-colonial struggles 41, 49
anti-racism 72, 116
anti-Semitism 20

Apel, Karl Otto 200, 201–5, 207, 217, 219, 221
Arendt, Hannah 99
Aristotle and Aristotelian thought 61, 126, 138–9
asceticism 41–2
asymmetries 195
atomism 116
Augustine, of Hippo 204
authenticity/inauthenticity 7–9, 10, 142, 194, 197, 198, 226 n.63
authoritarianism 21, 47, 138
    and responsibility 182, 200, 201, 203, 218
authority 105, 106, 181, 185, 186, 187, 192, 218
autonomy
    and freedom 4, 18, 27, 40–1, 44–6, 47, 57
    and inequality 77
    and law 98, 107
    and responsibility 175, 176, 188, 194, 195, 198, 200, 221
    and solidarity 116, 135
autopoietic systems 93–5, 100, 102, 108

Baudrillard, Jean 26
Bauman, Zigmunt 145
Beck, Ulrich 13, 14, 46, 146, 253 n.25
Bell, Daniel 209
Benhabib, Seyla 224 n.30, 230 n.42

Berlin, Isaiah 58
biotechnology 26
Bloch, Ernest 200
Bobbio, Norberto 61–3, 68, 70, 84
Boltanski, Luc 155, 194–8, 206, 210–11
Bourdieu, Pierre 73–5
Brazil
  citizenship 68
  inequality 72
  law 103, 104
  solidarity 123, 130, 137, 143, 144
Bull, Hedley 215
bureaucracy 14, 25, 32, 52, 87, 185
Burt, Ronald 195

Canada, solidarity 142
capabilities, and freedom 34, 43–4, 80–1
capital 73–4
  social 195, 217
capitalism
  and equality 64, 69, 73, 83
  and freedom 14, 15–27, 32, 47
  and responsibility 194–8, 200, 201, 210–12
  and solidarity 115, 155, 156, 158
Carter, Angela 193
Castel, Robert 149–50, 153, 196
Castells, Manuel 158–9
causality 11, 44, 48, 71, 175, 189–90, 204, 212
centred subjectivity 12
Chiapello, Eve 155, 194–8, 207, 210–11
Chile 33

choice 11, 13–14, 23, 26, 27, 30, 33, 36, 48, 51, 173–4
Christianity 40, 42
  love in 135
citizenship
  disembedding and real abstractions 35, 82–92
  and equality/inequality 57–8, 64, 66, 71–5, 77–9, 115
  and law 93–100, 102, 106, 108, 109, 111
  passivity of 88–90, 129, 191, 217
  and responsibility 180, 184, 185, 186–7, 191, 198, 203, 212, 215, 217–18, 221
  and rights 57, 60–70, 72, 77–8, 84, 89, 90–1, 92, 99, 140, 142–3, 150, 153
  and solidarity 115, 120, 121–2, 126, 129, 131, 134, 140, 142–3, 147–53, 164
civic virtue 59, 106
civil law 174
civil rights 61, 62–8, 93, 160, 191
civil society 75, 99, 133, 134, 151, 162, 184, 185, 216, 217
classes
  and equality/inequality 64, 69, 72–5, 85, 86
  and freedom 5, 11, 50
  and responsibility 209, 220–1
  and solidarity 121, 132, 139, 143–7, 150, 156, 164
  see also working class
closed systems 93–6, 108
cognitive aspects
  and equality 57, 110
  and freedom 4, 33, 40, 42, 46, 49

and responsibility 178, 179, 182
and solidarity 116, 154, 164, 167, 168
Cohen, Jean L. 60, 148–9
Cold War 216
collaboration 157, 158, 169, 210, 213, 214
see also networks
collective action 154, 204
collective conscience 118, 119, 120, 130
collective identities 145
collective responsibility 192, 199, 200–5
  new developments 209–22
  problems of individualism for 205–9
collective rights 64–5, 66–7, 68–9, 89, 142–3
collective subjectivities
  and equality 57, 67, 80, 90
  and freedom 12, 27, 29, 31, 36, 41, 48–53
  and responsibility 178, 182, 187, 188, 199, 200, 204, 212, 217, 219, 249 n.1
  and solidarity 116, 117, 119, 127, 130, 133, 151–3, 161–2, 164, 166
  see also classes; family; nation
collectives (Sartre) 12–13
collectivity and collectivities 27, 180
colonialism 83
command 101, 155, 214
commodification 20, 24, 25, 141
  of relationships 197
commodity fetishism 16, 17, 19, 83, 84, 85
common good 85, 197

common sense 102
communication 93, 101, 206, 213
communication society 101
communicative action 26, 96, 97, 100, 127, 129, 164, 204
communicative community 202
communicative power 98–9
communicative rationality and rationalization 31, 87, 102
communism 24, 60, 83, 86, 145
communitarianism 60, 98, 143
community 102–4, 143
competition 168
complexity 13, 32, 33, 39, 109, 111
  and responsibility 186–7, 219
  and solidarity 126, 128, 130, 132, 140, 141, 154, 155, 160–6
compulsion 39, 47, 169
compulsive monogamy 38, 39, 169
confluent love 136
Confucianism 51
Consensus-building 100
conservatism 38, 39, 174, 227
  law 105, 107
  projects 29, 31–4, 138
  and responsibility 179, 209, 255 n.45
Constant, Benjamin 58
Constitution, cult of 107
consumer choice 51
consumerism 14, 26
context 100–11
  see also disembedding
contingency
  and equality 58, 96, 154, 155
  and freedom 3, 5–15, 28, 32, 36, 37, 39, 48, 50, 53
  and responsibility 182, 210
  and solidarity 124, 169
contract(s) 64, 97, 155

see also sexual contract; social contract
contractarianism 76, 90, 98
conventionalism 184
corporations and corporatism 68, 119, 166
   and responsibility 210–12, 219
cosmopolitanism 103, 148
coupling concept 94, 95
creativity 11, 16, 20, 30–1, 53, 141, 178, 194, 198
crime 198
crisis, notion of 7–8
cultural industry 20
culture 125
   and solidarity 140–1, 145
   tragedy of 17
Czechoslovakia, invasion of 12

danger 36–8
decisionism 10, 22, 29
de-differentiation 63–4, 126, 128
Delanty, Gerard 218
democracy
   and equality/inequality 89
   and freedom 15, 21, 26, 33, 47
   and law 96, 99, 105, 106, 109, 110
   and responsibility 184, 185, 186, 187, 188, 200, 201, 202, 203, 213, 217–19, 220
   and solidarity 137, 152, 166
depression, as pathology of freedom 39, 206, 207
determinism 21, 22, 85
developmentalist approach 34
deviance 61–2, 128, 180
dialectical approach, need for 92
difference 20
   and equality 78, 115–18, 208
   and responsibility 208
   and solidarity 143, 156, 161
differentiation 32, 72, 85–6
   and solidarity 118–31, 132, 143, 160
   see also de-differentiation
dignity 40, 202
discourse ethics 127, 164, 203, 204–5, 216
disembedding 13, 34–46
   real abstractions 82–92, 104
   and responsibility 206, 215
   and solidarity 115, 116, 123, 124, 125, 126, 139, 141, 147, 163
disorder *see* order and disorder
division of labour, and solidarity 119, 120, 122, 123, 124, 125, 126, 129
divorce 136, 137
dogmatism 3, 39, 47, 115, 169
domestic justice 72
domination
   definition 4
   and equality 61, 69–70, 73, 80, 81, 86
   and freedom 3–5, 7, 12, 23, 27, 28–9, 30, 31, 33–4, 45, 46, 47, 49, 51, 57, 70, 92, 99–100, 115
   and responsibility 177, 186, 188, 207, 208, 221
   and solidarity 127, 163, 166, 167, 168
drives, life and death 24, 37–8
Durkheim, Émile 118–20, 124, 128, 130, 132, 140, 155–6, 160, 161, 179, 239 nn.2, 13
duty 175, 179, 190, 215, 218

INDEX 261

ecology
  crisis of 13
  and responsibility 211, 216, 218
  see also nature
economy
  and freedom 28, 31, 32
  and responsibility 204, 210–12, 221
  and rights 63
  and solidarity 161–2, 163
  see also capitalism; corporations and corporatism
Eder, Klaus 93, 101, 236 n.7
efficacy and efficiency 130
Ehrenberg, Alain 206
Einstein, Albert 74
elitism
  and equality 82, 96, 99
  and freedom 14, 15, 51
  and responsibility 178, 185, 186, 187, 188, 192, 199, 218, 219
  and solidarity 148
emotions 117, 127, 137, 138, 139
emotivism 126
Engels, Friedrich 144, 145, 147, 233 n.36
Enlightenment, the 6, 8, 15, 16, 20, 25, 28, 45, 46, 58, 74, 91, 140, 191, 249 n.4
equal liberty 77–8, 79, 81
equality
  and citizenship 57–8, 71–5, 77–9, 115
  difference and 78, 115–18, 208
  and freedom 40, 45, 57–60, 69, 70, 79–82, 91–2
  and history 57–60
  law and 57, 103, 104, 108, 109, 110, 111
  and responsibility 107, 174, 176, 177, 181, 186, 190, 192, 199, 207, 208, 213, 219, 220, 222
  and solidarity *see* solidarity
  see also inequality
equity principle 66, 69
Esping-Andersen, Goran 245 n.58
essentialism 139, 168
ethnicity 115, 121–3, 217
Europe, responsibility 216
European Community 157
evolutionary theories 65, 118–31, 132
Ewald, François 189–91, 249 n.4
exclusion 32, 115, 130, 146, 147, 149, 166, 167
Existentialism 9, 11, 22, 201
expert systems 13, 35, 46
expressive aspects
  and difference 116
  and equality 57, 88, 103
  and freedom 4, 33, 42, 46, 49
  and law 110
  and responsibility 182
  and solidarity 154, 164, 167, 168

facticity 7–8, 10, 97
fairness 94
family 32
  and responsibility 198, 209–10, 214
  and solidarity 115, 132–9, 156, 159, 163, 164
fantasy 24
fascism 19, 219
  see also Nazism; social fascism
fear 36–8, 39
feminism 25, 116, 231 n.14

feudal society 64
formal rationality 18, 19, 20, 50, 84
Foucault, Michel 46, 189
fragmentation 19, 115, 123
France 59, 68, 111
   solidarity 131, 149–53
Frankfurt School 5, 16, 19–27, 31, 45, 48, 84–7, 91, 224 n.30
Fraser, Nancy 208
fraternity 131, 189
free riders 197
freedom
   and contingency 3, 5–15, 28, 32, 36, 37, 39, 48, 50, 53
   definition 4
   and domination *see* domination
   and equality *see* equality
   history and meaning *see* history
   and law 105, 106, 107, 109, 110
   and projects 28–53
   and reflexivity 3, 13, 14–15, 29, 30–1, 33, 36, 39, 42, 43–4, 46, 50, 51, 81
   reification and rationalization 15–27
   and responsibility 6, 13, 17, 173–4, 175, 177, 178, 181, 183, 184, 185, 187, 189, 190, 192, 193, 194, 199, 201, 203, 205, 206–8, 213, 219, 220, 221, 222
   and solidarity 115, 133, 135, 136, 147, 153, 155, 161, 163, 166–9
French Revolution 59, 131
Freud, Sigmund 24, 36–8, 186, 206

Friedman, Milton 211
friendship 133, 136, 138–9, 197
functionalism 95, 120–3, 128, 129, 160, 161, 179–82, 233 n.8
fundamentalism 38, 39, 141
future 26

Garapon, Antoine 93, 104–6, 108
general will 96, 184
genetic engineering 123–4
Germany 68, 102, 143
   social theory 15–27, 49–50
   see also Frankfurt School
Giddens, Anthony 13, 14, 34–6, 46, 80, 129, 130, 135–6, 198, 242 n.19
global level 35, 36, 165–6
global order 162
global responsibility 216–17
globalization 35, 70, 88, 110, 126, 141, 142, 148, 156
glocalization 104
Great Britain
   citizenship and rights 64, 67, 68
   and responsibility 198
groups (Sartre) 12, 13

Habermas, Jürgen 16, 25–7, 28, 31, 50, 85–8, 91, 118, 124, 125, 127, 129, 130, 142–3, 149, 156, 160, 163, 164, 188, 202, 203, 204, 205, 224 n.30
   and law 86–8, 93, 94, 96–100, 101, 105, 108, 109, 235 nn. 4, 5
Hart, Herbert L. A. 254 n.34
Hayek, Friedrich 162, 163, 202
hedonism 209

Hegel, Georg Wilhelm Friedrich 5, 12, 16, 17, 18, 20, 48, 52, 91, 127, 185, 208
Heidegger, Martin 5, 7–9, 12, 13, 26, 36, 52, 226 n.63
helplessness 36–8, 39
Hemingway, Ernest 193
heterogeneity 117, 143, 161
  see also difference
hierarchy
  and responsibility 177, 178, 194, 199, 208, 214, 215, 222
  and solidarity 133, 137, 146, 154, 155, 156, 157, 158, 159, 160, 161, 163
Hilferding, Rudolf 154
history
  and equality 57–60
  and freedom 6, 7, 9, 12–13, 26, 29, 46–53
Hobbes, Thomas, and Hobbesian tradition 34, 74, 97, 151, 165, 181, 183–4, 214, 216
homogeneity 116, 143, 150, 208
homophobia 33
Honneth, Axel 208
Horkheimer, Max 19–21, 25, 28, 45, 47, 50, 84, 161, 227 n.74
human rights *see* rights
Husserl, Edmund, and Husserlian thought 9, 25, 77
hybridization 123

idealism 16, 48, 226 n.64
identification models 137
identity
  and equality 57, 73, 88, 105, 154
  and freedom 14–15, 22, 35, 36–41
  and responsibility 182, 205
  and solidarity 123, 132, 135, 138, 139, 141, 145, 146–7, 154, 159, 163, 169
identity logic 21
ideology 20, 168
  hierarchical 208
imagined communities 139
immigration 147
imperialism 83
imputation 174, 187, 190, 191, 212
inauthenticity *see* authenticity/inauthenticity
inclusion 121, 147, 150
individual and individualization 19, 21–2, 69, 119, 125, 133, 141, 146, 151
individualism
  and equality 71, 72, 76, 98
  and freedom 9, 14, 40
  and responsibility 173, 177, 183–99, 200, 201, 205–9, 213, 222
  and rights 61, 65, 66–7
  and solidarity 116, 126, 135, 146, 149–50, 152, 153, 168
inequality 57, 58
  and abstraction and power 76–82
  and citizenship 64, 66, 71–5
  disembedding and real abstractions 82–92
  and freedom 11
  law 110
  and responsibility 192, 207, 208, 212, 221, 222
  and solidarity 143, 146, 167
  see also equality
information, asymmetries of 195
injustice 78

insecurity *see* security and insecurity
institutions
  citizenship 71, 89, 90
  and freedom 3, 49, 52–3
  and inequality 79
  and responsibility 204, 205, 207, 208, 209, 212–14, 217–18, 219–20
  and solidarity 217
instrumental rationality 18, 19, 20, 21, 27, 33, 40, 50, 84, 130
integration 120, 126, 129–30, 132, 150, 160, 166
interactivity 201
interests 166, 249 n.4
International Monetary Fund 147
international networks 162
international organizations 217
international relations, and responsibility 215–17, 218, 200
internationalization, of rights 62
intersubjectivity 9, 10, 12, 30, 50, 99, 181, 200, 201–5
Iraq, Kurd crisis 216
irrationality 10
Italy 68, 137, 157

Jameson, Fredrick 26
Japan 157
Jonas, Hans 198, 200–1, 202, 203, 207, 221, 250 n.9, 253 n.22
Judaism 41
judicial systems 104–11, 116, 154
justice
  and equality 72, 76–80, 90, 94, 100, 103–4, 109

  and responsibility 107, 179, 194, 208, 213
  and solidarity 139

Kant, Immanuel and Kantianism 5, 6, 10, 41, 74, 77, 97, 127, 174, 175, 176, 187, 188, 201, 202, 235 n.40
Keynesianism 69, 148, 155
knowledge 5
Kohlberg, Lawrence 50, 253 n.18
Kritik 6
Kymlika, Will 142

labour 16
  and solidarity 149–50
  see also division of labour
labour market, individualized 13
Lasch, Christopher 209
Lash, Scott 145, 155
Latin America
  capitalism and citizenship 83
  equality/inequality 68, 72
  freedom 33, 41, 51
  law 103, 104, 130
  modernity 160
  responsibility 175, 176, 185
  solidarity 123, 130, 137, 143, 144, 162
law 57, 68, 72, 83, 86–8, 93–100, 238 n.47
  and plurality and context 100–11
  and responsibility 174, 175, 187, 188, 189, 192, 213–15
  and solidarity 116, 148, 149, 151, 154, 155, 160, 161, 163
  see also rights
lay agency 46, 110

Le Bon, Gustave 186
leadership 178, 181
learning 50, 101
left, the, and equality and freedom 59
legality concept 97
legitimation 188
leisure time 212
Lévi-Strauss, Claude 230 n.39
liberal modernity 15, 110, 117, 125, 155, 159, 165, 185
  and responsibility in 183–92
liberalism
  and citizenship 63, 64, 66, 68, 91
  and equality 58, 78, 79, 96
  and freedom 22, 52
  and responsibility 179, 183, 187, 212
  and solidarity 150
liberty 4, 23, 51
  equal 77–8, 79, 81
life world 25–6, 31, 96, 124, 163, 204
  colonization of 25, 26, 28, 33, 86, 96
lifestyles 14–15, 29, 138, 147
Lindholm, Charles 135, 241 n.7
local 141
Locke, John 151, 184
Lockwood, David 129–30
love relationships
  and freedom 38, 39
  and responsibility 197, 214
  and solidarity 115, 132, 133, 134–6, 163, 164
Luhmann, Niklas 93–6, 97, 100, 109, 163
Lukács, Gyorg 8, 18–19, 20, 48, 84, 161, 226 n.64

Machiavelli, Niccolò 187
MacIntyre, Alasdair 126
management, and responsibility 194–8, 210
Mann, Michael 80
Marcuse, Herbert 19, 20, 23–4, 28, 206
market, the 71, 90, 215, 217
  and law 102, 103
  third stage of modernity 155–6, 157, 159, 160, 161, 162, 163
marriage 133, 134, 135, 136, 138, 210
Marshall, Thomas Humphrey 63–5, 71, 85, 121, 148, 150, 180
Marx, Karl 5, 15, 16–17, 20, 21, 22, 27, 29, 35, 48, 52, 73, 83, 85, 86, 91, 99, 100, 108, 144, 145, 147, 185–6, 188, 208, 233 n.36
Marxism 11, 18–27, 31, 59, 83, 129, 200
masculinity, and responsibility 192–3
mass media *see* media
materialism, Marxist 16, 20
Mead, George H. 177, 181, 207, 253 n.18
meaning 38, 81, 88
  and history 13, 46–53
  loss of 27, 43–4, 47
  and responsibility 215
means testing 65, 66, 148
media 106, 141
Megill, Allan 6
Melucci, Alberto 13, 14, 36, 244 n.47
meritocracy 234 n.18

methodological individualism 176
mimesis 21, 24
Minkowski, Hermann 74
mixed articulated modernity 117, 118, 155–66, 167
  and individualism 192–9
  new forms of responsibility 209–22
modernity
  openness 14, 38–9
  and solidarity 117, 125–6
  stages of 154–60
  tensions of 3–5, 58–9, 169
  see also liberal modernity; mixed articulated modernity; state-centred modernity
modernization 83, 157
Molina, Luis de 176
Mondragón 157
morality
  and equality 94, 96, 235 n.40
  and freedom 6, 46
  and responsibility 174, 175, 176, 185, 187, 193, 194, 199, 201, 211, 212, 217
  and solidarity 116, 119, 126, 139
Morse, Richard 175
motivation 47, 51, 53, 165, 206
movement 234 n.24
multicultural movements 116, 132
multiculturalism 142–3, 156
mutual aid organizations 213
myth 45

narcissism 193
nation
  and inequality 82
  and solidarity 120–1, 139–47, 156, 164
nation-state 57, 87, 88, 90, 110, 125, 126, 140–1, 142, 148
  and responsibility 185, 215, 217
national culture 140, 141
national identity 140
nationalism 7
nationalization 63
natural law 61, 68, 76, 101, 143
nature
  domination of 16, 23, 45–6, 49, 69
  responsibility for 200, 221–2
Nazism 19, 45
  Heidegger and 9, 10, 52
needs 4, 23
negative freedom 4, 23, 24, 34, 43, 52, 58, 60, 70
Nelson, Benjamin 176
Neo-colonialism 141
neocorporatism 145, 219
neo-Darwinism 202
neofunctionalism 240 n.18
neo-Kantianism 248 n.10
neoliberalism 32, 33, 41, 66, 70, 85, 138, 160, 161, 162, 198, 212, 254 n.33
neo-Marxism 157
neo-realism 216
networks
  and responsibility 194, 195–6, 197, 210, 212, 213–15, 217
  and solidarity 138, 146, 155, 156, 157–60, 161, 162, 164, 165, 166–7, 169
new social movements *see* social movements
Newtonian time–space 74, 165

Nietzsche, Friedrich 5–7, 10, 36, 177, 178, 185
nihilism 6, 47
non-governmental organizations 162, 217
non-residents' rights 149
normative aspect
  and equality 57
  and freedom 4, 10, 23, 26, 33, 40–1, 42, 49
  and law 96–7, 100, 105, 110
  and responsibility 176, 178, 180, 181, 182, 207
  and solidarity 121, 123, 125, 126, 127, 128, 129, 154, 164, 167, 168
nostalgia for Being 7–9

obligation 174, 175, 184–5, 191, 192, 210, 215
Offe, Claus 145, 154–5, 227 n.3
opportunity concept, negative freedom as 43–4
order and disorder 34, 115, 126, 128–9, 155, 181
organic solidarity 140
Orwell, George 123
other, responsibility to 176–7

Parsons, Talcott 34, 74, 80, 94, 118, 120–3, 124, 125, 126, 127, 128, 129, 132, 140, 160, 163, 179–82, 193, 197
participation 103
particularism 108, 163, 166
Pateman, Carol 246 n.3
patriarchy 62, 131, 133, 136, 137, 160, 210
pauperism 190
penal law 87–8, 130, 174

personal relationships 13, 14, 132–9, 197
philanthropy 88, 150, 153, 212
philosophy 3–13, 14, 116
Piaget, Jean 50
pleasure 103
pluralism 7
  and law 100–11, 117
  and responsibility 208, 215, 219
  and solidarity 116–17, 119, 120, 122, 124, 125, 126–7, 128, 132, 140, 141, 142, 143, 145, 147, 151, 153, 154, 163
political economy 118
political rights 61, 62–8, 93
political systems, and freedom 28, 31, 32
politics 162, 176
positive freedom 4, 24, 34, 43, 52, 58, 60
positive rights 62, 68
positivism 25, 201
post-colonialism 72, 116
post-Fordism 194
postmodernity and postmodernism 51, 95, 117, 148–9, 155, 222
post-structuralism 95
post-Taylorism 194
'post-traditional' society 3
poverty 70, 146, 150, 189, 190
power
  and abstraction and inequality 76–82
  and freedom 31, 40, 45, 46, 50, 51–2, 53, 229 n.27
  and responsibility 181, 183–5
pragmatism 181, 223 n.4
praxis 12, 13, 18, 20, 205

privatism 14, 59, 60, 109
privatization 47, 69, 151
privilege 3, 29, 34, 57, 60, 79, 80, 81, 82
proceduralization, legal 102, 107–8, 110
production 83
　see also capitalism
progress 6, 15, 16, 202
project(s) 11–12, 23, 28–31, 195–6, 197, 206, 210
　conservative 29, 31–4
　of freedom 34–46
property rights 64, 97, 99
Protestantism 45, 123, 183, 229 n.23
　and responsibility 175–6, 209
Providence State 151, 152, 191
proximate relationships 13, 14, 132–9, 197
public opinion, and responsibility 222
public sphere 26, 96, 99, 101, 102, 162, 203
　and private sphere 69, 197, 210, 212–13
public virtue 59, 106
pure relationships 136, 139

quantification 19

racism 33, 115
rational mastery 45–6, 47, 166, 168, 200, 221–2
rationalism 29
rationality and reason
　and equality 74, 96
　and freedom 5, 16, 20–1, 50
　and responsibility 184, 185, 186–7, 192, 204–5, 219
rationalization 7, 15–27, 28, 31, 50–1, 53, 86, 125, 229 n.23
　and law 94–5, 101, 102, 106–7, 155
Rawls, John 73, 76–80, 85, 90, 92, 152, 202
real abstractions
　and citizenship 35, 191, 221
　and equality 57, 58, 70, 71, 72, 79, 82–92, 116
　and freedom 19
　and law 98, 100, 104, 108, 109
　and responsibility 251 n.27
　and solidarity 128, 129, 134, 147, 149, 164
realism 7, 185, 188, 192, 216, 221, 236 n.26
reason *see* rationality and reason
recognition
　politics of 72, 143
　and responsibility 200, 208, 209
redistribution 143, 146, 208
redress, principle of 234 n.18
re-embedding 38–40, 42, 57, 73, 88, 90
　and solidarity 115, 116, 141
reflexivity
　and freedom 3, 13, 14–15, 29, 30–1, 33, 36, 39, 42, 43–4, 46, 50, 51, 81
　and law 93, 102, 107–8
　and responsibility 198
　and solidarity 125, 168
regulation 4, 101, 102
reification and reification theory
　and equality 57, 84, 86–7

and freedom 8, 12, 15–27, 50, 53, 223 n.14
and law 109, 111
and responsibility 194
and solidarity 147, 161
relativism 5
Relativity Theory 74, 117
religion 6, 38, 39, 41–6, 176
and solidarity 144, 169
Renaissance 176, 183, 187
Renan, Ernest 140
representation 219–20
repression 181
resistance 22
responsibility
definition 173
and equality *see* equality
and freedom *see* freedom
individualism and mixed articulated modernity 192–9
movement from individualistic to statist modernity 183–92
possible new forms 139, 209–22
social theory 173–82
and solidarity *see* solidarity
see also collective responsibility
revolutions 24, 41, 49, 82, 144
rights
and citizenship *see* citizenship
and law 93, 98, 99, 102, 105, 109
and responsibility 179, 185, 189, 191, 212, 215, 216, 221
and solidarity 117, 128, 142–3, 149, 155, 160, 164, 185
see also social rights
risk 13, 146, 152, 222
Romanticism 16, 142
Rosanvallon, Pierre 149, 151–3

Rousseau, Jean-Jacques 97, 184, 188
Russell, Bertrand 136

Sartre, Jean-Paul 5, 9–13, 22, 23, 36, 37, 48, 168, 173, 174, 175, 181, 201, 206
Scandinavia 68
Schluchter, Wolfgang 248 n.10
Schumpeter, Joseph A. 186–7
science-conscience 40, 176
secularization 144
security and insecurity 53, 184, 190, 213
self 13, 14
self-conservation 204
self-control 195
self-creation 16
self-expression 4, 167
self-regulation and -management 107, 110–11, 152
self-responsibility 9
Sen, Amartya 34, 69–70
serial monogamy 136
sexism 33
sexual contract 133–4, 184, 193, 210
sexual harassment law 107–8
sexuality 136
and freedom 24, 32
Shaw, Martin 216
Simmel, Georg 7, 13, 17–18, 35, 36, 120, 127
Smith, Adam 118
Smith, Anthony 243 n.26
sociability 108
social capital 195, 217
social conflicts 100, 101–2, 105, 108

social contract 133, 184, 185, 187–8, 189, 191, 192, 193, 198, 202
social control 23, 24, 181
social democracy 59, 60, 107, 109, 148, 187, 189
social fascism 47, 162
social interaction 154
social memory 43, 44, 116, 140
social morality 119
social movements 14–15, 21, 49, 144, 145–6, 147, 162, 163, 217, 218, 221
social policy
  and equality 63–8, 88, 91
  and responsibility 212–14
  and solidarity 132, 142, 148–53, 156–7
social rights
  and equality 61, 62–70, 91, 93, 115, 117
  and responsibility 190, 191, 195
  and solidarity 115, 117, 128, 148, 152, 159
social space 74–5
social sphere of responsibility 213, 220–1
social systems 31, 75, 93–100, 179–82
social theory
  and freedom 3–5, 15–27
  and responsibility 173–82
socialism 59, 60, 67, 144, 145, 167, 208
  failure 13, 52, 96
sociology
  and freedom 3, 13, 14, 28–53
  of law 93–100, 116
  and responsibility 179–82, 188
  and social space 74

and solidarity 116, 125, 126, 132
solidarity
  definition 128
  and differentiation 118–31, 132, 143, 160
  and equality/inequality 60, 67, 68, 70, 88, 96, 103, 115–18, 143, 146, 166–9
  and freedom 115, 133, 135, 136, 147, 153, 155, 161, 163, 166–9
  fundamental forms 132–53
  in mixed articulated modernity 155, 156, 163
  and responsibility 152, 169, 174, 175, 176, 177, 180, 181, 183, 190, 191, 193, 198, 199, 201–5, 207, 210, 212, 213, 215, 217, 218, 220, 222
Sousa Santos, B. de 102–4, 108
space–time dimension *see* time–space
specialization 19, 32, 46
Spencer, Herbert 119, 239 n.5
Stalinism 19
state
  and freedom 47
  and inequality/equality 57, 69, 71, 72, 87–8
  and law 98, 102, 103, 107, 109, 238 n.47
  and responsibility 176, 180–1, 182, 183–92, 195, 215, 216, 217, 219, 220
  and rights 69, 89
  and solidarity 117, 119–20, 128, 131, 154, 155, 161, 162–3, 165, 239 n.13
  see also nation-state; welfare state

state-centred modernity 110, 117, 125–6, 145, 155, 159, 165
  responsibility in 183–92
state of nature 183, 184, 193, 216
structuralism 95, 230 n.39, 233 n.8
Strydom, Piet 179
Suárez, Francisco 176
subjective rights 97, 98, 99
subjectivity 12, 16
  see also collective subjectivities
substantive rationality 101, 102
superego 207, 209
symbolic interactionism 181
symbolic tokens, disembedding mechanism 13, 35
systems theory 93–100, 179–82, 188

Taylor, Charles 142
technology 23, 221–2
  see also biotechnology; genetic engineering
Teubner, Gunther 95
Thatcherism 198
Third International 18
Third Way politics 198, 209, 242 n.19
Third World, the 216
time 39, 94, 212
time–space
  and equality/inequality 73–5, 79, 87, 91, 117, 165
  of law 110
  and responsibility 202, 221
  and solidarity 117, 137, 164, 165
time–space distantiation 34–5
Tocqueville, Alexis de 58–60, 80, 81, 99, 104, 105, 108, 188

totalitarianism 20, 21, 23, 201
totalization, history as 13, 48
traditional societies (law) 105
transcendence 24, 27, 29, 38, 41–6, 51, 81, 135, 139, 168–9, 177
tribes 145
Trotsky, Leon 165
trust 214–15
truth 6, 13, 237 n.41
tyranny 59

Ulysses 45
uncertainty 5, 215
unfreedom 3, 16, 24, 31–2, 167
Unger, Roberto M. 106–7
United Nations 217
United States
  freedom 40
  networks 157
  responsibility 198, 216
  solidarity 121–3, 130, 143
universalism
  and freedom 5–6, 10, 68
  law 103, 107, 108, 109, 111
  and responsibility 202, 208
  and rights 63, 68, 92
  and solidarity 124, 142, 153, 163–4
Urry, John 145, 155
utilitarianism 58, 77, 90, 202
utopian perspective, and responsibility 200, 201, 202, 221

validity 97
value theory 22, 86, 87
values
  and equality 100
  and freedom 5, 7, 10, 11, 27, 47
  and responsibility 177, 180

and solidarity 121, 126, 127, 128, 129, 163
violence 38–9, 105, 193
voluntarism 10, 29, 184, 210, 213, 214, 215

Wagner, Peter 36, 155, 157, 194
Walzer, Michael 238 n.1
weapons race 216
Weber, Max 6–7, 10, 13, 17, 18, 19, 20, 27, 29, 35, 46, 47, 48, 51, 61, 80, 81, 91, 95, 100, 175, 177–8, 179, 181, 185–6, 188, 201, 228 n.21
Weeks, Jeffrey 242 n.14
welfare state
  and equality 68, 87, 93, 101, 102, 111
  and responsibility 182, 198–9, 254 n.33
  and solidarity 147–53, 155, 160
  typology 68
  unfreedom of 24
women
  equality 230 n.5
  responsibility 184, 193
  rights 64
  solidarity 131, 133, 136, 137
working class 16–17, 18, 19, 23, 24, 52, 220–1
  and responsibility 184, 185–6, 193
  and solidarity 144–7, 148
World Bank 66, 147
world society perspective 216

Yugoslavia, dissolution of 216